THE
LINCOLN LEGEND

By Roy P. Basler

AN analysis of the rise of our
greatest American hero-myth —
a study of Lincoln, the man, as
seen through his almost legendary reputation.

Poets, novelists, dramatists,
and biographers have, with the
help of the folk mind, built up a
Lincoln legend comparable to
the hero tales of mythology. It
is the achievement of Mr. Basler's book that it cuts the true
from the false, separates the poetical interpretation from the
historical fact, and gives us a
solid estimate of the true Lincoln buried beneath this amazing
weight of idolatrous hero-worship. By analyzing and clarify-
ing the existing knowledge of
Lincoln, the author has produced
a discriminating source book of
Lincolniana and an invaluable
guide for a better understanding
the man.

egend

Conceptions

SAINT-GAUDENS'S STATUE OF LINCOLN
IN LINCOLN PARK, CHICAGO

The

LINCOLN LEGEND

A STUDY IN CHANGING CONCEPTIONS

ROY P. BASLER

Boston and New York

HOUGHTON MIFFLIN COMPANY

The Riverside Press Cambridge

1935

The Riverside Press
CAMBRIDGE · MASSACHUSETTS
PRINTED IN THE U.S.A.

TO

JAY B. HUBBELL

PREFACE

THE river of Lincoln literature flows on undiminished. From 1860 to the present there have been few low-water marks, but numerous flood stages, testifying to the emotional, often idolatrous, hero-worship of writer and reading public. The bibliography of Daniel Fish, published in 1905, listed 1080 books. J. B. Oakleaf, bringing the Fish bibliography down to 1925, added 1600 new items. In addition to the works listed in these official bibliographies, there are the thousands of articles, stories, and poems which have appeared in periodicals. The portion listed in the *Readers' Guide* alone is enormous. But the student must wonder even more at the personality which is the source of so much genuinely significant narrative, speculation, and interpretation as appears in this most remarkable 'multiplication of books.' For certainly the wellspring of wonder is there, in Lincoln the man, as well as in Lincoln the mystery.

It has been a part of my study to attempt, at least, to keep Lincoln the man continually before the reader as he studies the legend, for nowhere is it easier to hang oneself upon the horns of historical dilemma than in the study of this man and this myth. It has not been my purpose to 'debunk' Lincoln, or to give, primarily, a definitive study of his character and achievement; but rather to show how poets, writers of fiction, dramatists, and occasionally biographers have, with the help of the folk-mind, created about Lincoln a national legend or myth which in conception is much like the hero-myths of other nations.

PREFACE

A study of literary treatments of Lincoln was first suggested to me by Professor Jay B. Hubbell, of Duke University. In many ways the present work has grown away from literature and might in part properly be called a study of Lincoln's reputation. As it was originally planned, the purely literary treatments were the principal materials with which I intended to work. As it proceeded, the overlapping of literature, biography, and folklore became more and more apparent, with the result that more non-literary matter was included than at first intended. The legendary aspect of Lincoln, which became the one important development uniting the entire mass, was quite as often apparent in biography and reminiscences as in literature; and, to differentiate still further, literary atrocities were often as significant in theme as the works of literary value. The reader is cautioned, therefore, not to expect every verse cited to be a masterpiece. On the other hand, he will not, I think, find any more verse that had better never been written than he would find in an exhaustive study of many an accepted literary figure. Generally the poetasters who wrote of Lincoln found in him some inspiration which exalted their verse beyond its customary level. Those poets who are admittedly of some importance composed, with few exceptions, in their better vein when they wrote of him. Similarly writers of fiction and drama have often done their best work in a Lincoln novel or play. If the student of Lincoln finds quotations inflicted too often and too long, I hope that the average reader, unacquainted with the mass of Lincoln literature, may find them interesting. It has been my purpose to let the legend speak for itself wherever possible.

During the course of my study I encountered two items which deal particularly with the legendary significance of

Lincoln. I acknowledge with pleasure my indebtedness to them for suggestions. The first is an editorial by Carl Van Doren entitled 'The Poetical Cult of Lincoln,' which appeared in *The Nation*, May 17, 1919. Mr. Van Doren, in reviewing the better-known poems on Lincoln by the poets of the so-called 'new movement' in American poetry, discusses very briefly the significance of Lincoln as a symbol and the tendency of poets to treat him as a purely legendary figure. The other work is Lloyd Lewis's *Myths After Lincoln* (1929), which vividly narrates the popular apotheosis of Lincoln during the period of terror, grief, and brigandage which followed the assassination. The present study may be said to begin where Mr. Lewis left off; the materials with which I have been concerned are practically untouched by him.

I wish to acknowledge further the assistance of Professor Hubbell, whose suggestions and criticisms have been stimulating and constructive. To Professor P. F. Baum, also of Duke University, and to Mr. Carl Sandburg, I am indebted for reading and criticizing the manuscript. Mr. Paul M. Angle, Secretary of the Lincoln Centennial Association, has kindly given his opinion and additional information on moot points. Several persons connected with the Duke University Library and the Library of Congress have been of assistance in many ways.

R. P. B.

CONTENTS

ILLUSTRATIONS

The Lincoln Legend

A Study in Changing Conceptions

The Lincoln Legend

I

A Survey of Lincoln Literature

I

IT IS difficult now to comprehend the wave of hero-worship which swept over the country after Lincoln's assassination. In reality the tide had already set in before, and his death was but an opening of the floodgates of emotion. The state of the public mind was then, as it has always been, exceedingly delirious after a period of war and national stress. The populace must, it seems, have its periods of emotional unbalance even during quiet times. So at a period when the nation's emotions were all but out of control, when half a million soldiers were dead in their uniforms and thirty millions of people were so spent with grief that no man could be quite sane any more, it is not surprising that the entire populace reverted in its mental processes to something common to the childhood of a race — the creation of a hero-myth. Drunk with success, the North was ready to apotheosize the leader who had preserved the Union and abolished slavery.

Lloyd Lewis has given, in *Myths After Lincoln* (1929),

3

a vivid account of the hysteria that reigned during the days of 'Black Easter' and the reaction of the popular imagination to the assassination. Lincoln was suddenly lifted into the sky as the folk-hero, the deliverer, and the martyr who had come to save his people and to die for them. There is a striking similarity between this popular conception of Lincoln as the dying god and the similar myths of many lands and peoples. In the chronicle of folk-beliefs the list of dying gods is long and their stories are longer. Sir James George Frazier has traced, in *The Golden Bough*, the myth of the dying god through many ancient and modern religions. Osiris died each year to bring life to the dormant grain. Adonis was a parallel divinity in Greek mythology. In addition to these there were, to mention only a few, Apollo, Attis, Balder the Beautiful, and we might add King Arthur. As had the dying gods of older times, Lincoln came up from the people. He was mocked and unrecognized for what he was until he had died. As Osiris carried his evil brother Set into myth as his slayer, and King Arthur took with him the dark Sir Modred, so Lincoln snatched John Wilkes Booth from oblivion.

In the years that followed the assassination, the folk-mind was enraptured with the stories of how Lincoln had suffered, prayed, dreamed, and loved mankind and conquered his enemies. How he had doubted, despaired, cunningly schemed, and contrived to effect his ends, no one wanted to hear. His kind face and sad smile were infinitely more appealing than the cool, slow brain that thwarted the enemies of the Union and brought order out of chaos. To have done what he had, he must have been superhuman, a mysterious symbol of the god of the common humanity in whose flesh he had lived. Man has always felt, somehow, that a divine guide is required to help him through the thorny thicket of life. He has felt, likewise, that a chosen one must die in retribution for the sins of the race or of the world. It is a doubly significant myth that combines the deliverer and the dying god. So the myth of Lincoln grew in its various phases. In one phase it was primarily mystical and religious; in another it was intensely national.

Day by day the impression grew that Lincoln had been the chosen one of God. Those who had known him told everything they had known which was in keeping with the memory of the martyr. We cannot call into question here all of the reminiscences that were printed, but one of the least highly colored will suffice as an example. Francis B. Carpenter, who had painted the historical 'First Reading of the Emancipation Proclamation,' published *The Inner Life of Abraham Lincoln* (1867) based on a six months' acquaintance with Lincoln while painting his portrait. The spiritual figure as he is portrayed in this book is, in the words of the author, 'grounded in righteousness, as immovable as one of the giant ranges of our own Rocky Mountains.' Carpenter's opinions are modest and critical when compared with many others.

America was badly in need of a folk-hero. In the brief course of her history as a nation, several candidates for the office had been put forward. Washington, as the father of his country, came nearer to being 'canonized' than any other. But there was a remoteness about him which repelled genuine personal affection. 'Parson' Weems presented him with the necessary sanctity, but not even Weems could make Washington the homely, lovable personal saint that the popular mind needed to have in its household deity. The romance of the self-made man and the homely attraction of kindly, solicitous Father Abraham went together to form the requisite appeal to all classes. The accomplishments of Lincoln in his official capacity equaled those of Washington. The two aspects made him at once honored and loved.

Parallel to the popular reaction to the assassination there arose simultaneously the praise and symbolization of Lincoln by the poets. Shortly after the assassination, a volume of *Poetical Tributes* appeared which included nearly two hundred poems collected from newspapers and periodicals all over the United States, Canada, and England. These poems were unanimous in acclaiming Lincoln as the Emancipator and Savior of the nation. Second only to this praise was the execration of the American Judas, John Wilkes Booth, and the cry of vengeance upon the South. Even a respectable Virginian poet and clergyman, Christopher Pearse Cranch, sent out the clarion call to exterminate the devils.

THE MARTYR

No, not in vain he died, not all in vain —
Our good, great President. This people's hands
Are linked together in one mighty chain,
Knit tighter now in triple woven bands,
To crush the fiends in human mask, whose might
We suffer, oh, too long! The devils we must fight
With fire. God wills it in this deed. This use
We draw from the most impious murder done
Since Calvary. Rise, then, O countrymen!
Scatter the marsh-light hopes of Union won
Through pardoning clemency. Strike, strike, again!
Draw closer round the foe a girdling flame!
We are stabbed whene'er we spare. Strike, in God's name!

The better poets who wrote of Lincoln — and there were few who did not write — were occupied chiefly with the theme of justice, mercy, and liberty as represented by the martyred President. Whitman wrote of the 'sweetest wisest soul'; Bryant, of him who was 'slow to smite and swift to spare'; Lowell, of the 'brave, foreseeing first American.' Eventually these poets had as much influence in forming the lasting conception of Lincoln as the biographers. Later an historian, F. J. Turner, was to lament, 'How can one speak of him except in the words of Lowell's great "Commemoration Ode"?' Even those who had ridiculed Lincoln came tardily to lay, as did Tom Taylor in the London *Punch*, a wreath on Lincoln's bier and contribute to the swelling mass of eulogy a few other words of love and adoration:

> Yes, he had lived to shame me from my sneer,
> To lame my pencil and confute my pen —
> To make me own this hind of princes peer,
> This rail-splitter, as true-born king of men.

This myth that sprang up overnight influenced history and biography to such an extent that they have not to this day rid themselves of the effect. The popular idolatry of Lincoln still exists, and even those legends which biographers have exploded continue to pass current in popular literature, which largely moulds the general conception of Lincoln. As a background for the study of the legend, we may first consider the biographical accounts and the nature of the mass of literature which has grown up about Lincoln. The biographies should present the more critical appreciation of the man for approximately what he was, as contrasted with what the legend-makers have made of him, and at the same time present an outline of Lincoln's growing reputation.

II

The first biographies of Lincoln were published shortly after his nomination in 1860. They were very brief and generally of little significance. Most of them show very little acquaintance with Lincoln's life previous to the Lincoln-Douglas debates. The two best are those by John L. Scripps and by William Dean Howells and John L. Hays. Scripps obtained from Lincoln an autobiographical sketch which he simply elaborated. Howells and Hays worked from materials collected by an agent who was sent to Springfield for the purpose of interviewing Lincoln and some of his associates. The autobiographical sketch of Lincoln is printed in his complete works and may be consulted as a general summary of all the campaign biographies.

The first widely read biography was William M. Thayer's *The Pioneer Boy* (1863). It is ninety per cent fiction, having little more fact than the briefer campaign biographies. In the 'Parson' Weems tradition, it is important as the first biography to make use of many anecdotes in connection with Lincoln's traditional honesty and poverty in his uphill struggle. Thayer expanded this biography several times, and in 1882 published the most complete form under the title *From Pioneer Home to White House*. All of his biographies of Lincoln were very popular, each passing through many printings.

After Thayer, the most widely read author was Josiah Gilbert Holland, editor of *Scribner's Monthly*, whose *Life of Abraham Lincoln* appeared in the fall of 1865. Over one hundred thousand copies of this book were eventually sold. Holland added much material to what was known, but most of it was comprised of such anecdotes and folk-tales of the popular hero of the backwoods as agreed with the conception of the sainted martyr. The total portrait presented Lincoln as a model youth and 'a Christian gentleman.' There is nothing but eulogy in its opinions, and facts out of keeping with eulogy are excluded from its pages.

Lincoln's status as a Christian gentleman was unassailed until Ward H. Lamon published the first volume of his biography in 1872. For the early life of Lincoln, Lamon used the materials collected by William H. Herndon, but of the period when he was himself familiar with Lincoln in Springfield and on the circuit he wrote from his own knowledge. Lamon had been closely associated with Lincoln for years and was at one time his law partner. Thus the main contribution of his biography was a realistic account of the Illinois circuit-riding lawyer and his bare, uncultured, crude existence. He attempted to disprove Holland's contention that Lincoln was a Christian and told some of the more unpalatable details of his life. The result was that the book met with extreme disapproval, and it was said that some of Lincoln's friends bought up as many copies as they could and destroyed them. The second volume was never published. The controversy over Lincoln's religion which began with Lamon's book is not yet stilled, and the later biographers have not yet found an entirely satisfactory mean between the unreal picture by Holland and the generally bald and dense realism of Lamon.

In *The World's Work*, for February, 1911, Lamon's daughter, Dorothy Lamon Teillard, gives some interesting extracts from contemporary reviews and other comments upon her father's book. Josiah Gilbert Holland, whose biography has been discussed, denounced it as 'a shameless book' and described Lamon's Lincoln as 'a half-lunatic infidel.' But Herndon wrote to Lamon in 1885:

> Lamon's first life of Lincoln is the truest life that was ever written of a man, as I think.... No life will succeed permanently in this world that is bottomed on a lie and sustained by a fraud. Why, Lamon, if you and I had not told the exact truth about Lincoln, he would have been a myth in a hundred years after 1865.

Dorothy Lamon Teillard's analysis of the causes which led to the unfavorable reception of her father's book is illuminating:

> It was thought his fame would suffer if all the ugly facts were known. But it was prompted in part also by the timid and the conventional cowardly notion that opinions of the time about social standing, about education, and about religion would somehow suffer if all his experiences and opinions were frankly told.... The reading public regarded it as an offense to trace his wonderful growth from so humble an origin. Then there was the religious world, which was shocked that he was described as unorthodox. What may be called the sectional public took exception to the unprejudiced attitude toward the South.... Then there was what might be called the social public that was shocked by the truth about Lincoln's humble and hard bringing up.

Furthermore, as the author hints, the political party to which Lincoln belonged — and which was even then refusing to carry out his magnanimous policy for reconstructing the South — resented Lamon's humanizing of Lincoln. It wanted Lincoln's memory kept sacred so that it could be most effectively used for party purposes and ends.

It was this attitude on the part of the public in general that caused Donn Piatt, when asked a number of years after the assassination to write a reminiscence of the

Lincoln that he had known, to lament the despotic tyranny of public opinion among a free people — public opinion which had created, with the aid of a select group of biographers in the 'Parson' Weems tradition, an anaemic myth from the fondly remembered Martyr President. This public had demonstrated on the publication of Lamon's biography that any picture which was not in keeping with the impossible popular deity was not fit for public sight. The Lincoln that Donn Piatt had known — homely, skeptical, lacking in the finer sensibilities, and more often harsh than meek and mild — had passed from human knowledge: 'I hear of him, read of him in eulogies and biographies, and fail to recognize the man I encountered, for the first time, in the canvass that called him from private life to be President of the then disuniting United States.'

Napoleon defined history as 'lies agreed upon.' In the matter of biography Lincoln concurred. Herndon tells us that after reading a biography of Edmund Burke, Lincoln commented:

Biographies as generally written are not only misleading but false. The author of this life of Burke makes a wonderful hero out of his subject. He magnifies his perfections — if he had any — and suppresses his imperfections. He is so faithful in his zeal and so lavish in praise of his every act that one is almost driven to believe that Burke never made a mistake or a failure in his life. I've wondered why book publishers and merchants don't have blank biographies on their shelves, always ready for an emergency; so that, if a man happens to die, his heirs or his friends, if they wish to perpetuate his memory, can purchase one already written, but with blanks. These blanks they can at their leisure fill up with rosy sentences full of high-sounding praise. In most instances they commemorate a lie, and cheat posterity out of the truth.

In 1884 Isaac N. Arnold's biography was published. Arnold, a close friend and admirer of Lincoln, had written an earlier study of him in connection with the history of the antislavery movement, which was published in 1867. His biography is marked by considerable candor, but he did not present the more dismal details of Lincoln's early life, and the agnosticism which Lamon had stressed, he denied. The chief bias aside from general admiration was in the account of Lincoln's attitude toward slavery. Arnold presented all the evidence and anecdote available to prove that Lincoln had burned with zeal from his boyhood to liberate the slaves.

In 1888 came the notable biography wherein William H. Herndon, Lincoln's law partner, set forth the mass of documents, reminiscences, and impressions that had been used by Lamon. This was the height of realistic biography. For years Herndon had collected, wherever he could, bits of information from many people who had known Lincoln in Illinois. He did not make any attempt to cull his material, and it seemed to many who relied on his accuracy that much might have been omitted. Later students argue that his account is extravagant in presenting Lincoln's melancholy and the harsh details of his early life and later domestic infelicity. The reminiscences of Lincoln's boyhood are largely sprinkled with folk-tales, but the account of the years in which Herndon knew him is relatively accurate in spite of overemphasis on the drabness and unrelieved crudity in his life. Lord Charnwood says of Herndon that he

> ... was like Boswell, of the opinion that a great man is not best portrayed as a figure in a stained-glass window. He had lived with Lincoln, groaned under his odd ways, and loved them, for sixteen years before his Presidency, and after his

death he devoted much research, in his own memory and those of many others, to the task of substituting for Lincoln's aureole the battered tall hat, with valuable papers stuck in its lining, which he had long contemplated with reverent irritation. Mr. Herndon was not endowed with Boswell's artistic gift for putting his materials together, perhaps because he lacked that delicacy and sureness of moral perception which more than redeemed Boswell's absurdities. He succeeded on the whole in his aim, for the figure that more or less distinctly emerges from the litter of his workshop is lovable; but in spite of all Lincoln's melancholy, the dreariness of his life, sitting with his feet on the table in his unswept and untidy office at Illinois, or riding on circuit or staying at ramshackle western inns with the Illinois bar, cannot have been so unrelieved as it is in Mr. Herndon's presentation. And Herndon overdid his part. He ferreted out petty incidents which he thought might display the acute Lincoln as slightly too acute, when for all that can be seen Lincoln acted just as any sensible man would have acted. But the result is that, in this part of his life especially, Lincoln's way of living was subjected to so close a scrutiny as few men have undergone.

In 1890 John G. Nicolay and John Hay, who had been private secretaries to Lincoln during the war, published their ten-volume *Abraham Lincoln: A History*, parts of which they had published serially in the *Century* over a period of years. In this biography Lincoln is often buried beneath the facts of history, inasmuch as most of the important historical material of the period 1860–65 is included. As a source book it is invaluable, but as biography it lacks unity. Lincoln is somewhat intemperately eulogized and presented in his every act as wise and righteous. In the account of his early life every effort is made to gloss over the unbecoming and emphasize that which was in keeping with the later Lincoln. Furthermore, the account lacks a great deal and must be supplemented with the later works of Beveridge and Sandburg. In spite of the fact that many biographies of Lincoln have been written since, these ten volumes remain the best source of general information, especially concerning his later life. They are very probably quoted oftener than they are read, but they are readable history.

To Nicolay and Hay, Lincoln was a hero, and unavoidably their sentiment tended to present him as a hero. The legend naturally influenced their expression, but there is no evidence that they wilfully misrepresented the man they had known. The facts presented speak for themselves. At the worst, facts are omitted which might have spoken otherwise. The chief proof of the merit of their work is that the Lincoln who emerges through its many volumes is, for the most part, the same Lincoln that remains after forty years of new evidence and reinterpretation.

Their squeamishness in glossing over the more unpleasant details of such affairs as the Shields duel and Lincoln's strange courtship of Mary Todd does not commend their treatment of Lincoln's early life to the careful student, but it must be remembered that at the time of their writing much of the material on Lincoln's early life was unauthenticated and very little of it certain enough to merit complete acceptance. Their best course was to take what seemed correct, and, like others, they made mistakes. They did not err, however, as the romantic-realist Herndon did, in crediting the most melodramatic accounts as the truth.

Whoever wishes to study Lincoln as President cannot stop with the biography of Nicolay and Hay, but he cannot find a work that will take its place. The intimate knowledge and understanding which these biographers possessed of Lincoln in his last years gave to their study a unity of conception, if not of execution, which is unique in Civil War histories. It is as if Lincoln himself were ordering again the affairs of a nation submerged in enormous problems and significant events. The largeness of the time and the man is nowhere revealed more sweepingly. Yet the dust collects on the ten large volumes, and Lincoln is known through the short biographies.

Abraham Lincoln by John T. Morse, Jr., appeared in 1893. The Herndon biography and the history of Nicolay and Hay had a few years before presented two widely divergent accounts. Morse proceeded to evaluate the material in each and gave, as a result, the first account that dealt with Lincoln's entire life in an approximately unbiased manner. His early Lincoln was based on Herndon, the later, chiefly on Nicolay and Hay. Morse's biography marks the beginning of a period of critical study which attempts to evaluate Lincoln from the materials collected by Herndon, Nicolay, and Hay.

Morse recognized the divergence between the two phases of Lincoln as a problem difficult to explain. He considered the frontier product revealed by Herndon to be true, and yet Lincoln the statesman and executive was in his mind somewhat colored by the popular myth. In order to resolve the two, he offered the following hypothesis:

> The very quality which made Lincoln, as a young man, not much superior to his coarse surroundings was precisely the same quality which, ripening and expanding rapidly and grandly with maturing years and a greater circle of humanity, made him what he was in later life. It is through this quality that we get continuity in him; without it, we cannot evade the insoluble problem of two men — two lives — one following the other with no visible link of connection between them;

without it we have physically one creature, morally and mentally two beings.

What this quality was, Morse does not further specify, but the impression may be left that Lincoln was little more than a human sponge that absorbed the characteristics of the society in which he moved.

Like many others, Morse could not conceive that the rough-and-tumble frontier was aught else than a retarding influence. Environment may be important, but Lincoln cannot be explained, it seems to me, by his place any more completely than by his time. Morse, however, sees in the greatness of Lincoln an exotic quality which could not have developed under other circumstances.

> One can hardly conceive that in any age of the world or any combination of circumstances a capacity and temperament like that of Caesar or Napoleon would not force itself into prominence and control. On the other hand, it is easy to suppose that if precisely such a moral question and peculiar crisis as gave to Lincoln his opportunity, had not arisen contemporaneously with his years of vigor, he might never have got farther away from obscurity than does the ordinary member of Congress.

Morse hastens to add that, though this be true, the conditions did exist, and Lincoln's greatness is none the less.

As a solution to the character of Lincoln, Morse's biography is not, perhaps, as good as it is in presenting a vivid account of Lincoln's life, but the early life of Lincoln is not so well done as the later. Morse could see nothing but the bald crudeness of the frontier society, the dull routine of ill-paid labor and hard living. The mass of folklore concerning these early years he thought 'not worth recounting.' The statesman was so far removed from the farmhand who slaughtered hogs at thirty-one cents a day that the latter was insignificant. The fact that the statesman had done rough work did not lend any dignity to the lowly occupation.

The heyday of frontier interpretation of American society had not yet come when Morse wrote of Lincoln.[1] From it he might have benefited by taking a middle path. For although the frontier cannot explain everything, it was not so insignificant as Morse considered it to be, on the one hand, as a permanent influence in Lincoln's character; nor so largely significant, on the other hand, of mediocrity and narrowness in his early character.

In reality, Morse did not solve Lincoln. He was ready at the end of his biography to admit his particular failure, but, perhaps, he came in most things closer to the real Lincoln than any of his predecessors. He realized the reality as well as the enigma and saw clearly what Lincoln accomplished if not always the exact force which moved him.

In 1895 Ida M. Tarbell's biography was published. The chief contribution of this book was a mass of material of the same variety as that upon which Herndon's was based, but it was much brighter in color than Herndon's. The reminiscences which were given presented a fresher, more wholesome view of Lincoln's early life, which had been pictured by Herndon and Lamon as drab and miserable beyond the fact. These reminiscences are as reliable as those collected by Herndon; and if there is any value in either, they should only be considered together.

In 1899 appeared Norman Hapgood's *Abraham Lincoln*,

---

[1] F. J. Turner's first essay on the frontier, 'The Significance of the Frontier in American History,' was read to the American Historical Association in 1893.

the Man of the People. Like Morse, Hapgood attempted
to portray the Lincoln of Herndon and the Lincoln of
Nicolay and Hay as one and the same. It seemed quite
logical to the author that Lincoln might 'reach as high
as the saints in one direction and as high as Rabelais in
another'; and that he might be 'the prairie male as well
as the sage and martyr, the deft politician as well as the
generous statesman.' But Hapgood did not any more
than Morse picture a coherent Lincoln. He left what little
of the prairie male he presented on the prairie and presented in his later chapters the traditional sage and man
of sorrows. Furthermore, in the early chapters there was
more of the budding prophet than there was of the
Rabelaisian joker.

III

Short biographies have a way of being good in some
particular fashion, without being good enough to last.
This is especially true of the biography which is written
'in the light of what we now know.' The latest discovery
or fad is the 'open sesame' to character. Perhaps this
may be in the form of actually new material concerning
the subject, but more often it is in the form of a psy-
chological, historical, or philosophical fad. There is, however, a combination of sympathy and detachment, appreciation and criticism, which often produces a short
biography of as much merit as a long one ever attains.
There are two short biographies which, possessing the
balanced effects, are unsurpassed as interpretations of
Lincoln.

Passing over several biographical interpretations which
appeared from year to year after 1900 and were alike only
in the conclusion that Lincoln was our greatest man, we

come to the two primarily synthetic biographies of most worth — Lord Charnwood's biography and Nathaniel Wright Stephenson's study of the growth of Lincoln as an artist.

Charnwood's *Abraham Lincoln* (1917) is the best combination of criticism and admiration yet to appear. This author, more than any other, successfully weighs the historical importance of each event and incident in the mass of facts, and hence the critical reader is more willing to agree with him in the end that Lincoln is to be credited for certain things and condemned for others. The credit far surpasses the condemnation, however, and the absence of any specific eulogy in the biography only leaves the reader free to phrase his own. One is convinced for the first time in reading this book of what he thought all along; namely, that Lincoln was neither a spiritual genius nor a low clown of tricky mind, but that he was rather a quiet man who generally bent all his powers to the vindication of certain principles. We observe his mistakes and questionable doings, but we perceive that they are outweighed by his accomplishment.

This biography is unique among Lincoln biographies in some ways, though quite ordinary in others. It was written for Englishmen, and one of its greatest values is that it is not American. It cannot be held sectional or national, though it is in a sense partisan. From its viewpoint Lincoln belongs not to one nation and one period, but to the world and to all time.

Charnwood is a partisan in that he believes in the ideals of a democracy and in that he is, like Lincoln, a hater of slavery, sectionalism, and pretense. Above all, he admires and loves Lincoln. Many biographies of Lincoln have been all but ruined by the fact that their authors possessed these same beliefs, but Charnwood has a consciousness of his bias. He seems to overstress Lincoln's faults in order to correct his own tendency toward hero-worship. His interpretation of Lincoln results in the vindication of the democracy of common men, and, coming from an Englishman, it cannot be American complacency. Lincoln's commonness is almost without vulgarity. Without glossing over Lincoln's crudeness and sins against decorum, Charnwood perceives the nobility of Lincoln's intellect and the dignity of his spirit. His mistakes and failings are shown, but they enhance, rather than detract from, his habitual clear thinking and right acting. His Lincoln is ambitious without being selfish, humble but strong, intelligently persevering, and sublime without being spectacular.

This is not a new interpretation. Charnwood's chief merit is that he has grasped all that is genuine and sound in past Lincoln biography. The reader may value as he chooses, appreciate as he chooses, but he never escapes the greatness of Charnwood's conception. There is a balanced proportion in the treatment of historical topics which is seldom found in Lincoln biographies; all the historical matter introduced is in direct connection with Lincoln. The hero is not buried among facts.

But however much Charnwood admires Lincoln and, as it is given to him, understands him, he does not by his method get at the whole man. Lincoln is drawn as Charnwood sees him, and Charnwood does not see him whole. Lincoln, it would seem, means different things to each biographer, and even when he means the same things, only apparently are they the same. For example, to Charnwood, Lincoln is at once a common man and an extraordinary literary artist and statesman, but it is the literary artist and statesman that engrosses. The homely and democratic Lincoln is really an outer shell, a superficial earthly housing of genius that is best represented by the achievement of the statesman. To Morse, on the other hand, Lincoln is an extraordinary statesman as well as a common man. His greatness is not something superior to his homely character, but it is the result of the very elements which make him a common man — his slow, clear thinking, his right acting, his belief in democratic principles, his conservatism, and so on. This common greatness, however, required an especial time and a certain crisis in which to make itself manifest. In still a third instance, to Carl Sandburg, whose work I shall discuss later, Lincoln's greatness is in being homely. His lowliness and greatness are of the same piece of cloth. He is a cross-section of humanity, just as other men are, each quite an individual in the exact lineaments of his grain, yet possessing the same ordinary qualities of humanity in general. Sandburg has not yet published his study of the President, however, and how well he may be able to make his later character one and the same with the prairie Lincoln remains to be seen.

Contemporary with Charnwood's biography there appeared the most important literary interpretation of Lincoln since Whitman's poem; namely, John Drinkwater's *Abraham Lincoln: A Play* (1919). Like Charnwood, whose biography served as the chief inspiration of the play, Drinkwater was interested in Lincoln as the statesman who made war and governed nobly. The British interest in Lincoln, as it appeared in such men as Charnwood, Drinkwater, and Lloyd George, was chiefly marked by admiration for Lincoln's conception of statesmanship. The period of the World War brought the example of Lincoln's unselfish devotion to principles, his utter lack of vindictiveness, and his plain honesty of purpose, before men who thought on the ills of government as never before. They saw in him a message of spiritual values to their age. Similarly the poets who were writing of Lincoln in the United States during the war called in all seriousness upon his shade to look down with pity on a strife-torn world. The general tendency was to call up Lincoln's name in behalf of every movement and project, with the result that one's ears were tired as were those of the nameless Athenian who was sick of hearing Aristides called 'the just.'

Nathaniel Wright Stephenson's *Lincoln* (1922) is, more than the biographies hitherto discussed, a study of the character that made the statesman and literary artist, rather than a study of the statesman and literary artist. The subtitle may, perhaps, signify wherein it differs: 'An Account of his Personal Life, Especially of its Springs of Action as Revealed and Deepened by the Ordeal of War.' Stephenson works, not in the traditional biographical or historical manner, but with the feeling of an artist toward his materials. Perhaps 'imagination' and 'insight' are good words to describe the qualities which chiefly characterize this work, but possibly it is, as some may claim, just another interpretation, better than most and written with warmth and gusto. The reader perceives, while he reads, that Stephenson is no mere chronicler, but that he has lived in and with Lincoln until he has come naturally to tell a story which is his own as well as his character's. Whether this Lincoln is the final explanation we may doubt, but it is easily the most appealing study of character that has yet been done.

Lincoln's literary expression is the best key to his character; so, apparently, Stephenson thinks. Lincoln is first of all an artist in temperament. His view of life is in all essentials poetic. Perhaps therein lies the explanation of what we shall so often notice in these pages — the living of a legend or a myth. Throughout Lincoln's life in Illinois we see the evidence that inwardly he differed vastly from the ugly, humorous country lawyer. Every accomplishment of his life seems to have come from an inward inspiration, and for years there are lulls which are fraught with pathos in their descent into the depths of futility.

In politics as in the practice of law Lincoln is the artist, and as an artist he has the defects of his qualities. Systematic study is unknown to him. He has little conception of economic laws or of the science of government, but he has a keen perception into human nature and a grasp of moral principles, combined with a power of creative expression. The creative artist becomes evident early in literary expression, but it is not until he has been president for some months that the artist as an executive becomes apparent. Under the necessity imposed by circumstance Lincoln emerges. In successive struggles with Congress, his Cabinet, and his generals he gains a growing confidence in himself and his ability. He begins to translate his intuitive knowledge into action and free himself, more and more, from subservience to advisers. 'The outer and inner Lincoln had fused. He was now a coherent personality, masterful in spite of gentleness, with his own peculiar fashion of self-reliance, having a policy of his own devising, his colors nailed upon the masthead.' The dreamer is transformed into a man of action.

The fusion of the outer and inner person was the result of a profound interior change. Those elements of mysticism which were in him from the first, which had gleamed darkly through such deep overshadowing, were at last established in their permanent form. The political tension had been matched by a spiritual tension with personal sorrow as the connecting link. In a word, he had found his religion.

Henceforward Lincoln achieves each successive goal set before him by what means he can, relying upon his faith and his intuitive knowledge. Even at the end his unfinished task of creating a sentiment of charity and brotherhood is so nearly complete that the vindictives, so long his enemies, cannot enjoy more than a brief triumph after his death. 'The transitoriness of their evil triumph, the eventual rally of the nation against them, was the final victory of the spirit of Lincoln.'

At the last there comes victory and the final achievement of his task and with it a change in Lincoln:

> His mood underwent a mysterious change. It was serene and yet charged with a peculiar grave loftiness not quite like any phase of him his friends had known hitherto.... It was as if the seer in the trance had finally passed beyond his trance; and had faced smilingly toward his earthly comrades, imagining he was to return to them; unaware that somehow his emergence was not in the ordinary course of nature; that in it was an accent of the inexplicable, something which the others caught and at which they trembled; though they knew not why.

Thus Stephenson deals with the mystic Lincoln. Were a poet writing history to his own liking, he could not much improve the conception or the manner. Stephenson acquires biographical unity by the use of the key-word 'artist.' Yet does this solve the problem of Lincoln? Perhaps for some people.

IV

Within the last decade three biographers have contributed much new material and have done especial service in the critical examination of many questionable statements. Although their names will appear often in later pages, some brief mention may be made here. William E. Barton in his numerous books has laid to rest some of the popular fables and controversies. His research has established something like order in Lincoln genealogy and has reduced to the bare facts some of the popular legends, such as, the paternity legends, the Ann Rutledge legend, the William Scott episode, and Lincoln's infidelity. Carl Sandburg's *Abraham Lincoln: The Prairie Years* (1926) gives an adequate literary treatment of the early life of Lincoln against its proper background. Sandburg has realized what others have not — that knowledge of the early life of Lincoln is based so largely on the popular opinion of those who knew him that if any of it is to be credited, all of it has the same claim to worth until proved false. Albert J. Beveridge's biography (1928) covers the same period in Lincoln's life in an entirely different and more scholarly manner.

In spite of the good intentions of many biographers, the early life of Lincoln never received understanding treatment until more than fifty years after his death. Carl Sandburg's biography gave for the first time the story of Lincoln's rise from poverty and obscurity in a manner that comprehended the true epic significance of the subject matter. There is much of the obviously legendary material, and the spirit of the Lincoln legend pervades the entire work. It is the epic of the prairie combined with the epic of Lincoln, and they are for once successfully made into one. Sandburg does not hesitate to throw in a free-verse poem whenever the mere prose of narration is unsuited to the occasion. The growing corn of the prairie possibly meant much to Lincoln, and in the story of his life the poetry of the corn gives a contact with reality which the ordinary methods of biography do not attain. Sandburg apparently believes in the soundness of folklore when taken *en masse* as evidence of the true Lincoln; and, although the student may have doubts about the verbal accuracy of many accounts, when he has finished the whole, he is impressed with the truth as well as the beauty of the story. It is not, however, the kind of study which will serve as an authority on disputed points.

There have been those biographers and poets who saw, or thought they saw, epic material in the early life of Lincoln. They have failed to grasp or present it, chiefly because they have attempted to make it epical in some classical fashion. Other biographers have seen nothing except the commonplace and morbid and have presented either a bald or a softened account, both incorrect. Sandburg knows the prairie and the people that Lincoln knew. For him there is not so much incongruity in Lincoln as other biographers have found, because he knows and understands the Middle West. Much of the misunderstanding of Lincoln has been due to exaggeration of superficial matters.

In 1928 came Albert J. Beveridge's biography, which gives an account of Lincoln up to 1858. It is the best critical examination of all the sources from which the early life of Lincoln has been pieced together, part by part, by many biographers from the widely diverging Holland and Herndon on down to the present. Covering the same period as Sandburg's study, it offers just what

Sandburg's book does not, and taken together these two works give, respectively, an adequate scholarly and an adequate literary treatment. It is worthy of notice that they result after all in much the same Lincoln. The conclusion is that the Lincoln of Illinois was in himself one of the most interesting characters that our country has produced. Had he never become president, his life would have been one of our most enigmatical, most human, and most beloved sectional memories.

Beveridge went over the original manuscripts from which Herndon's biography was compiled; he visited the Lincoln country and sifted the local legends; and he attempted to include in his work every fact that research could uncover. This method combined with the machinery of scholarly footnoting makes the study, as far as it goes, the one best authority. Beveridge's theory that 'facts when justly arranged interpret themselves' explains his work well. He does not add up his facts and discoveries and draw conclusions as much as one would like to have him do; but he reasons well, perhaps, that in the end his readers will be as far from agreeing with him as with each other, except in generally admiring Lincoln.

Naturally enough, considering the difficulties, of the three outstanding biographies, each falls short of being the *magnum opus* which we have awaited so long. Nicolay and Hay did not comprehend the significance of Lincoln's early life in either its poetry or its fact. Sandburg and Beveridge do not carry it on. Perhaps we may yet hope for a definitive work by one man covering both periods.

V

In all of the biographies one may search in vain for an entirely acceptable conception which embodies both the private and the public Lincoln. Agreement is far more commonly found in the assessments of the public Lincoln. After all, as Charnwood has put it, Lincoln proved a very useful president and accomplished certain ends, which, even though one may not agree that they were right, have once and for all settled the questions of slavery and the Union.

In considering Lincoln's purposes and actions, there are two points of view from which one never sees the same result; namely, that of the sovereign and sacred individuality of the State which Lincoln supposedly destroyed, and the sovereignty of the Federal Government. There are still many who maintain that though established by force of arms Lincoln's entire political philosophy was wrong. To their arguments there is no answer, except that generally Lincoln's position has been sustained by opinion. Then, too, the South's position on the issue of slavery still beclouds the question when we are told that Lincoln might have prevented the Civil War by designating, during the fitful months that followed his election, his position as open to compromise. All questions of moral issues aside, still Lincoln's position was one of political fairness. He had been elected by a portion of the people violently opposed to the extension of slavery. He was himself opposed to it. On what grounds save weakness could he have deserted his position? Expediency Lincoln never failed to consider, but the inexpediency of compromise was established by the fact that what little support Lincoln had was dependent upon his avowed opposition to the extension of slavery. To hold that he might have pacified the fire-eating element in the South is, of course, as foolish as to contend that he might have stopped the frantic chorus of Abolitionism.

In spite of all the controversy and conflict, Lincoln has steadily risen in the opinion of his biographers as a man who surmounted the difficulties of his task and solved the problems of his day. His methods are not, however, so easily agreed upon; to some they were eccentric but farsighted; to others they were simply an astute brand of opportunism.

All criticism of the public Lincoln turns eventually on one question: Was he a mere opportunist? Can his management of national affairs be interpreted as an abject following of the course of events with no further view than to preserve his own political head? There is a timeliness about all of his important moves that is, to say the least, remarkable. He seemed to many of his contemporaries like a ship's cable that always swings easily with the tide, but holds fast at both ends. Thus the radicals never believed him. He seemed to be playing fast and loose, and always luck turned with him at the critical points of his administration. Lord Charnwood, in an article which appeared in the *Anglo-French Review* in 1920, undertakes to discuss the problem and arrives, like most of the later critics, at the conclusion that Lincoln cannot be intelligently explained as an opportunist. Some of his observations are worth quoting:

> The strength, of which many signs will become apparent upon any candid examination of this part of his conduct, is not that of a man with some kind of special faculty for administrative office, or with quick intuition into novel circumstances and into men whom he had not studied; it is the

slightly eccentric but none the less effective strength of a man in whom ordinary candor, patience, and desire to do the right thing, however it might appear to others, habitually rose to that level just above our ordinary reach, which amounts to heroism and genius.

. . . .

It is pretty evident that he proved a very serviceable president; he kept the North together; but his services have been attributed to opportunism of a very common kind and the cheap and negative virtue of the sort of man who can never plunge.... Of the author of the speeches and sayings which make Lincoln familiar to most of us it is only common sense to expect something very far removed from common politics in the main motive of his policy.

. . . .

There is indeed no alternative to this relatively disparaging view of him (as at the highest a second-class statesman, a shrewd and a conscientious opportunist and nothing more) except the extreme opposite view which ascribes to him an originality, an undeviating consistency, and a philosophic grasp of facts in relation to a deeply thought-out principle, such as few others, if any, of the world's great statesmen have shown.

This latter is my own view.

In dealing with the same question Nathaniel Wright Stephenson arrives at a similar conclusion, but with a more direct consideration of the elements which seem to prove it.

It is difficult for the most objective historian to deal with such questions without obtruding his personal views, but there is nothing merely individual in recording the fact that the steady drift of opinion has been away from the conception of Lincoln as an opportunist. What once caused him to be thus conceived appears now to have been a failure to comprehend intelligently the nature of his undertaking. More and more, the tendency nowadays is to conceive his career as one of those few instances in which the precise faculties needed to solve a particular problem were called into play at exactly the critical moment. Our confusions with regard to Lincoln have grown out of our failure to appreciate the singularity of the American people, and their ultra-singularity during the years in which he lived. It remains to be seen hereafter what strange elements of sensibility, of waywardness, of lack of imagination, of undisciplined ardor, of selfishness, of deceitfulness, of treachery, combined with heroic ideality, made up the character of that complex populace which it was Lincoln's task to control. But he did more than control it: he somehow compounded much of it into something like a unit. To measure Lincoln's achievement in this respect, two things must be remembered: on the one hand, his task was not as arduous as it might have been, because the most intellectual part of the North had definitely committed itself either irretrievably for, or irreconcilably against, his policy. Lincoln, therefore, did not have to trouble himself with this portion of the population. On the other hand, that part which he had to master included such emotional rhetoricians as Horace Greeley; such fierce zealots as Henry Winter Davis of Maryland, who made him trouble indeed, and Benjamin Wade; such military egoists as McClellan and Pope; such crafty double-dealers as his own Secretary of the Treasury; such astute grafters as Cameron; such miserable creatures as certain powerful capitalists who sacrificed his army to their own lust for profits filched from army contracts.

The wonder of Lincoln's achievement is that he contrived at last to extend his hold over all these diverse elements; that he persuaded some, outwitted others, and overcame them all. The subtlety of this task would have ruined any statesman of the driving sort. Explain Lincoln by any theory you will, his personality was the keystone of the Northern arch; subtract it, and the arch falls. The popular element being as complex and powerful as it was, how could the presiding statesman have mastered the situation if he had not been of so peculiar a sort that he could influence all these diverse and powerful interests, slowly, by degrees, without heat, without the imperative note, almost in silence, with the universal, enfolding irresistibility of the gradual things in nature, of the sun and the rain. Such was the genius of Lincoln — all but passionless, yet so quiet that one cannot but believe in the great depth of his nature.

We are, even today, far from a definitive understanding of Lincoln's statecraft, but there is perhaps justification for venturing upon prophecy. The farther from him we get and the more clearly we see him in perspective, the more we shall realize his creative influence upon his party. A Lincoln who is the moulder of events and the great creator of public opinion will emerge at last into clear view. In the Lincoln of his ultimate biographer there will be more of iron than of a less enduring metal in the figure of the Lincoln of present tradition. Though none of his gentleness will disappear, there will be more emphasis placed upon his firmness, and upon such episodes as that of December, 1860, when his single will turned the scale against compromise; upon his steadiness in the defeat of his party at the polls in 1862; or his overruling of the will of Congress in the summer of 1864 on the question of reconstruction; of his attitude in the autumn of that year when he believed that he was losing his second election. Behind all his gentleness, his slowness, behind his sadness, there will eventually appear an inflexible purpose, strong as steel, unwavering as fate.

But we have already seen how clairvoyant Stephenson becomes when he tries to analyze this man that did

> bestride the narrow world
> Like a Colossus.

The more fully Lincoln's varied career is traced and the magic of his words studied, the more his genius grows and passes beyond each interpretation. He cannot be explained by the rule of thumb which fits a Daniel Webster or a Stephen A. Douglas. There was in him none of the energy or the magnetism which traditionally belongs to the hero. When the interpreter is through, he says, in effect — that man was not a genius; he was genius.

ABRAHAM LINCOLN IN 1860

John T. Morse, Jr., concluded his biography with a statement of what he believed he had accomplished, and perhaps it might yet fit the sum total of Lincoln biography. He wrote:

> For myself, having drawn the picture of the man as I see him, though knowing well that I am far from seeing him all, and still farther from seeing inwardly through him, yet I know that I cannot help it by additional comments. Very much more than is the case with other men, Lincoln means different things to different persons, and the aspect which he presents depends to an unusual degree upon the moral and mental individuality of the observer. Perhaps this is due to the breadth and variety of his own nature. A friend once said to me: Lincoln was like Shakespeare, in that he seemed to run through the whole gamut of human nature.

VI

In addition to the biographies there is a mass of popular narrative which has grown up about Lincoln and has considerably influenced the conception of the hero. These tales are of two varieties — stories supposedly told by Lincoln and anecdotes about him. The first group is a combination of stories which Lincoln possibly told and tales which have been credited to him. As a story-teller he was famous wherever he went. There is abundant testimony in the biographies and reminiscences to his facility for mimicry and impersonation and to the fact that he never forgot a joke which he heard. He was habitually reminded of some story when he saw an opportunity to point his argument or to avoid a difficult situation without antagonizing an importunate office-seeker or self-appointed adviser. Often the stories were very broad, but even those who testify to their broadness make it clear that he told them only to illustrate a point. This reputation as a humorist is the basis for what has become through the years the legend of a Rabelaisian Aesop. The second group of stories — those about Lincoln — range from the folk-tales of the wild frontier days of cock-fighting and wrestling matches to the saintly stories of the martyr's later days.

Although most of the biographies contain a considerable amount of this material and no biography is entirely free of it, it is best represented by books which claim to be nothing more than Lincoln yarns and stories. Early collections of jokes appeared before Lincoln's death, purporting to be Lincoln's, though most of those included were certainly not his. His fame as a story-teller merely gave enterprising publishers an opportunity to sell their joke-books. After the assassination newspapers and magazines were continually printing reminiscences which varied in length from a paragraph to several pages. These, together with the stories credited to Lincoln, were collected from time to time and published in book form. The most interesting collection of both varieties was made by A. K. McClure and published as '*Abe*' *Lincoln's Yarns and Stories* (1901). The best collection of stories about Lincoln, S. G. Pratt's *Lincoln in Story*, was published in the same year.

In more or less original form, these are the legends that have been used over and over in poetry, fiction, and drama. Interest in these stories has become now somewhat a thing of the past. From Lincoln's death their popularity grew until about 1909, when the Lincoln Centennial brought out every old story from its nook. Since then interest has steadily waned as Lincoln has become more and more fixed in his dignified posture as America's greatest statesman and leader.

VII

I have already spoken of the popular deification of Lincoln which took place after the melodramatic assassination. The part which the poets played in eulogizing the martyr has been barely hinted. In addition to the Virginian poet Christopher Pearse Cranch, whose sonnet has been quoted, there were poets in every section of the country who published verses in memory of Lincoln. In the volume of *Poetical Tributes* published in 1865 there are represented poets from every Northern State and from seven Southern States, not to mention numerous others in Canada, England, and France. Most of the better known American poets of the day wrote and read their tributes along with the host of lesser hero-worshiping versifiers.

Walt Whitman and James Russell Lowell wrote the poems which are still admired above the rest. Whitman's 'O Captain! My Captain!' and 'When Lilacs Last in the Door-Yard Bloom'd' were composed shortly after Lincoln's death. The first is probably the most popular poem that praises Lincoln as the statesman and leader, the captain of the ship of state. The second is a personal elegy in which Whitman expresses the sorrow and hysteria that swept over the nation —

For the sweetest, wisest soul of all my days and lands.

Lowell's tribute was written during the summer of 1865 as a part of the 'Harvard Commemoration Ode.' The Ode was read on July 21, but the passage on Lincoln was added later. The most famous line is the last, which praises Lincoln as

New birth of our new soil, the first American.

Of the New England poets several besides Lowell wrote

tributes. Oliver Wendell Holmes read a hymn 'For the Services in Memory of Abraham Lincoln' at the services held in Boston on June 1. As a Lincoln poem it is insignificant, but as a hymn it expresses well the righteous horror of New England at the crime of the assassin. Herman Melville, who had forsaken his novels during the war to write war poems, wrote 'The Martyr' in which he reflects with satisfaction that, though Lincoln is dead,

> The avenger takes his place,
> Who in righteousness shall do
> What the heavens call him to.

William Cullen Bryant's 'The Death of Abraham Lincoln' summarized Lincoln in the last stanza:

> Pure was thy life; its bloody close
> Hath placed thee with the sons of light,
> Among the noblest host of those
> Who perished in the cause of right.

The younger New England poets were represented by Richard Henry Stoddard, Edmund Clarence Stedman, and Henry Howard Brownell. Stoddard's poem 'Abraham Lincoln: An Horatian Ode' is one of the better poems among this early group. It is quite different from the merely pretty verse which he habitually wrote and attains occasional dignity as it describes the funeral train and praises the mighty dead:

> Ay! And his genius put to scorn
> The proudest in the purple born,
> Whose wisdom never grew
> To what, untaught, he knew.

Stedman, war correspondent for the New York *World*, author of many war poems, and later stockbroker, poet, and critic of leisure, wrote a sonnet extolling Lincoln as a second Christ who died for his people:

> And when the morning opened Heaven's gate
> There passed the whitest soul a nation knew.

Brownell, one of the most popular war poets, whom Oliver Wendell Holmes dubbed 'our Battle Laureate,' wrote a lengthy poem which recounted in martial strains Lincoln's review of the Grand Army and then effectively described in contrast the ghost of Lincoln reviewing the army of the dead.[1]

It is impracticable to enumerate here all the poets and poems of Lincoln during this year, but a few others should be mentioned briefly. George Henry Boker, a Pennsylvania dramatist and poet, read his 'Our Heroic Themes' before the Harvard Phi Beta Kappa Society within a few days after Lowell had read his 'Commemoration Ode.' Julia Ward Howe, the author of 'The Battle Hymn of the Republic,' wrote several poems praising Lincoln and scorning Booth. Robert Henry Newell, better known as Orpheus C. Kerr, wrote at length to show

> 'Twas needed — the name of a martyr sublime,
> To vindicate God in that terrible time.

John James Piatt, an Indiana poet who had written a good Lincoln poem in 1862, 'Stern be the Pilot in the Dreadful Hour,' wrote 'The Dear President,' a poem not quite so saccharine as its title.

When the feverish admiration which inspired so many poets to write of Lincoln had subsided, a Western poet

---

[1] Bret Harte has a poem of similar plan and execution, 'A Second Review of the Grand Army.'

Edward Rowland Sill wrote 'The Dead President' (1867) in which he asked well:

> Were there no crowns on earth,.
> No evergreen to wreath a hero wreath,
> That he must pass beyond the gates of death,
> Our hero, our slain hero, to be crowned?

Although there is no year which has since produced so many Lincoln poems as 1865, there is no year in which many have not been written. There is a stream of Lincoln verse which has been running steadily ever since his death. To mention only a few of the more important poems which appeared from year to year until 1900: there is Bayard Taylor's 'Gettysburg Ode' (1869), which paraphrased Lincoln's 'Gettysburg Address,' and *The Ballad of Lincoln* (1870) by the same author; John Greenleaf Whittier's 'Emancipation Group' (1879) read at the unveiling of the replica of Thomas Ball's statue in Park Square, Boston; Rufus Blanchard's *Abraham Lincoln; the Type of American Genius* (1882), a long allegory depicting the spiritual forces which moulded Lincoln; a heavy elegy read at Lincoln's tomb on the nineteenth anniversary of the assassination, 'Abraham Lincoln' (1884), by Samuel Francis Smith, the author of 'America'; the two sonnets 'On the Life Mask of Abraham Lincoln' (1886) and 'To the Spirit of Abraham Lincoln' (1888) by Richard Watson Gilder, who succeeded Lincoln's biographer J. G. Holland as editor of the *Century*; the passages on Lincoln in the 'Columbian Ode' (1892) by Harriet Monroe, an Illinois poet and editor of *Poetry: a Magazine of Verse*; 'At Lincoln's Grave' (1894) by Maurice Thompson, a Confederate veteran and Hoosier poet who is better known as the author of *Alice of Old Vincennes*; Lyman Whitney Allen's 'Abraham Lincoln,' an historical poem which was awarded the New York *Herald* prize in 1895; and a second poem, 'Lincoln's Birthday' (1898), by Richard Henry Stoddard. These are a few of the better poems written during this period. In spirit they agree with the sonnet by Richard Watson Gilder in recognizing Lincoln as the patron saint of America.

TO THE SPIRIT OF ABRAHAM LINCOLN
(Reunion at Gettysburg, 1888)

Shade of our greatest, O look down today!
    Here the long, dread midsummer battle roared,
    And brother in brother plunged the accursed sword; —
    Here foe meets foe once more in proud array
Yet not as once to harry and to slay
    But to strike hands, and with sublime accord
    Weep tears heroic for the souls that soared
    Quick from earth's carnage to the starry way.
Each fought for what he deemed the people's good,
    And proved his bravery with his offered life,
    And sealed his honor with his outpoured blood;
But the eternal did direct the strife,
    And on this sacred field one patriot host
    Now calls thee father — dear majestic ghost!

At the beginning of the twentieth century new developments are apparent in Lincoln poetry. The publication of the biographies by Herndon and Nicolay and Hay gave to the poets, as to other biographers, the first comprehensive collection of Lincoln materials. As critical biographers attempted to draw a consistent picture of Lincoln from these sources, so the poets realizing the wealth of materials began to write the epics of Lincoln. The material in Herndon was of especial use. It was with the frontier phase of Lincoln's life that many of the poets were chiefly concerned. Interest in the frontier was becoming more apparent in literature in general. As has already been noted, F. J. Turner's essay 'The Significance of the Frontier in American History' (1893) had given a new bias to historical interpretation. The revival of the historical novel brought the frontier much into vogue in fiction.

Edwin Markham's 'Lincoln, the Man of the People' (1901), is the first good poem of the new group. Following up the strain of praise begun by Lowell and Richard Henry Stoddard, Markham praised Lincoln as the symbol of Americanism and democracy, the product of new forces working in a new world, the elemental genius of America —

> A Man to match the mountains and the sea.

The group of epic poets begins with the publication of Ernest L. Staples's *A Man of Destiny* (1902). This poem, as uneven as it is long, succeeds in giving the story of Lincoln coherence by exalting the theme of Abolition. Lincoln is singled out by divine Providence to liberate the slaves and preserve the Union. The early books, the matter of which is from Herndon, glorify the trials and hardships of the frontier in heroic measures and emphasize the prophetic mission of Lincoln by all manner of idealization. A second epic of considerable length, *The Burden Bearer* (1908), by Francis H. Williams, is generally better verse than its predecessor, but is not so compactly executed. The early books give an ideal treatment of the frontier and a good conception of Lincoln as the growing Titan of the time. In the later books happenings become chaotic, and Lincoln is lost in the resounding praise of battles and generals. It is neither an epic of Lincoln nor an epic of the war, but smatterings of both printed altogether. The title is significant of the Atlantean Lincoln, whose shoulders are, to paraphrase Milton, fit to bear the weight of a mighty government.

A SURVEY OF LINCOLN LITERATURE

The Lincoln Centenary, February 12, 1909, brought out a host of poems, as well as tributes of every other variety. Poets who had written of Lincoln before wrote of him again. Julia Ward Howe read the last of her several tributes to the martyr at a centenary celebration held in Symphony Hall, Boston. Edwin Markham wrote another poem 'The Coming of Lincoln,' in which the birth of Lincoln is paralleled with the birth of Christ. Bliss Carman wrote of 'The Man of Peace' to whose tomb men journey as of old to the tombs of saints —

> Where men may come as to a shrine
> And temple of the good,
> To be made sweet and strong of heart
> In Lincoln's brotherhood.

Percy MacKaye read his lengthy, solemn 'Centenary Ode' before the Brooklyn Institute of Arts and Sciences. The poem passes from the comparison of the births of Lincoln and Christ through a saga of the longshank boy to a eulogy of the hero as

> The mystic demi-god of common man —
> The patriarch of peoples still to be,
> Blending all visions of the promised land
> In one Apocalypse.

James Oppenheim's 'The Lincoln Child' in a similar vein traces the growth of America's prophet and finds in his life the solution to human ills —

> Oh, to pour love through deeds —
> To be as Lincoln was! —

Edwin Arlington Robinson celebrated 'The Master' as one of the enigmatical mysteries that can be worshiped, but never told.

> The love, the grandeur, and the fame
> Are bounded by the world alone;

The calm, the smouldering, and the flame
Of awful patience were his own:
With him they are forever flown
Past all our fond self-shadowings,
Wherein we cumber the Unknown
As with inept Icarian wings.

Several poems were written comparing Lincoln with Darwin and Felix Mendelssohn, who were likewise born in 1809. The numerous memorials and statues called forth other poems. Nancy Hanks was celebrated as the Madonna of the Backwoods, and Hodgenville, Kentucky, as the American Bethlehem. Magazines devoted entire issues to Lincoln. Some idea of the enormous amount of tribute may be had from the fact that forty large volumes of newspaper clippings were collected by the Chicago Historical Society during the Centennial. There was no abatement in the steady flow of Lincoln verse after the Centennial. Another epic poet, Denton J. Snider, published from 1910 to 1914 four ponderous poems of a 'Lincoln Tetralogy' which narrated in many varieties of verse the spiritual epic of the centuries.[1] George W. Bell, a far better poet, published in 1913 a long interpretative poem, *Abraham Lincoln: A Poetical Interpretation*, in which Lincoln is extolled as a great philosopher and spiritual leader.

The so-called 'new movement' in American poetry came just before the World War. One of its chief characteristics naturally was an exalted sense of nationalism. Amy Lowell described it in *Tendencies in Modern American Poetry* (1917) by commenting: 'Hyphens are submerged in the solid over printing of the word "America." We

---

[1] These works are as follows: *Lincoln in the Black Hawk War* (1910), *Lincoln and Ann Rutledge* (1912), *Lincoln in the White House* (1913), *Lincoln at Richmond* (1914).

are no more colonies of this or that other land, but ourselves, different from all other peoples whatsoever.' In this new movement Lincoln was recognized by nearly every major poet as the one American and was glorified into a symbol of nationalism and democracy.

Edwin Arlington Robinson, from whom Amy Lowell traces the new movement, had already written of Lincoln in 1909. In 1914 Witter Bynner published his 'A Farmer Remembers Lincoln.' Vachel Lindsay's 'Abraham Lincoln Walks at Midnight,' published in the same year, solemnly lamented that the ghost of the great American democrat could not rest while the tyrants of Europe sent their peasants to war.

James Oppenheim's second Lincoln poem, 'Memories of Whitman and Lincoln' (1916), wove together the praise of the two American brothers who guard the land in the strength of democracy. Edgar Lee Masters's best Lincoln poem is 'Ann Rutledge,' which appeared in *Spoon River Anthology* (1915). He has others, the most notable being 'Autochthonous' (1916), which compares, as several other poets have done, Lincoln and Darwin, and emphasizes Lincoln's common American qualities. There is little of the legendary Lincoln in Masters's poems, if 'Ann Rutledge' be excepted. John Gould Fletcher's rhetorical 'Lincoln' (1917) followed in the trend of Robinson's 'The Master,' making Lincoln even less a man and more a national symbol. Carl Sandburg's *Cornhuskers* (1918) contained several Lincoln poems, none of which are notable, with the possible exception of 'A Tall Man,' which is not certainly about Lincoln; although 'Fire Logs' is a delicate and tender tribute to Lincoln's mother Nancy Hanks. Arthur Guiterman's 'He Leads Us Still' (1919) is well titled. All of these poets have adopted Lincoln as the hero who best exemplifies their conception of America. If there is something which they admire that was not in the living Lincoln, they endow him with the quality *gratis*. His real genius they admire as typically American. His philosophy of freedom and equality, charity and justice, love and tenderness, they extol.

Since 1920 poems which deal with Lincoln have not been generally so notable. Edwin Markham has added two to his list, 'Lincoln Lives' and 'Ann Rutledge,' both published in 1926. Stephen Vincent Benét's *John Brown's Body* (1927) is perhaps the most significant poem in which Lincoln figures since Robinson's 'The Master,' but Lincoln is not Benét's main theme. Sandburg's *Good Morning, America* (1928) has one good poem on Lincoln, 'Lavender Lilies,' which evokes the memory of Lincoln as a plea for charity and amity between white men and negroes. *An Epic Trilogy* (1929) by Lyman Whitney Allen contains an expanded version of a poem first published in 1895, which has been noticed above. A sonnet sequence *Lincoln Remembers* (1930) by Edna Davis Romig contains some good pieces. The number of poems being written has not decreased, however, and the popularity of Lincoln as a poetic subject is overshadowed only by his popularity as a subject for biography and fiction.

Poems about Lincoln have been collected and published in anthologies from time to time. The earliest of these was the volume *Poetical Tributes* published in 1865. The best are *The Praise of Lincoln* (1911) edited by A. Dallas Williams and *The Book of Lincoln* (1919) edited by Mary Wright-Davis. As anthologies go, these contain poems of more than ordinary merit, but they are worth notice chiefly for the testimony they bear to the interest in Lincoln. When a hero has attained the dignity of more than a half-dozen anthologies composed solely of poems about him, he has enjoyed more fame than most of his composers. Probably no European except Napoleon, and of course the great legendary figures, has had more good poems, or more bad ones, written about him.

VIII

In 1901 there appeared the first notable Lincoln novel, Winston Churchill's *The Crisis*. Novelists had been much slower to find Lincoln than the poets. Only two early novels of any merit had presented him as a character, *The McVeys* (1888) by Joseph Kirkland and *The Graysons* (1888) by Edward Eggleston. In neither novel a major character, Lincoln moves through a few chapters in each, a vague, elusive, mysterious figure, whose very appearance is uncertain. Both novels are stories of the early days in Illinois. Eggleston does not give, as in *The Hoosier Schoolmaster*, a realistic picture of frontier life. Perhaps it is significant that the story was written at Nervi, near Genoa. Furthermore, the plot is founded on the romantic legend of how Lincoln procured the acquittal of Duff Armstrong in the famous 'almanac trial,' on the evidence that the moon was not in a position to enable the chief witness to see the act which he described.[1] Considering the tendency to realism in Eggleston's other novels of the Middle West, the story of Lincoln is oddly romantic. In the pre-

[1] It is interesting to note that this story is in the biographies, somewhat trimmed down by the investigations of W. E. Barton, with very little emphasis on the use of the almanac. Professor Jay B. Hubbell of Duke University tells me that the same story of the almanac is told of Patrick Henry in some places in Virginia.

face the author explains his attitude toward his materials in words that may fit the attitude of the later novelists and of some biographers:

> I could not by any possibility have verified the story I had received about 1867 from one of Lincoln's old neighbors. To have investigated the accuracy of my version of the anecdote would have been, indeed, to fly in the face and eyes of Providence, for popular tradition is itself an artist rough-hewing a story to the novelist's hands.

In *The Crisis* Lincoln appears first as the rough, crude frontier lawyer who tells Rabelaisian stories in the height of his glory to a group of politicians gathered in a dingy hotel room. One of the characters describes him as the ugliest man imaginable. The reader is assured that in spite of this roughness Lincoln is a noble soul, and before many pages are passed the traditional melancholy of the martyr begins to settle about Lincoln, enveloping him completely in a nimbus of sanctity at the Freeport Debate with Douglas. In the later chapters he has completely changed into the piteous martyr — sad Father Abraham whose heart was pierced daily by the ingratitude of his people while he strove on, trusting in divine guidance, in his work of saving the nation and liberating the slaves.

After *The Crisis* the novel of the most literary merit is Francis Grierson's *The Valley of Shadows* (1909). Grierson presents with romantic imagination the story of Illinois life in the fifties when the prairie was illuminated by the genius of Lincoln and the people were stirred by a mystic impulse to rise up against slavery.

In the revival of the historical novel in which Churchill participated there came several other Lincoln narratives, the most important of which is Thomas Dixon's *The Southerner* (1913).[1] In an earlier novel by the same author, *The Clansman* (1905), which was later adapted to the cinema by D. W. Griffith as *The Birth of a Nation*, Lincoln had figured very briefly as the merciful President whose love for the South was in direct contrast with the hatred of the vindictive Reconstructionists. *The Southerner* Dixon wrote to develop the statement made by Walt Whitman that 'Lincoln, though grafted on the West, is essentially, in personnel and character, a Southern contribution,' which is quoted by Dixon on the title page. By making Lincoln a Southern gentleman, Dixon at once vindicates his hero and Southern chivalry. Dixon is himself a Southerner, *bien entendu*.

Short stories are scattered through the February issues of many periodicals from year to year. Most of them are based on a significant legend or an important incident in Lincoln's life. Thus 'The Perfect Tribute' (1906) by Mary R. S. Andrews is the story of what a wounded Confederate said of Lincoln's 'Gettysburg Address,' and 'The Counsel Assigned' (1912) by the same author tells a story of Lincoln's self-sacrifice in order to assist a poor youth arraigned for murder. Elsie Singmaster's 'Gettysburg Stories' (1907–13) make the most of the romance that hallows the famous dedication service. Eleanor Atkinson's 'Lincoln's Love Story' (1909) is a sentimental account of Lincoln's love for Ann Rutledge. Honoré Willsie Morrow's 'Benefits Forgot' (1917) is a romance of Lincoln's kindness to a mother who wrote to him asking about her son from whom she had not heard after his enlist-

[1] Some of the less significant novels of this type are H. Butterworth's *In the Boyhood of Lincoln* (1892), M. H. Catherwood's *Spanish Peggy* (1899), L. Boyd's *The Sorrows of Nancy* (1899), H. Green's *A Lincoln Conscript* (1909), and O. M. Gale's and H. M. Wheeler's *The Knight of the Wilderness* (1909).

ment. These stories are typical of the many others that may be found in the bibliography.

Irving Bacheller's *A Man for the Ages* (1919) presented for the first time in fiction a realistic picture of the strong, awkward Lincoln who split rails and did odd jobs around New Salem, Illinois, during the early eighteen-thirties. Although there is a general preponderance of realism, the romantic creeps into the picture in the form of Lincoln's elemental wisdom. Even in these early years the hero is a sage who speaks in parables. Being an Easterner, Bacheller draws his Lincoln with Yankee outlines. A later novel by the same author, *Father Abraham* (1925), presents Lincoln as President with a superabundance of homely qualities and hardly as much wisdom as he evinced in the New Salem days.

Maria Thompson Davies, a Kentucky novelist, gave in *The Matrix* (1920) the romance of Nancy Hanks and Thomas Lincoln. Dixon had portrayed Nancy in the prologue to *The Southerner* as an unusual woman, frail, sad, and mystical. *The Matrix*, based on the more romantic Kentucky legends collected by the author, presented Nancy as a strong, self-reliant woman combining the qualities of a modern athlete and a Lucy Stoner.

Another novelist, Bernie Babcock, has written four romantic novels on different phases of Lincoln from his courtship of Ann Rutledge to his peregrinations as a spirit who haunts the American Wandering Jew, John Wilkes Booth, who, according to the story, was not captured and killed by the authorities, but has wandered over the surface of the earth tormented by the memory of his deed.[1]

[1] Babcock's novels are as follows: *The Soul of Ann Rutledge* (1919), *The Soul of Abe Lincoln* (1923), *Booth and the Spirit of Lincoln* (1925), *Lincoln's Mary and the Babies* (1929).

A SURVEY OF LINCOLN LITERATURE

The most significant novels since 1920 compose the 'Lincoln Trilogy' by Honoré Willsie Morrow. *Forever Free* (1927) is a novel of the first two years of Lincoln's administration and the Emancipation Proclamation, from which the author takes the title. *With Malice Toward None* (1928) carries the action up to the second inauguration. *The Last Full Measure* (1930) recounts the last few weeks of Lincoln's life. These novels may be called dramatized biography, and in many respects give the most living picture of Lincoln to be found in fiction. Historical accuracy in dealing with the major figures is approximate. In the first novel of the series inaccuracies are more damaging than in the latter two because of the melodrama for which they are introduced. Although Lincoln as he appears in the first novel is a lovable, ordinary, fatherly man, he becomes gradually transfigured throughout the trilogy. His spiritual halo becomes most radiant just before the assassination, during the period of victory and achievement.

Although there are a number of dramas in which Lincoln is a character, there are few that have value either as stage plays or as literature. John Drinkwater's *Abraham Lincoln: A Play* (1919) is the only one which is meritorious in both respects. Plays written earlier than Drinkwater's are either laborious or ephemeral. Only a few need be mentioned. The earliest is *The Royal Ape* (1863), a satire in blank verse and heroic couplets which was published in Richmond, Virginia. Most of the early plays are melodramas replete with spies and plotting assassins of which the following are examples: *Assassination* (1879) by D. C. Vestal, *Madame Surratt* (1879) by J. W. Rogers, and *J. Wilkes Booth; or, the National Tragedy* (1880) by W. A. Luby. *The Tragedy of Abraham Lincoln* (1876) by Hiram

D. Torrie is a serious blank-verse attempt to portray the Illinois frontiersmen in the language of exiled courtiers in the Forest of Arden and official Washington in the language of Shakespeare's Romans. *Lincoln and Humanity* (1916) by Walter M. Zink is a morality play in which Lincoln is the type of Christian hero who possesses all the virtues and no vices.

Drinkwater is the only dramatist who has successfully imposed an artistic unity on the materials of Lincoln's life and portrayed with any dignity either Lincoln's character or the historical events of his time. It is essentially a drama of character, with no continual action to unite the several independent scenes in which the character of Lincoln is the single interest. Although Drinkwater's Lincoln is not without a number of very human qualities, he is implicitly a figure of supernatural proportions designed as an ideal hero in whom are all things noble and grand.

Since Drinkwater's drama there have been several plays of some theatrical success, only a few of which require mention here. Thomas Dixon's *A Man of the People* (1920) depicts Lincoln as the savior of the Union. The action is confined to a period of eleven days during August and September, 1864, when the Union is secured by the fall of Atlanta. *The Mantle of Lincoln* (1926) by Test Dalton is a play of the modern Lincoln, in which the chief character, by acting always as Lincoln would have acted, achieves success through his honesty, perseverance, charity, and so on. *Spirit of Ann Rutledge* (1927) by H. W. Gammans is a spirit play in which Lincoln is guided and inspired by the shade of Ann Rutledge.

In addition to these, *The Haunted Biographer* (1927) by Gamaliel Bradford, while hardly to be classed as drama, should be mentioned for an interesting series of conversations — Dialogues of the Dead — between the spirit of Lincoln and the spirits of Shakespeare, Charles Lamb, Mark Twain, Dwight L. Moody, and John Wilkes Booth. The conversations hinge upon questions of genius, reputation in history, and religious belief. The title is oddly suggestive. Bradford, who splendidly interpreted in his 'psychographies' so many American heroes, never attempted a portrait of Lincoln. I have checked his numerous comments on Lincoln scattered through several volumes. Together with this work they indicate an interest that is profound, and at the same time, an amount of uncertainty that is not common to Bradford's work as a whole. It is interesting to speculate that for the great 'psychographer' as for so many Lincoln biographers, Lincoln was too complex a soul. To quote Bradford's own phrase, 'He still smiles and remains impenetrable.'

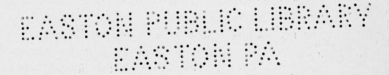

II

The Diviners of Lincoln

I

It is indeed a far cry from the Lincoln of 1861 to the Lincoln who was eulogized in 1865 as the martyr. Men who were disappointed in the ugly Illinois lawyer and thought him of very mediocre caliber when he was nominated were to praise him as the greatest American. As much as his martyrdom had to do with this change in opinion, it is possible that there were other forces which gradually brought about a different conception from that held in 1861. Then, too, it is possible that our general impression of what Lincoln's contemporaries considered him to be in 1861 is somewhat inaccurate. In this chapter are presented the views which certain prominent men expressed concerning Lincoln during the years of his presidency. There is considerable material, but representatives of every class and section are not available because only in the case of more prominent men have letters and other documents written at the time been published. Intimate associates of Lincoln have been excluded because their opinions have not the requisite detachment. A considerable number of the men represented are primarily men of letters. Their papers have been more fully published than those of other men, and hence it is possible to trace the development of their opinions. Furthermore, since it was the men of letters who eventually praised and idealized Lincoln as the great American genius, their contemporary opinions may be significant as a background for their later eulogies. Before these facts are presented, however, it may be well to consider the general condition of public opinion during Lincoln's presidency.

From the day that he was nominated as the Republican candidate, Lincoln became naturally a partisan hero to one portion of the people and a quasi-villain to another portion. Between the two extremes there were estimates of varying bias. Until his assassination these two conceptions ran parallel, and then one practically disappeared. There have been since many assessments of the man which are not by any means heroic, but there is none which descends into complete hatred to make him a monster.

Lincoln had many calumniators and detractors, not all in the Democratic party, and they descended as low for their material as their like has ever gone. His personal appearance was ridiculed by cartoonists the country over. 'Ape,' 'baboon,' 'gorilla,' 'buffoon' were common epithets. His fame as a teller of stories not always above reproach enabled his political enemies to hang on his name every foul yarn that came along. There were whispers of his illegitimacy and of his immorality. Not content with vilifying the man, his enemies circulated gossip concerning his wife — among other things that she was a Copperhead and a Southern spy. The peak of this scurrility was reached during the campaign of 1864. There is more evidence of hatred in the campaign literature of this year than in all the scattered libels previous.[1]

---

[1] Typical examples of the worst sort are two pamphlets entitled respectively, *Abraham Africanus I, His Secret Life as Revealed Under the Mesmeric Influence*, and *Book of Prophet Stephen, Son of Douglas*.

THE LINCOLN LEGEND

In March, 1861, William H. Russell, correspondent of the London *Times*, took occasion to jot down an observation on public opinion at the time which gives a fair index to the true value of newspaper opinion of Lincoln and, at the same time, of representative and sane observation:

> I was astonished to find little sympathy and no regard for the newly installed Government. They were regarded as obscure or undistinguished men. I alluded to the circumstance that one of the journals continued to speak of 'The President' in the most contemptuous manner.... 'Oh, yes,' said the gentleman with whom I was conversing, 'that must strike you as a strange way of mentioning the Chief Magistrate of our great Republic, but the fact is, no one minds what the man writes of anyone, his game is to abuse every respectable man in the country in order to take his revenge on them for his social exclusion and at the same time to please the ignorant masses who delight in vituperation and scandal.'

Newspapers and periodicals are filled with contradictory evidence of Lincoln's reputation. Partisan sentiment renders the average newspaper practically worthless as a source of unbiased opinion. There is little attempt to maintain more than approximate accuracy in assessing public men in staid and ordinary periods; but during the stress of war and national upheaval, saneness and accuracy are seldom apparent. In the following pages there appear some general references to newspaper and periodical opinions of Lincoln, chiefly in relation to personal opinion of some one man who dictated the general policy of the publication. There has been no attempt to present a systematic study of newspapers as such, and, after surveying a considerable number of the more important papers of the North, one may well doubt whether much would be gained by further study. Opinion varied directly with the success of the Northern armies and with the success of executive policies, with modification or exaggeration according to partisan sentiment.

Nowhere is the changing sentiment of the people of the North, their likes and dislikes, their alternate hopes and fears, their hasty and often unjust judgments of men and measures, more vividly reflected than in the cartoons of Lincoln which appeared in the various periodicals of the time. *Frank Leslie's Illustrated Newspaper*, *Harper's Weekly*, and *Vanity Fair*, the American counterpart of the London *Punch*, liberally represented Lincoln in caricature. Interesting cartoon histories of Lincoln have been compiled from these sources by Rufus R. Wilson and Albert Shaw. *Abraham Lincoln and the London Punch*, by William S. Walsh provides an interesting account of the treatment Lincoln received at the hands of the official jester of Britain. Lincoln was savagely cartooned. Physically he was a subject which lent itself to the most extravagant caricature. Even ordinary types can be unmercifully ridiculed by the cartoonist, but the man who is odd in the slightest physical feature is doomed. Lincoln was a choice subject for the accomplished cartoonist and a blessing to the novice. In surveying the mass of caricature, one may be impressed chiefly by the brutality and injustice which are typical of the average cartoon. On the other hand, if one forgets for the moment the martyr, saint, and savior, it is evident that Lincoln was not dealt with more harshly than other public men of his time. The imbecility of James Buchanan in caricature is, one feels, more disparaging than the uncouthness of the cartoon Lincoln. Douglas is far more ridiculous as a sort of Mellin's Food Baby than Lincoln as the aboriginal monster with bushy hair. In caricature Lincoln appears a giant among pigmies; he is more often terrible than ridiculous; and it is not impossible to perceive that the cartoonists could not avoid something elemental and awe-inspiring in his makeup. All things considered, Lincoln is, as a caricature, the most interesting figure of the time. If one had nothing but the cartoons of the period, from which to write history, he could not fail to see in Lincoln the unique figure among American leaders.

Among the Confederates it might be expected that the man who symbolized all that they were fighting against would be grossly misrepresented, but all the satire and propaganda that reached the printed page did not surpass in scurrility the Copperhead pamphlets of the North. The worst of the South's contribution is a dramatic satire entitled *The Royal Ape*, which represents Lincoln as a drunkard and unfaithful husband and the White House as a scene of debauchery.[1]

Private opinion in the South conceived Lincoln to be just the sort of animal that he was represented as being in the most scurrilous campaign literature. There are few letters or journals of Southern writers that cover the period which have been printed without deletions. The aim of editors and literary executors has been to assist the world to forget the horrors of those bitter years, and rightly so, perhaps. But it is not amiss to give examples of Southern opinion from two gentlemen of admitted tranquillity and dignity of mind.

---

[1] *The Royal Ape* is by far the most interesting and clever piece of satire on Lincoln that I have seen. In spite of its scurrility it has literary value. The verse is better than that of most Lincoln eulogies. The title page is dated Richmond, 1863, but it was printed in Columbia, South Carolina. The incidents and certain acute satiric jabs at President Lincoln and Mrs. Lincoln and the Cabinet members seem to indicate that the anonymous author was personally acquainted with official Washington during the first two years of the war.

THE FEDERAL PHOENIX

A JOB FOR THE NEW CABINETMAKER

CONTEMPORARY CARTOONS OF LINCOLN

THE DIVINERS OF LINCOLN

On March 1, 1861, Sidney Lanier wrote to his father:

> ... What a *disgusting* Scene was the Lincoln *hand*-Shaking affair —— ! I think the disgrace of the United States had its fit culmination therein: the scene ought to go into History under the title of 'The Great Apotheosis of the Great Hog —— '

Some years after the war these violent opinions still existed in their most virulent form. On December 15, 1871, Paul Hamilton Hayne wrote to Margaret J. Preston apropos of Richard Henry Stoddard's poems on Lincoln:

> ... There are, however some 4 or 5 productions in S[toddard]'s book, which as a Southerner, I find it hard to peruse with anything like patience.
>
> These 'Homeric lines' on *Lincoln*, for instance, *may* be good, but I see continually between each stanza, the gawky, coarse, not-over cleanly, whisky drinking, and whisky smelling Blackguard, elevated by a grotesque *Chance* (nearly allied to *Satan*) to the position for which of all others, he was most unfit; — and whose memory has been *idealized* by the Yankee fancy, & Yankee arrogance, in a way that *would* be ludicrous, were it not *disgusting*, and calculated, finally, to belie the facts of History, and hand down to future times as Hero and Martyr, as commonplace a *Vulgarian* as ever patronized bad Tobacco, and mistook *blasphemy* for *wit*.

But there were writers doing Lincoln valiant service during these years when the final achievement of his ambition was greatly in doubt. Most noteworthy of these was W. M. Thayer, whose *Pioneer Boy* (1863) set the fashion in Lincoln biography which lasted until years after his death. If this notable book has now little claim to worth because of its lack of facts, it was in 1863 an important interpreter of the President of the United States. Thayer took his lesson in biography from 'Parson' Weems and then surpassed his master. In 1864 Thayer again sent to press a vindication of Lincoln entitled *The*

Character and Public Services of Abraham Lincoln, in which he portrays Lincoln as 'the model President, the champion of Freedom, and the EMANCIPATOR.' This is the continuation of the thesis of his earlier work:

> The child is ever father of the man. It is our purpose to show, in this volume, how the inherent qualities of industry, honesty, perseverance, and cheerful devotion to duty, which characterized the PIONEER BOY, and were the means, under Providence, of his elevation to the PRESIDENCY, have sustained him in that high office, and enabled him to bear the unequalled cares and responsibilities it entailed upon him.

A 'dime novel' biography by J. O. Victor, published in 1864 in the famous 'Beadle' series, is second only to Thayer's portraits in acclaiming Lincoln. Here was a perfect treatment of the theme which was later to make Horatio Alger, Jr., famous. The most appealing fact to Victor was that Lincoln's 'Greatness was not thrust upon him — he achieved it. Step by step, line by line — "through long days of labor, and nights devoid of ease," he forced his way from obscurity to renown.' It was the one appeal that would reach the heart of every poor man, and every rich man who had been poor. It was the philosophy of democracy vindicated by a living example whom it was every man's duty to admire. If there is any significance in the scurrilous attacks on Lincoln, it is balanced by such works as these. Both are propaganda rather than opinion and are not significant of Lincoln's reputation beyond that. But the adulation of Thayer and Victor is marked by a sincerity which the bitterest attacks on Lincoln do not have.

The differences of opinion which prevailed between Lincoln and nearly every member of Congress at some time or other during his presidency gave rise to numerous and often bitter denunciations of Lincoln's policies and methods, not only of conducting the war, but also of conducting international and civil affairs. The criticism of the conduct of the war varied with the fortunes of the several armies. If there were defeats, everything was wrong; if there were victories, silence or praise was in order. Partisan feeling brought about opposition to certain generals and the undue advancement of others. The suspension of the writ of *habeas corpus* created much opposition. Lincoln's failure to uphold Frémont's emancipation order made enemies on one side; the Emancipation Proclamation later made enemies on the other. Every Congressman and every citizen had his own idea of how everything should be done, and all could not have been pleased.

The popular conception of Lincoln as the bearer of the calumny and woe of the period is true. But it must be remembered that from the standpoint of his critics he was often justly condemned. The suspension of the writ of *habeas corpus* and the wholesale program of arrest and imprisonment could not be forgiven by a free people on the grounds of 'military necessity.' Much of his trouble he brought upon himself by doing and taking the responsibility for autocratic measures which might have been avoided. The contrast, as made by J. G. Randall, between Lincoln's method of assuming authority and Woodrow Wilson's method of gaining the co-operation of Congress before undertaking extreme measures reveals the possibility that Lincoln was not as tactful an executive as he might have been.

Within the Republican party, Lincoln did not have unanimous support at any time during the first two years of his administration. Not even the members of his Cabinet thought him capable of handling the difficult situation which confronted him on his inauguration in 1861. Thus Lincoln was forced to fight and maneuver himself into the position of recognized supremacy that is generally accorded a president on his election. Even when his supremacy was established, there continued to be opposition on various issues. Generally speaking, the leaders of the Republican party, in Congress and out, followed the trend of public opinion. When there were no Union victories, there was much carping, and committees were formed whose function it was to instruct the President in matters of war and state. The radical element was never satisfied with Lincoln's conservative policies in regard to emancipation and, later, reconstruction. But, as a whole, the party leaders realized that the general success of the war depended on how well the Administration was supported, and, however grudgingly, they lent their support.

The many expressions of bitter opposition or friendly agreement which were uttered concerning Lincoln from time to time during the years of war do not give an accurate picture of the reputation of the man. There are examples of the admiration of political enemies, and there are examples of condescension and praise that bordered on ridicule among his supposed friends. Lincoln wrote to the actor James Hackett, who had submitted to the newspapers a letter from Lincoln containing certain critical remarks on Shakespeare:

My note to you I certainly did not expect to see in print; yet I have not been much shocked by the newspaper comments upon it. Those comments constitute a fair specimen of what has occurred to me through life. I have endured a great deal of ridicule without much malice; and have received a great deal of kindness, not quite free from ridicule.

THE DIVINERS OF LINCOLN

It is very necessary to keep in mind the bitterness of feeling prevalent in the mildest souls of the period. Even Emerson does not always keep his sweetness. In a time of much less stress and greater national unity Woodrow Wilson received a hammering that occasionally equaled the ferocity of Rebellion times. It is hard to forget the speeches, meetings, memorials, rage, and outcry — the voice of the people as it hammered its will into the President — as well as the expressions of such popular leaders of the period as Roosevelt, Lodge, and Reed. And yet there was a general confidence in the ability and motives of Woodrow Wilson, which was expressed not only at the polls, but every day on the street. The opinion of the common man of the sixties has been lost, but there remain a few sources of information that can be cited as contemporary evidence of the reputation of the man which have not the bias of partisanship in the same degree that it is found in the newspapers and on the platform. The private letters, journals, and diaries of the period are invaluable. From these sources some of the following accounts have been extracted with the hope that they may reveal something not hitherto recognized in any degree of completeness.

The most complete accounts of personal opinion on Lincoln, written from 1861 to 1865, appear in the letters and journals of literary men who were primarily observers rather than participants in public affairs. These men privately assessed Lincoln as they understood him from a more or less detached point of view. Lord Charnwood in his biography of Lincoln comments that it was only among the American men of letters who are recognized today that Lincoln received anything like a just appraisal. Relatively speaking, this is true if we except a few of those men in public affairs who were intimate enough with Lincoln really to appreciate his ability. Much of this chapter is gathered from these sources. In view of the fact that so many of these men eulogized Lincoln after his death as the type of the American demos, these contemporary accounts are significant indices to the value of the later intemperate expressions.

II

It has often been popularly assumed that Lincoln was in 1861 — to quote Charles Francis Adams, Jr. — an 'absolutely unknown, and by no means promising, political quantity.' Albert J. Beveridge in his biography of Lincoln has, it may be hoped, destroyed this unhistorical opinion once and for all. It is true that there were many persons who did not know Lincoln in 1861 — some who had never heard of him — but he enjoyed the national reputation of the average presidential candidate. The Lincoln-Douglas debates had made Lincoln a national figure in spite of his defeat at the polls. In 1858–59 he was in continual demand as a speaker in the Northern States.[1] It was not mere flattery that Charles H. Ray wrote to him on July 27, 1858: 'You are like Byron, who woke up one morning and found himself famous. People wish to know about you. You have sprung at once from the position of a capital fellow, and a leading lawyer in Illinois, to a national reputation.' There is another unhistorical opinion which still exists; namely that Lincoln was in 1861 an incompetent man who grew to a majestic

[1] Nicolay and Hay (pp. 177 ff.) give an account of the numerous invitations extended by Republican State Committees and organizations in many of the large cities. The Cooper Union invitation was only one of many.

figure in four years by means of his serious endeavor. Charles Francis Adams, Jr., may again be quoted: 'During the years intervening between 1861 and 1865 the man developed immensely; he became in fact another being. History, indeed, hardly presents an analogous case of education through trial.' Even so recent a work as Stephen Leacock's *Lincoln Frees the Slaves* (1934) upholds this idea with some persuasion. Leacock's theme is that Lincoln was, when he became President, ignorant and incompetent, without plan or policy; only his love for humanity was remarkable, and only by it was he redeemed. The Emancipation Proclamation, Leacock feels, set free Lincoln as well as the slaves.

But we have a phenomenon even more curious in the opinions of many men who, writing years after the death of Lincoln recall that they saw nothing of promise in the new President in the early days following his election, when in fact they did see and record many evidences of power. Henry Adams is a case in point. In *The Education of Henry Adams* (1906) he wrote that he 'looked anxiously for a sign of character,' but saw only a 'lack of apparent force.' But on December 8, 1860, he had written to Charles Francis Adams, Jr.: 'Lincoln is all right. You can rely on that. He has exercised strong influence through several sources on this committee [a special committee on the state of the Union, of which Charles Francis Adams, Sr., was the head] and always right.' Again on December 22, 1860: 'The President elect has signified, too, in more ways than one, what the committee had better do and what leave undone. General Scott is reported as saying that Mr. Lincoln is a man of power.' The basis for these opinions was the fact that Lincoln was acting according to what Henry Adams conceived as correct judgment. Within a month, however, Lincoln had passed over Charles Francis Adams, Sr., in selecting his Cabinet, and Henry Adams wrote on January 24, 1861: 'Lincoln's position is not known, but his course up to this time has shown his utter ignorance of the right way to act, so far as his appointments go. It is said, too, here, that he is not a strong man.'[1] Such are the influences which determine the reputation of a man who has the power to appoint men to high office. In recalling his impressions of Lincoln in after years, Henry Adams forgot his early conception of Lincoln and remembered the impression based on personal difference of opinion. It will be observed that the most accurate estimates quoted in the following pages were made on the consideration of the qualities of the man rather than his acts. The correct judgment of character cannot be based on whether the person in question acts in accordance with one's personal opinion. The men who were unable to conceive of any course of action as right except that which they had hatched in their own minds were the ones who never saw ability in Lincoln.

III

Of the newspaper men of the period who have claim to literary significance, Horace Greeley and William Cullen Bryant are possibly the greatest, and their opinions of Lincoln will be fully presented below.

The course of Greeley's opinion and treatment of Lincoln was peculiar and tortuous. In 1858, the year of the

[1] There is a letter written by Henry Adams on January 11, 1861, too long to quote sufficiently, which is a revelation of the jealousy and disappointment at the appointment of Cameron and the ignoring of Charles Francis Adams.

Lincoln-Douglas debates, he strove for the acceptance of Douglas as the Republican candidate for United States Senator from Illinois. In April, 1859, he hoped that 'Seward or Chase will be nominated' in 1860. He attended the National Republican Convention of 1860 and did all in his power to prevent Seward's nomination and to bring about Lincoln's, ostensibly favoring Bates of Missouri until he came out openly for Lincoln, posing the while as Seward's ardent admirer. A bitter wrangle ensued between Greeley and Seward's friends, and Lincoln's consideration for the advice of Thurlow Weed may have been somewhat responsible for Greeley's persistent attacks on Lincoln himself. From his inauguration to his death Lincoln had to face the meddling, shouting, impetuous pronouncements of Greeley's paper and still more meddling and personal affronts in the form of letters and interviews. In 1864, not content with fighting harder to prevent Lincoln's renomination than he had fought to bring about his nomination in 1860, Greeley went so far as to attempt to force Lincoln's withdrawal and the selection of a new candidate. Edward Everett Hale relates that on the day that Lincoln was shot, Greeley had written an editorial, 'a brutal, bitter, sarcastic personal attack.' It was withheld by the managing editor of the *Tribune*, whom Greeley assailed the next morning for not printing it. Greeley did not choose, however, to order the printing or to mention the affair thereafter.

Erratic is the only word which fitly describes the judgment of Horace Greeley. The years from 1860 to 1865 are the most erratic of his life. In December, 1860, he was advocating the right of secession. In January, 1861, he wrote, 'I deny to one State, or to a dozen different States, the right to dissolve the Union.' In February, 1861, he was again advocating the right of secession. In January, 1862, in an address at the Smithsonian Institution, he declared against compromise because it implied concessions to armed treason. In less than a year he was in correspondence with the notorious Vallandigham about mediation.[1] Vehement and bitter, he struck out at everything not in keeping with his idea of the moment. He had no consistency himself and blamed it in others. In his own panic and distraction he could not abide calmness.

Unlike the criticisms of such men as Wendell Phillips and William Lloyd Garrison, who were men with a single thought, those made by Greeley have no guiding principle, unless we take the often cited — and denied — hatred of Seward and belief that Seward was responsible for Lincoln's opinions and purposes, as the inspiration of the unending criticism of the Administration.

Perhaps in no other place is Greeley's real opinion of Lincoln so apparent as in the letter which Greeley wrote to him shortly after the first battle of Bull Run. It reveals an utter lack of respect and confidence and without a blush dictates what the President of the United States must do. It is pathetic in its panicky queries:

Dear Sir: This is my seventh sleepless night — yours, too, doubtless — yet I think I shall not die, because I have no right to die. I must struggle to live, however bitterly. But to business. You are not considered a great man, and I am a hopelessly broken one. You are now undergoing a terrible ordeal, and God has thrown the gravest responsibilities upon you. Do not fear to meet them. Can the rebels be beaten after all that has occurred, and in view of the actual state of feeling caused by our late awful disaster? If they can — and it is your business to ascertain and decide — write me that such is your judgment, so that I may know and do my duty.

[1] H. J. Raymond's 'Journal,' *Scribner's Monthly*, xix, 703-10, March, 1880.

And if they *can not* be beaten — if our recent disaster is fatal
— do not fear to sacrifice yourself to your country. If the
rebels are not to be beaten — if that is your judgment in
view of all the light you can get — then every drop of blood
henceforth shed in this quarrel will be wantonly, wickedly
shed, and the guilt will rest heavily on the soul of every pro-
moter of the crime. I pray you to decide quickly, and let
me know my duty....

If it is best for the country and for mankind that we make
peace with the rebels at once, and on their own terms, do not
shrink from that. But bear in mind the greatest truth: 'Who-
so would lose his life for my sake shall save it.' Do the thing
that is the highest right, and tell me how I am to second you.

Yours, in the depth of bitterness.

Greeley's opinion of Lincoln may be summed up as an
excellent expression of the unreasonable, discontented
complaint of a large number of patriotic and devoted
citizens who did not know at any time what the real purposes and abilities of Lincoln were. It was not until Lincoln had been dead for several years that Greeley attained
any real conception of his power, and then it was not without the old erratic bias.

William Cullen Bryant was, like Greeley, from the day
of the Cooper Union Address more or less in touch with
Lincoln until the assassination.[1] Considerably interested
in politics, Bryant had observed Lincoln with more care
than many of the men who came to pass judgment upon

[1] Bryant's first acquaintance with Lincoln was much earlier than that enjoyed
by other prominent men of the time. During the Black Hawk War, while he
was visiting relatives in Illinois, he encountered a company of raw recruits led
by a 'tall, awkward, uncouth lad whose appearance particularly attracted
Mr. Bryant's attention, and whose conversation delighted him by its raciness
and originality....' (Parke Godwin, *A Biography of William Cullen Bryant*,
I, 238.)

The meeting was remembered long after, but the recollection may signify the
absence of any aversion in Bryant to the frontier crudities which were supposedly the basis for the aversion affected by many Easterners.

him in 1860. From his brothers in Illinois he had learned
something of the local respect for the man and of his significance as a leader. Consequently, it is not strange that
after he heard the Cooper Union Address he was convinced
of Lincoln's ability and recognized, partially, his genius.
His confidence in 'the excellence of his intentions and
singleness of his purposes' was unwavering, but he did not
hesitate to criticize some aspects of Lincoln's official acts
which he did not approve, such as the annulment of Frémont's proclamation.[1]

The justness with which he viewed the early Lincoln
remained to prevent any extravagance in his eulogy. In
announcing the assassination the *Evening Post* said:

> But Mr. Lincoln, who had none of Washington's elevation,
> or none of Jackson's energy, yet by his kindliness, his integrity,
> his homely popular humor, and his rare native instinct of the
> popular will, has won as large a place in the private heart,
> while history will assign him no less a place in the public
> history of the nation.

Bryant's poem written on the occasion is characterized
by the same reserve, which may give an impression of
perfunctoriness unless the complete story of his opinion
of Lincoln is understood. Furthermore, Bryant realized
with his usual reserve that his conception of Lincoln was
not a final assessment, which is more than can be said of
many of those who knew Lincoln. When approached by

[1] It is a question how much Bryant had to do with the movement in 1864 to
prevent Lincoln's renomination. Parke Godwin had, apparently, more to do
with the politics of the *Evening Post* than Bryant had, but Bryant must have
generally concurred in the spirit of its criticisms. The *Evening Post* merely
advocated the postponement of the Republican Convention with a view to another candidate and did not go to the lengths of Greeley's paper, the *Tribune*.
Bryant joined with a committee to request the Republican National Committee
to postpone the convention. But that does not necessarily mean that he wished
to prevent Lincoln's renomination.

several acquaintances on the possibility of his preparing Lincoln's memoirs, he wrote to Oliver Wendell Holmes:

> There are various reasons, however, some of which are personal to myself, and others inherent in the subject, which discourage me from undertaking the task of writing Mr. Lincoln's life.... Who that has taken part like myself in the controversies of the time can flatter himself that he shall execute the task worthily and impartially?

IV

From the Abolitionists Lincoln suffered much criticism, unjust in most cases, but for all that was said against him there was more appreciation from their pens than is generally supposed. One of them, however, seldom found a good word for him.

Wendell Phillips was a man of one dominating idea, and that idea gives him almost his only consideration in history. The antislavery cause became quite by accident the purpose in a life that had known no other purpose than the pleasures of fashionable society. Phillips had manifested no interest in the cause until suddenly, in November, 1837, at an indignation meeting presided over by Dr. Channing he felt called upon to speak. Twenty-five years later he recalled the incident, with particular reference to his fine appearance:

> I went there without the least intention of making a speech or taking any part in the proceedings. My wife and Mrs. Chapman wished to go, and I accompanied them. I remember wearing a long surtout, a brand-new one, with a small cape (as was the fashion of the day), and after the attorney-general made his speech denouncing Lovejoy as a fool, I suddenly felt myself inspired, and tearing off my overcoat, started for the platform. My wife seized me by the arm, half terrified,

and said, 'Wendell, what are you going to do?' I replied, 'I am going to *speak*, if I can make myself heard.'

Throughout the addresses which were printed in a form revised by Phillips from the shorthand notes of an admirer there is continually the stamp of the agitator who has one idea and does not hesitate to distort facts and misinterpret motives in order to sway the audience with him. As an orator he was brilliant. As an agitator he was devoted to an ideal principle. As a judge of men he was, perhaps, unwise. There were elements of contradiction in his very adherence to his one idea. From 1843 until the firing upon Fort Sumter he was a disunionist, believing it 'the only righteous path, and the best one for the white man and black.' He succeeded in making it clear that the North would be purified by severing relations with the slaveholding South, but the beneficial result to the slave, neither he nor other disunion Abolitionists ever made clear. It is hard to avoid the implication that his first ideal was the spotlessness of a Northern Union rather than the freedom of all slaves. When it became evident after the firing on Sumter that the Union would be preserved if the strength of the North were sufficient for the task, his criticism of the Administration was based on the fear that the Union would be saved, still contaminated by slavery.

In his judgments on Lincoln and other prominent men of the time there is to be observed but one consistent criterion — their attitude toward the immediate abolition of slavery and complete social and political equality for the negro. For him there were no great men except in the ranks of the Abolitionists, and every Abolitionist was a great man. Thus General Butler was 'one of the ablest of the very few able men this war has thrown to the surface.' Hamilton, Butler, Phelps, and Frémont were 'the sound national element of civil and military purposes.' In this light Lincoln was, of course, at best a very mediocre man. 'He is not a genius; he is not a man like Frémont, to stamp the lava mass of the nation with an idea; he is not a man like Hunter, to coin his experience into ideas. I will tell you what he is. He is a first-rate second-rate man.' Further, it was evident in August, 1862, that Lincoln 'has no mind whatever. He has not uttered a word which gives even a twilight glimpse of any antislavery purpose. He may be honest — nobody cares whether the tortoise is honest or not; he has neither insight nor prevision, nor decision.' Not content with this low rating, Phillips felt called upon to impugn Lincoln's motives, even after the Emancipation Proclamation. 'The President is an honest man; that is, he is Kentucky honest, and that is necessarily a very different thing from Massachusetts or New York honesty. A man cannot get above the atmosphere in which he is born.' As Lincoln was hopeless, so were all of his Cabinet. 'I do not believe there is in that Cabinet — Seward, Chase, Stanton, Wells — enough to make a leader.'

It is of no use to multiply these acrid statements. They began before Lincoln was elected and continued with some abatement until his death. In 1861–62, however, Phillips delivered addresses intended as patriotic flourishes for the inspiration of the mob, in which he expressed confidence and respect for Lincoln's ability and purposes; but he lived to regret them, when at the New England Convention in March, 1864, Garrison used them as arguments for Lincoln's support in the face of later and, if possible, more bitter denunciations of the Administration by Phillips.

William Lloyd Garrison, while no less an ardent Abolitionist than Phillips, never wholly condemned Lincoln, and after the Emancipation Proclamation practically abandoned his policy of personal criticism. He was, on the whole, a man of larger views than Phillips and realized the difficulties which beset Lincoln upon his elevation to the presidency. In 1861, however, he was as unsparing in his criticism of the early days of Lincoln's Administration as any Abolitionist or Southerner in the country. At the fall of Sumter he united with the general public to support the Government and lent his influence to stop criticism. He wrote to Oliver Johnson on April 19, 1861, 'It is no time for minute criticism of Lincoln, Republicanism, or even the other parties, now that they are fusing for a death grapple with the Southern slave oligarchy; for they are instruments in the hands of God.' By fall, however, Lincoln had revoked Frémont's proclamation of freedom and Garrison was criticizing at length. In December Garrison characterized the message to Congress suggesting colonization for the freed people as 'wishy-washy,' wondering whether Lincoln was capable of 'uttering a humane or generous sentiment respecting the enslaved millions.' In January, 1862, however, he was making allowances and admitting the possible wisdom of Lincoln's hesitancy on the ground that the North was not sufficiently united in a desire for emancipation. This course of criticism and sympathy continued until Lincoln's death with a growing faith in his purpose and ability. In 1864 Garrison was able to state in defense of Lincoln against Phillips, 'Since that event [Emancipation Proclamation], and in view of what has followed in the enrollment of tens of thousands of colored soldiers, I have changed my opinion of Abraham Lincoln. In proportion as he has fallen in the estimation of the disloyal portion of the North, he has risen in my own.'

THE DIVINERS OF LINCOLN

John G. Whittier, as well as Garrison, was sadly tried by President Lincoln's cautious and conciliatory measures as to slavery.

In September, 1861, Whittier wrote to Lydia Maria Child, apropos of Frémont's proclamation of freedom:

> I am afraid the Government will tie up the hands of Frémont. I was just thinking of trying to thank him for his noble word 'free,' when, lo! the papers this morning bring us Lincoln's letter to him, repudiating the grand utterance. Well, if the confiscated slaves are *not* free, then the Government has turned slaveholder, that is all.
>
> I am sick of politicians. I know and appreciate the great difficulties in the way of the Administration, but I see neither honesty nor worldly wisdom in attempting *to ignore the cause of the trouble.*
>
> They tell us we must trust, and have patience; and I do not like to find fault with the Administration, as in so doing *I seem* to take sides with the secession sympathizers of the North.

It is interesting to notice, however, that Whittier began to appreciate Lincoln's literary style at an earlier date than did most of his contemporaries. He wrote to James T. Fields on December 2, 1862, 'Abraham's message to Congress is a great improvement in point of style. Its conclusion is really noble.'

In contrast with the Abolitionists, there were many men who, like Oliver Wendell Holmes, had little interest in affairs. Holmes we might expect to be distrustful of a frontier President. In matters of family and caste he was the most undemocratic of the Brahmins. He said before Lincoln was elected: 'It has happened hitherto, so far as my limited knowledge goes, that the President of the United States has always been what might be called in general terms a gentleman. But what if at some future time the choice of the people should fall upon one on whom that lofty title could not by any stretch of authority be bestowed' — this was a horrible possibility to him. When it happened, even if not loud in praise, Holmes was not among the detractors. In February, 1862, he wrote to John Lothrop Motley concerning the Virginia Abolitionist, Moncure D. Conway: 'M. D. Conway has talked with father Abraham, who, as he thinks, is honest enough, but simply incompetent and without a plan. I don't know that his opinion is good for much. He is an out-and-out immediate emancipationist.'[1] If there is any virtue in a negative statement it may be assumed that Holmes did not, at least, despair. On the day of Lincoln's death, however, he philosophically observed that 'more than likely Lincoln was not the best man for the work of reconstruction.' His hymn written on the occasion is marked by a perfunctoriness that denies any marked appreciation of Lincoln.

V

James Russell Lowell, like most of the people of the East, did not know much of Lincoln in 1860. He lamented in an article in the *Atlantic* for October, 1860, the fact that Seward had not been chosen as the Republican candidate. But he accepted Lincoln with confidence on the basis of his record. 'He has proved both his ability and his integrity; he has had experience enough in public affairs to make him a statesman, and not enough to make him a politician.' By June, 1861, Lowell had had time to be-

[1] In his *Autobiography* M. D. Conway admits that he never came to believe Lincoln competent, much less a great man. Lincoln's Union policy was never sound to Conway, in spite of the fact that it worked. Conway saw in Lincoln a unique character, humorous and oddly original, but he saw no sign of intellect or leadership.

come, along with most of his contemporaries who wished an aggressive and dashing leader, disappointed in Lincoln. In an article, 'The Pickens-and-Stealins' Rebellion,' which appeared in the *Atlantic* for June, 1861, he expressed his impatience with Lincoln's caution, and disappointment in his public utterances. Another article in the December issue of the *Atlantic* still found nothing to praise. It is from these essays written for the public that we must glean whatever of Lowell's conception of Lincoln we get, for his published letters are singularly free of references that reveal his attitude.[1] Not until January, 1864, did Lowell give another essay to the public, when there appeared in the *North American Review* 'The President's Policy,' which was later combined with a eulogy written after Lincoln's death and published under the title 'Abraham Lincoln' in *Political Essays*. There is a poem of the autumn of 1863, however, which reveals something of the change that had taken place since December, 1861, in Lowell's attitude toward Lincoln. In its final form there are two parts, but the first was submitted to the *Atlantic* some time before the second was written. 'Two Scenes From the Life of Blondel' is a contemplation upon the frustration of hopes and the impossibility of attaining ideals. In the first part Lincoln is conceived as the ideal prince, and there is a ring of sincere admiration that is not surpassed by the lines written after Lincoln's death for the 'Harvard Commemoration Ode.' Some time later Lowell sent Fields the second part, which, half-serious and half-humorous, sighs over the

> ... infinite odds 'twixt a hero to come
> And your only too palpable hero *in esse*!

[1] Chiefly because of editorial deletions in the Norton edition, which was edited from the standpoint of Lowell's literary pursuits.

THE LINCOLN LEGEND

Precisely the odds (such examples are rife)
  'Twixt the poem conceived and the rhyme we make show of,
  'Twixt the boy's morning dream and the wake-up of life,
  'Twixt the Blondel God meant and a Blondel I know of!

But the spirit of Scene One attains a conception of Lincoln which we cannot expect even a poet to hold for long if his hero continues to live and act. Entirely ideal, the poem remains one of the finest, and probably least noticed, of tributes. It is the only remarkable poem on Lincoln written before his death.

TWO SCENES FROM THE LIFE OF BLONDEL

SCENE I

'Twere no hard task, perchance to win
  The popular laurel for my song;
'Twere only to comply with sin,
  And own the crown, though snatched by wrong;
Rather Truth's chaplet let me wear,
  Though sharp as death its thorns may sting;
Loyal to Loyalty, I bear
  No badge but of my rightful king.

Patient by town and tower I wait,
  Or o'er the blustering moorland go;
I buy no praise at cheaper rate,
  Or what faint hearts may fancy so;
For me, no joy in lady's bower,
  Or hall, or tourney, will I sing,
Till the slow stars wheel round the hour
  That crowns my hero and my king.

While all the land runs red with strife,
  And wealth is won by peddler-crimes,
Let who will find content in life
  And tinkle in unmanly rhymes;
I wait and seek; through dark and light,
  Safe in my heart my hope I bring,

Till I once more my faith may plight
   To him my whole soul owns her king.

When power is filched by drone and dolt,
   And, with caught breath and flashing eye,
Her knuckles whitening round the bolt,
   Vengeance leans eager from the sky,
While this and that the people guess,
   And to the skirts of praters cling,
Who court the crowd they should compress,
   I turn in scorn to seek my king.

Shut in what tower of darkling chance
   Or dungeon of a narrow doom,
Dream'st thou of battle-axe and lance
   That for the Cross make crashing room?
Come! with hushed breath the battle waits
   In the wild van thy mace's swing;
While doubters parley with their fates,
   Make thou thine own and ours, my king!

O, strong to keep upright the old,
   And wise to buttress with the new,
Prudent, as only are the bold,
   Clear-eyed, as only are the true,
To foes benign, to friendship stern,
   Intent to imp Law's broken wing,
Who would not die, if death might earn
   The right to kiss thy hand, my king?[1]

'The President's Policy' recognized for the first time something more than an unconscious drifting in Lincoln's management of affairs. There was a purpose and a mind at work which had not been appreciated because it had not been understood. 'Mr. Lincoln, as it seems to us in reviewing his career, though we have sometimes in our impatience thought otherwise, has always waited, as a

---

[1] H. E. Scudder has pointed out the fact that this poem was written of Lincoln. See *James Russell Lowell*, II, 43.

wise man should, till the right moment brought up all his reserves.' Frankly confessing his own misjudgment of both the purpose and ability of the man to manage the affairs of state, he presented a worthy appraisal of what Lincoln had accomplished:

> Mr. Lincoln's perilous task has been to carry a rather shaky raft through the rapids, making fast the unrulier logs as he could snatch opportunity, and the country is to be congratulated that he did not think it his duty to run straight at all hazards, but cautiously to assure himself with his setting pole where the main current was, and keep steadily to that. He is still in wild water, but we have faith that his skill and sureness of eye will bring him out right at last.

As an observer of affairs Lowell was keen, but, like most supporters of Lincoln, he had periods of depression in which the course of events seemed quite without any guiding hand. It would be too much to expect that his faith in and opinion of Lincoln should never waver, for Lowell as well as Lincoln was human. He wrote to Charles Eliot Norton in the summer of 1864: 'The war and its constant expectation and anxiety oppress me. I cannot think. If I had enough to leave behind me, I could enlist this very day and get knocked in the head. I hear bad things about Mr. Lincoln and try not to believe them.'

The famous lines which were to become a part of the 'Harvard Commemoration Ode' express the fullness of his respect and reverence for the memory of the 'first American,'[1] which must wait for consideration until a

---

[1] The origin of this idea with Lowell was probably much earlier than the 'Commemoration Ode.' Scudder points out the use of a similar phrase in 'Scotch the Snake or Kill it,' which Lowell submitted for the July *Atlantic* several weeks before the 'Ode' was composed. There it stood 'the most American of Americans.' The idea of Lincoln symbolizing Americanism was common, however. Emerson said on April 19, 1865, 'He was thoroughly American' (*Works*, xi, 330, 'Abraham Lincoln'). See also Hawthorne's comment below, and Motley's.

later chapter. It is significant that the fullness of appreciation of Lincoln was approximately reached by Lowell before the assassination. In spirit, either 'Blondel' or 'The President's Policy' is an exceedingly high tribute to a living man. That a Brahmin could reach such a judgment of Lincoln merely as a careful student and critic of his actions and policies, with nothing of the regard engendered by personal contact, which enabled those close to Lincoln both to admire and love, is a tribute to his perception.

Parallel with the course of impressions which are portrayed in the writings of Lowell run the estimates of Lincoln in the letters of Charles Eliot Norton. At the time of Lincoln's first inauguration Norton thought that he had 'shown great courage and dignity' up to that time. But on April 29, 1861, his doubts had commenced. He wrote on that date to George William Curtis: 'I more than ever wish he [Seward] could have been our President. I am not satisfied that Mr. Lincoln is the right man for the place at this time.' On December 5, 1861, he wrote again to Curtis:

> ... We are very serious over the President's message. We think it very poor in style, manner and thought — very wanting in pith, and exhibiting a mournful deficiency of strong feeling and of wise forecast in the President. This 'no policy' system in regard to the conduct of the war and the treatment of the slavery question is extremely dangerous, and must at the best produce very unfortunate divisions of opinion and of action among the people; — it is truly a very sad thing to see each successive opportunity for great decisive, *right* counsels thrown away and worse than lost.[1]

On March 8, 1862, he answered an optimistic letter from Curtis:

[1] Contrast this with Whittier's view of the same message, above.

... All you say is very interesting. But can I quite agree with you in confidence in Mr. Lincoln's instincts? His message on Emancipation is a most important step;[1] but could anything be more feebly put, or more inefficiently written? His style is worse than ever; and though a bad style is not always a mark of bad thought — it is at least proof that thought is not as clear as it ought to be....

... As for Lincoln's suggestions, I am sure that good will come of them.

In September, 1862, Norton's letters were filled with rejoicing over the Emancipation Proclamation, but unlike Emerson, he did not perceive in it the revelation of all the statesmanship and ability which had moulded the policy of the Administration from the beginning. Lincoln was still an uncertain quantity to him. On November 12, 1862, he again wrote to Curtis:

... Were it not for one or two *ifs*, I should feel much better about the state of affairs than I have for some time. The worst of the *ifs* is the one concerning Lincoln. I am much afraid that a domestic cat will not answer when one wants a Bengal tiger....

By September, 1863, Norton had become educated to the new style in letters and thenceforward was to remain an admirer of a literary excellence which he had not comprehended at the outset. In a letter to Curtis dated September 3, 1863, he referred to Lincoln's letter to J. C. Conklin as follows:

... We might congratulate each other on the extraordinary excellence of the President's letter. He rises with each new effort, and his letters are successive victories. Indeed the series of his letters since and including the one to the Albany Committee are, as he says to General Grant of Vicksburg,

[1] The special message urging 'a gradual abolishment of slavery' was sent to Congress March 6, 1862.

'of inestimable value to the country' — for they are of the rarest class of political documents, arguments seriously addressed by one in power to the conscience and reason of the citizens of the commonwealth.... There is in them the clearest tone of uprightness of character, purity of intention, and goodness of heart....

On December 10, 1863, he wrote concerning Lincoln's Proclamation of Amnesty:

...How wise and how admirably timed is his Proclamation. As a state paper its naïveté is wonderful. Lincoln will introduce a new style into state papers; he will make them sincere, and his honesty will compel even politicians to like virtue. I conceive his character to be on the whole the great net gain from the war....

The last sentence is to be noted, for it expresses the height of Norton's appreciation. From this time on there is no sign of even the slightest doubt as to Lincoln's greatness. One further quotation will serve for all the later references.

On December 28, 1864, Norton wrote to Aubrey de Vere:

Mr. Lincoln is constantly gaining in popular respect and confidence. He is not a man whose qualities are fitted to excite a personal enthusiasm, but they are of a kind to inspire trust. He is an admirable ruler for our democratic republic. He has shown many of the highest qualities of statesmanship, and I have little doubt that his course and his character will both be estimated more highly in history than they are in the main, by his contemporaries.

This is a fair estimate, but how odd it seems to find an admirer admitting that Lincoln 'is not a man whose qualities are fitted to excite a personal enthusiasm.' Such an admission makes the tribute from Norton all the more valuable, but how could he have imagined what Lincoln would come to mean within a few months as an inspiration of personal enthusiasm? It was an intellectual appeal that reached Norton, as well as Lowell and Emerson. The popular appeal of the frontier hero never reached them, but the gradual awakening to his genius they were not able to escape.

VI

The gradual awakening to the real Lincoln which took place in the minds of intelligent and unbiased observers is nowhere more amply recorded than in the works of Emerson. Apparently Emerson knew little of Lincoln, if anything, before his nomination. Like the Abolitionists who felt that they alone were responsible for the success of the new Republican party, Emerson expected the incoming Administration to busy itself immediately with the problem of emancipation. There were few men of his acquaintance who recognized the chief problem as the preservation of the Union, and he was not vitally concerned with the problem, either. He recognized, however — what many did not — that the President could not bring the country to an ideal by waving his hand. To Wendell Phillips expediency and tact were unknown except as concessions to the powers of evil. To Emerson they were the necessary implements for working a change. In April, 1861, when the Abolitionists were crying for emancipation to an Administration faced with hundreds of problems such as had never before confronted any President on his inauguration, Emerson wrote:

> If Mr. Lincoln appear slow and timid in proclaiming emancipation, and, like a bashful suitor, shows the way to deny him, it is to be remembered that he is not free as a poet to state what he thinks ideal or desirable, but must take a con-

sidered step, which he can keep. Otherwise his proclamation would be a weak bravado, without value or respect.

If Emerson had been more or less uninterested in the conduct of political America up to 1861, he became a reasonably careful student of the trend of national affairs. By the end of the year he was noting Lincoln's messages with critical acumen. In December, 1861, there appears in his *Journals* an observation to the effect that 'President Lincoln said well, that the rebels "carried only the ruin of their own country as ground to invoke the aid of foreign nations."' A month later he again commented favorably on the content and, also, the style, of the December message to Congress:

> President Lincoln has proposed to Congress that the government shall co-operate with any State that shall enact a gradual abolishment of slavery.... He speaks his own thought in his own style. All thanks and honor to the Head of the State! The message has been received throughout the country with praise, and we doubt not, with more pleasure than has been spoken.

The latter part of January Emerson went to Washington, where he was scheduled to give a lecture before the Smithsonian Institution on the thirty-first. Remaining in the city several days, he was carried to the various officials by Sumner and finally, on February 2, to President Lincoln. The account of the visit is frank and appreciative, but reveals that this personal contact did not bring about any conception of Lincoln's ability or any recognition at all that he was a man of genius:

> The President impressed me more favourably than I had hoped. A frank, sincere, well-meaning man, with a lawyer's habit of mind, good clear statement of his fact; correct enough, not vulgar, as described, but with a sort of boyish cheerful-

ness, or that kind of sincerity and jolly good meaning that our class meetings on Commencement Days show, in telling our old stories over. When he has made his remark, he looks up at you with great satisfaction, and shows all his white teeth, and laughs. He argued to Sumner the whole case of Gordon, the slave trader, point by point, and added that he was not quite satisfied yet and meant to refresh his memory by looking again at the evidence. All this showed a fidelity and conscientiousness very honourable to him.

When I was introduced to him, he said, 'Oh, Mr. Emerson, I once heard you say in a lecture, that a Kentuckian seems to say by his air and manners, "Here am I; if you don't like me, the worse for you."'

A second visit at the White House was made with Seward a few days later, and the account given in the *Journals* is detailed as to what was said, but quite barren as to impressions. It is in an amiable and entirely friendly tone, which at least indicates no disappointment on the further acquaintance. In the account of a visit with Sumner to the British Embassy, Emerson noted with pleasure that Baron Gerolt, the dean of the diplomatic corps, 'was enchanted with the expression of the President.'

The preliminary Emancipation Proclamation of September 22, 1862, was for Emerson the turning-point in his understanding of Lincoln's intelligence and executive ability. It became apparent that there was something more than drifting in the policy which had put off the act until the right moment. While others deemed it mistimed, if not entirely unfortunate, Emerson perceived that it was the logical climax of Lincoln's increasing endeavors toward an eventually complete emancipation. There are still those who maintain that Lincoln was forced into emancipation by popular opinion. The world in general has come to perceive with Emerson that there was a wisdom in Lincoln that directed the course of affairs far better than his critics knew. The comment written in the *Journals* at the time remains one of the best contemporary judgments of the Executive.

The extreme moderation with which the President advanced to his design — his long-avowed expectant policy, as if he chose to be strictly the executive of the best public sentiment of the country, waiting only till it should be unmistakeably pronounced — so fair a mind that none ever listened so patiently to such extreme varieties of opinion, so reticent that his decision has taken all parties by surprise, whilst yet it is just the sequel of his prior acts — the firm tone in which he announces it, without inflation or surplusage: — all these have bespoken such favor to the act that, great as the popularity of the President has been, we are beginning to think that we have underestimated the capacity and virtue which the Divine Providence has made an instrument of benefit so vast. He has been permitted to do more for America than any other American man. He is well entitled to the most indulgent construction. Forget all that we thought shortcomings, every mistake, every delay. In the extreme embarrassments of his part, call these endurance, wisdom, magnanimity; illuminated, as they are now, by this dazzling success.

In November, however, Emerson expressed further mild disappointment in Lincoln's appointments.

Mr. Lincoln thinks Emancipation almost morally wrong and resorts to it only as a desperate measure, and means never to put radicals into power. When he puts one into office, as Frémont, or Phelps, or Lane, he takes care to neutralize him by a Democrat or a Kentuckian who will thwart him. And prudent people say, 'Quite right, for these hotheads have no administrative talent.' Perhaps, also, they have a great deal. They respect principles, which it may still be believed, have a certain force if not in the Whig Club, yet in the Universe of men.

THE LINCOLN LEGEND

With all his growing appreciation of Lincoln's genius, Emerson could not reconcile Lincoln's unconventional habits with the traditional conception of what a President of the United States ought to be. Two notations in the *Journals* reveal a superior impatience with Lincoln's willingness to degrade his position by a lowly but worthy act. It is interesting that the second incident which Emerson objected to has been proved a myth, pure and simple, of which more will be said in another chapter.

November, 1863. *Lincoln.* We must accept the results of universal suffrage, and not try to make it appear that we can elect fine gentlemen. We shall have coarse men, with a fair chance of worth and manly ability, but not polite men, to please the English or French.

You cannot refine Mr. Lincoln's taste, extend his horizon, or clear his judgment; he will not walk dignifiedly through the traditional part of the President of America, but will pop out his head at each railway station and make a little speech, and get into an argument with Squire A and Judge B. He will write letters to Horace Greeley, and any editor or reporter or saucy party committee that writes to him, and cheapen himself.

But this we must be ready for, and let the clown appear, and hug ourselves that we are well off, if we have got good nature, honest meaning, and fidelity to public interest, with bad manners — instead of an elegant *roué* and malignant self-seeker.

March, 1863. President Lincoln should remember that humanity in a ruler does not consist in running hither and thither in a cab to stop the execution of a deserter, but, as Napoleon said, 'justice is the humanity of kings.'

But finally even the manners of Lincoln were accepted. The last comment on Lincoln in the *Journals*, written but a few days before the assassination, admits that this man attained by his very simplicity of manners a perfection in deportment unknown to polished society. Lincoln was, it seems, educating Emerson in practical democracy.

Why talk of President Lincoln's equality of manners to the elegant or titled men with whom Everett or others saw him? A sincerely upright and intelligent man as he was, placed in the chair, has no need to think of his manners or appearance. His work day by day educates him rapidly and to the best. He exerts the enormous power of this continent in every hour, in every conversation, in every act; — thinks and decides under this pressure, forced to see the vast and various bearings of the measures he adopts; *he* cannot palter, he cannot but carry a grace beyond his own, a dignity, by means of what he drops, e. g. all his pretension and tricks, and arrives, of course, at a simplicity which is the perfection of manners.

VII

If Edward Everett, Senator, President of Harvard, former Secretary of State, and bearer of many honors, was still in 1865 surprised by Lincoln's equality of manners in the presence of great men, as Emerson indicates, he had progressed by this time to a high estimate of Lincoln's executive ability. In February, 1861, he wrote in his journal, 'He [Lincoln] is evidently a person of very inferior cast of character, wholly unequal to the crisis.' Such estimates were made on the basis of what his friends had told him of Lincoln. When he met Lincoln, he was, like Emerson, surprised and pleased to find him 'much better than I expected.' To condense his own account as given in his journal, it became more clear to him, week by week, that Lincoln was the man of the hour. Everett had been for years an ardent supporter of the Union and a conservative on the slavery question. Hence, when he observed the caution with which Lincoln avoided antagonizing the border States and drew all forces together with his one prime object to save the Union, he could but admit the wisdom of a policy so like his own. In connection with the congressional election in 1862, at a period when Lincoln's popular favor was at its lowest ebb, Everett wrote to a group of political grumblers in New York, 'It is my purpose to continue to support the President, to the best of my ability.' At this time he gave in the course of an address an estimate of Lincoln which seems singularly free from bias and frankly appreciative when compared with what some of Lincoln's early supporters were crying against him at the time:

> The President gave ample proof of his intellectual capacity, when he contested a seat in the senate of the United States with Judge Douglas.... He is one of the most laborious and indefatigable men in the country; and that he has been able to sustain himself under as great a load of care as was ever laid upon the head or the heart of a living man is in no small degree owing to the fact that the vindictive and angry passions form no part of his nature and that a kindly and playful spirit mingles its sweetness with the austere cup of public duty.
>
> The most important objection urged against Mr. Lincoln is that personally he lacks fixedness of purpose, and that his Cabinet and Administration have wanted unity of counsel. I think I shall offend no candid opponent (I certainly am no partisan myself) if I remind you, that precisely the same charge, on the same grounds, might be brought against General Washington and his Administration.

In the election of 1864, Everett campaigned for Lincoln and in doing so became alienated from many of his former Democratic associates. Lincoln's victory in Massachusetts was conceded to be due largely to these endeavors. This support in 1864 means much when it is considered that Everett was personally friendly toward McClellan and had disapproved when Lincoln removed him from command.

One other point is worthy of mention. Everett was among the first to realize the real merit of Lincoln's literary style. The day following the dedication at Gettysburg, at which Everett was the principal orator, he wrote to Lincoln:

> ... Permit me to express my great admiration of the thoughts expressed by you, with such eloquent simplicity and appropriateness, at the consecration of the cemetery. I should be glad if I could flatter myself that I came as near the central idea of the occasion in two hours as you did in two minutes.

This is certainly first of all a polite appreciation sent as a matter of form, but that it was sincere is not to be questioned. In his journal Everett made favorable comments on Lincoln's writing which were not intended for Lincoln's eye. A few weeks later he said of the current message to Congress, 'The President's message appeared yesterday afternoon. A very remarkable document.'

Another man of letters, who, like Everett, belonged to the Democratic party, and, unlike Everett, was very little interested whether the South went or stayed or whether slavery was abolished or let alone, was Nathaniel Hawthorne. His observations on Lincoln were made in an article, 'Chiefly about War Matters,' which was printed in the *Atlantic* for July, 1862. This is the only source from which we may draw Hawthorne's opinion, for his interest in governmental affairs, if he had any, did not find much place in his letters. Mrs. Hawthorne does, however, speak of Lincoln occasionally in her letters in a very favorable tone. At one time she writes, 'I suspect the President is a jewel. I like him very well.'

THE LINCOLN LEGEND

Hawthorne's description of Lincoln was not printed entire by the *Atlantic* because Fields, the editor, felt that, however valuable it might be as an unprejudiced portrait, it was not reverent enough. Hawthorne felt that the portrait was of historic value and said so in his reply to Fields's letter suggesting the deletions. In many respects the picture is the most accurate that we have of the Lincoln of 1862. If Hawthorne was impressed with the oddity of the physical Lincoln, he was no less impressed with an underlying, 'powerful character.'

Unfortunately Hawthorne did not have the opportunity for extended conversation with Lincoln that Emerson had on his visit, and hence it is important to note the brevity and the nature of the occasion on which he saw him. There was a delegation from a Massachusetts whip factory which had an appointment at the White House for the purpose of presenting Lincoln with a handsome whip. Lincoln was at the time much in seclusion because of the death of his son, and Hawthorne had to attach himself to this formal group in order to be received. Thus on short acquaintance and with little previous interest Hawthorne sketched the following character, of which all but the last paragraph was omitted by the *Atlantic*:

> By and by there was a little stir on the staircase and in the passage-way, and in lounged a tall, loose-jointed figure, of an exaggerated Yankee port and demeanor, whom (as being about the homeliest man I ever saw, yet by no means repulsive or disagreeable) it was impossible not to recognize as Uncle Abe.
>
> Unquestionably, Western man though he be, and Kentuckian by birth, President Lincoln is the essential representative of all Yankees, and the veritable specimen, physically, of what the world seems determined to regard as our characteristic qualities.... There is no describing his lengthy awk-

wardness, nor the uncouthness of his movement; and yet it seemed as if I had been in the habit of seeing him daily, and had shaken hands with him a thousand times in some village street; so true was he to the aspect of the pattern American, though with a certain extravagance which, possibly, I exaggerated still further by the delighted eagerness with which I took it in. If put to guess his calling and livelihood, I should have taken him for a country schoolmaster [the Ichabod Crane type] as soon as anything else....

The whole physiognomy is as coarse a one as you would meet anywhere in the length and breadth of the states; but, withal, it is redeemed, illuminated, softened, and brightened by a kindly though serious look out of his eyes, and an expression of homely sagacity, that seems weighted with rich results of village experience. A great deal of native sense; no bookish cultivation, no refinement; honest at heart, and thoroughly so, and yet, in some sort, sly, — at least, endowed with a sort of tact and wisdom that are akin to craft, and would impel him, I think, to take an antagonist in flank, rather than to make a bull-run at him right in front.

His manner toward us was wholly without pretense, but yet had a kind of natural dignity, quite sufficient to keep the forwardest of us from clapping him on the shoulder and asking him for a story....

However, lest the above allusions to President Lincoln's little peculiarities (already well known to the country and to the world) should be misinterpreted, I deem it proper to say a word or two in regard to him, of unfeigned respect and measurable confidence. He is evidently a man of keen faculties, and what is still more to the purpose, of powerful character. As to his integrity, the people have that intuition of it which is never deceived.... The President is teachable by events, and has now spent a year in a very arduous course of education; he has a flexible mind, capable of much expansion, and convertible towards far loftier studies and activities than those of his early life; and if he came to Washington a backwoods humorist, he has already transformed himself into as good a statesman (to speak moderately) as his prime-minister.

All things considered, this portrait from the pen of a Democrat, at an early and unpromising period in Lincoln's Administration, is not without considerable historical value. There were many Republicans — Abolitionists, in particular — who at this time were of the opinion that Lincoln was hopelessly mediocre. It may be recalled that neither Emerson nor Lowell, nor any of their group came to any considerable appreciation of Lincoln until a date even later. John Hay charged this sketch with being one of contempt, but it is so only if one suppose all discussions of Lincoln not done in the sacred vein to be contemptuous. The result of a brief and casual acquaintance, it has none of the depth that can come only through long and careful observation, but it is marked by a detached and careful etching of the qualities which were apparent on the occasion. Anyone who is familiar with Hawthorne's *Note Books* realizes the perception with which he drew characters from life. Even if no allowance is made for Hawthorne's political and sectional bias, this must be admitted as one of the earliest recognitions of the fundamental elements of character which were later to be recognized as genius.

VIII

Like the aristocratic Francis Parkman, who, although a Republican and a supporter of Lincoln, thought him 'a man whose undeniable worth and usefulness were due to circumstances more than inherent ability,' George Bancroft held an unfavorable opinion of Lincoln at the start, and there is no evidence that he ever radically changed his view until he became the official eulogist after Lincoln's death. There is a passage in his 'Memorial

Address' which, although meant for Great Britain, fits Bancroft's own attitude just as well. 'They had not,' he said, 'one word of sympathy for the kind-hearted poor man's son whom America had chosen for her chief.'

In September of 1861, he wrote to his wife: 'We suffer for want of an organising mind at the head of the government. We have a president without brains; and a cabinet whose personal views outweigh patriotism.' A few days later he wrote again: 'the only trouble of mind I have springs from my want of confidence in our present administration.'

On August 15, 1861, he wrote to Dean Milman:

...Mr. Lincoln's administration came in and was not for the moment equal to the emergency. It had been chosen in the midst of unexampled prosperity, and was hardly more than suited for summer wear. The plan of seducing the Northern States failed from the beginning through the rightmindedness and honesty of the people; but the confederacy which meantime had been formed, was confident of asserting their independence. Mr. Lincoln's administration wavered, seemed even inclined to let them go. Their influence in the National councils has for the last twenty years been very pernicious; many persons inclined to let them go; some were even glad of their going. But on reflection it was plain that they could not go peaceably....

The best that Bancroft could say of Lincoln before his assassination appears in a letter written to the Republican nominating committee of a New York district which had nominated Bancroft for Congress in the fall of 1862. He admonished them that although

Complaints are made against the Administration; there never was and never will be an administration that does not require to be watched. But the people have chosen their President; and we who preferred another public servant must now consent to give vigour to the man who is the President under the

Constitution. To harp upon what is past and gone and irre-
mediable, would be useless; the graver question affecting
personal liberty must be settled in such a way as to leave no
dangerous precedent. Meantime, we cannot suffer the country to go to pieces because the President has committed
errors. Let, then, the voice of this district and this city be
distinctly heard in favour of an immediate, vigorous pro-
secution of the war.

IX

There was one man in Washington while Lincoln was
President who might be expected to appreciate him above
all others. After Lincoln's death Walt Whitman came to
admire his genius, and in after years he was the recognized
expounder of what Lincoln was. Whitman wrote little,
however, concerning Lincoln's greatness until after his
death.

Whitman has become so closely associated with the
worship of Lincoln that it is commonly assumed that he
was one of the earliest diviners of Lincoln's genius.
Probably he was, but there is very little evidence of it in
the letters which he wrote while he was in Washington
during Lincoln's Administration. Years later he remembered truly that he had admired Lincoln, but he admitted
that at first he was quite as doubtful as others. W. E.
Barton has stripped the fanciful pictures of Whitman and
Lincoln to a few facts, which are evidence only of the
slightest acquaintance, and he has shown how the false
ideas of Whitman's intimacy with Lincoln grew in the
last years of the Good Gray Poet.

For want of any written opinion of Whitman on Lincoln
prior to 1863, it is necessary to take a conversation with
Horace Traubel dated November 11, 1888, for information

on Whitman's earliest opinion: 'We talked of Lincoln; "What was your first impression of Lincoln?" W.: "I did not enthuse at the beginning, but I made up what I may call a prophetic judgment from things I heard of him: facts, stories, lights that came in my way."'

The significant statements are that he did not immediately realize the greatness of Lincoln, and that he obtained his knowledge of Lincoln from others.

By March, 1863, Whitman had attained a definite and genuine conception of Lincoln, which, although it bears the stamp of popular opinion at the time, shows some real divination. He wrote on March 19, to Nat and Fred Gray:

> I think well of the President. He has a face like a Hoosier Michael Angelo, so awful ugly it becomes beautiful with its strange mouth, its deep cut, criss-cross lines, and its doughnut complexion. — My notion is, too, that underneath his outside smutched mannerism, and stories from third-class county barrooms (it is his humor) Mr. Lincoln keeps a fountain of first-class practical telling wisdom. I do not dwell on the supposed failures of his government; he has shown, I sometimes think, an almost supernatural tact in keeping the ship afloat at all, with head steady, not only not going down, and now certain not to, but with proud and resolute spirit, and flag flying in sight of the world, menacing and high as ever, I say never yet captain, never ruler, had such a perplexing dangerous task as his, the past two years. I more and more rely upon his idiomatic western genius, careless of court dress or court decorum.

Thus Whitman was voicing a conception in 1863 that was to become poetry in 1865. The captain of the ship was not merely the poetic figure of a moment to be used or discarded, but the one metaphor which fit Whitman's Lincoln.

On June 30, 1863, Whitman wrote of Lincoln in a letter to his mother:

> Mr. Lincoln passes here (14th Street) every evening on the way out. I noticed him about half past 6 — he was in his barouche, two horses, guarded by about thirty cavalry. The barouche comes first under a slow trot, driven by one man on the box, not servant or footman beside; the cavalry all follow closely after with a lieutenant at their head. I had a good view of the president last evening. He looks more care-worn even than usual, his face cut with deep lines, seams, and his complexion gray through very dark skin — a curious looking man, very sad. I said to the lady who was looking with me, 'Who can see that man without losing all wish to be sharp upon him personally?' The lady assented, though she is almost vindictive on the course of the administration (thinks it wants nerve, etc., — the usual complaint).[1]

Although he presents himself here as to a certain extent the champion of the President, his words can hardly be called enthusiastic.

In a letter to his mother, October 27, 1863, he said, 'I have finally made up my mind that Mr. Lincoln has done as good as a big human man can do. I still think him a pretty big President.' One other reference to Lincoln Whitman made in a letter to his mother written in March, 1864, in which he simply stated, 'I believe in Grant and Lincoln too.'

In the description of Lincoln as he appeared after the inauguration on March 4, 1865, we have the last of those written before Lincoln's death. This sketch appeared in *Specimen Days*:

> ... He was in his plain two-horse barouche, and look'd very much worn and tired; the lines, indeed, of vast responsibilities,

---

[1] There is a similar description in *Specimen Days*, dated August 12, 1863, neither so interesting nor so revealing as this.

ABRAHAM LINCOLN IN 1864

upon his dark brown face; yet all the old goodness, tenderness, sadness and canny shrewdness, underneath the furrows. (I have never seen the man without feeling that he is one to become personally attach'd to; for his combination of purest, hardiest tenderness, and native western ever rudest forms of manliness.) By his side sat his little boy, of ten years....

These are the statements on which any opinion of Whitman's contemporary estimate of Lincoln must be based. They are meager enough when the later writings of Whitman are considered in their sympathetic adoration. When Lincoln was alive, Whitman judged him to be 'a pretty big President'; after Lincoln was dead, he appeared to Whitman 'the grandest figure yet on all the crowded canvas of the nineteenth century.'

X

If there was one true diviner of Lincoln, that one was John Lothrop Motley. Of Brahmin rank, he had not been, apparently, so badly bitten by the pride of caste as had Holmes, Bancroft, or even Lowell. If the personal equation in opinion were capable of being solved, Motley and Emerson would offer interesting and contrasting problems in their opinions of Lincoln. Both men met Lincoln twice and talked with him somewhat at length. Both were gratified to find him not the boor they had expected. Emerson went away pleased, but in no way convinced of the real character of the man, and did not perceive for some months any evidences of his genius. Motley went away satisfied that there was in the man a nobility and courage of character and a considerable native wisdom which were far more significant than his apparent ignorance in military and state matters. Not until he perceived in September, 1862, the true genius with which

Lincoln had been marshaling his forces from discordant elements, did Emerson realize his greatness. It had to be demonstrated to him. Motley arrived by some intuition, or by a genuine perception of character, at a high estimate of Lincoln on the second visit to the White House. Thereafter, Motley came within less than a year to venerate Lincoln as the type of all that was good in America. What sympathetic chords were touched in those brief interviews? Their story is told by Motley in two letters written to his wife.

June 20, 1861. My dearest Mary, — I told you that I went with Seward in the evening of Monday to see the President. He looks younger than I expected — less haggard than the pictures — and on the whole, except for his height, which is two or three inches above six feet, would not be remarked in any way as ill- or well-looking. His conversation was commonplace enough, and I can hardly remember a single word he said except when we were talking — all three — about the military plans in progress, he observed, not meaning anything like an epigram, 'Scott will not let us outsiders know anything of his plans.' He seemed sincere and honest, however, and steady, but of course it is quite out of the question for me to hazard an opinion on so short an acquaintance as to his moral or intellectual qualities.

June 23, 1861. I went and had an hour's talk with Mr. Lincoln. I am very glad of it, for had I not done so, I should have left Washington with a very inaccurate impression of the President. I am now satisfied that he is a man of very considerable native sagacity; and that he has an ingenuous, unsophisticated, frank, and noble character. I believe him to be as true as steel, and as courageous as true. At the same time there is doubtless an ignorance about State matters, and particularly about foreign affairs, which he does not affect to conceal, but which we must of necessity regret in a man placed in such a position at such a crisis. Nevertheless, his very modesty in this respect disarms criticism....

THE DIVINERS OF LINCOLN

... Afterwards he took up his message, which was lying in loose sheets upon the writing table, and read me nearly the whole of it, so far as it was written. On the whole, the document impressed me very favourably. With the exception of a few expressions, it was not only highly commendable in spirit, but written with considerable untaught grace and power.

On June 22, 1862, Motley wrote his second daughter concerning Lincoln:

... I have the most profound respect for him, which increases every day. His wisdom, courage, devotion to duty, and simplicity of character seem to me to embody in a very striking way all that is most noble in the American character and American destiny. His administration is an epoch in the world's history, and I have no more doubt than I have of my existence that the regeneration of our Republic for a long period to come will date from his proclamation calling out the first 75,000 troops more than a year ago.

That proclamation was read 'amid bursts of laughter by the rebel Congress'; but people do not laugh at Abraham Lincoln now in any part of the world, whatever else they may do or say.

Again, he wrote to his mother on August 2, 1864.

... I venerate Abraham Lincoln exactly because he is the true honest type of American Democracy. There is nothing of the shabby genteel, the would-be but couldn't-be fine gentleman; he is the great American Demos, honest, shrewd, homely, wise, humorous, cheerful, brave, blundering occasionally, but through blunders struggling onward towards what he believes the right.

On learning of Lincoln's assassination, Motley wrote to the Duchess of Argyll that he could not trust himself to speak of the man in death for whom he had so great reverence in life. He had loved the man as he had admired and venerated the President.

THE LINCOLN LEGEND

XI

In addition to these accounts, which present a comparatively continuous growth of the general esteem in which Lincoln was held, there are countless stray references in the letters and works of other writers which reveal a generous respect and, occasionally, adoration. George William Curtis was a staunch believer in Lincoln's ability, even at times when Lowell and Norton were doubtful. Henry James, Sr., held a high opinion of Lincoln, and when Sumner and many other friends were in 'despond with regard to the Civil government... Mr. James believed in Lincoln.' Young William James wrote to his father: 'Poor old Abe! What is it that moves you so about his simple, unprejudiced, honest career? Is it that he seems the representative of pure, simple human nature against all conventional additions?' Henry James, Jr., wrote in after years of the respect and veneration for Lincoln under his father's roof. Young John Fiske thought in 1862, '"Old Abe" the most glorious ruler we ever had.' Without multiplying instances, there is, in general, the evidence of respect for Lincoln's ability and appreciation of his accomplishment, which grows from month to month — now at a standstill, now leaping ahead — until, to the divining intellects he becomes an extraordinary figure of genius and power even before his assassination.

The evidence of all the men admitted to Lincoln's intimacy is that he maintained, without the least effort or assumption, a singular dignity and reserve in the midst of his easiest conversation, but among these men there is much variety of opinion as to Lincoln's character as has appeared in the accounts of the men of letters who knew him chiefly by his deeds and writings and only occasionally in a personal degree. In the individual judgments the differences may be assigned, generally, to evident personal bias. Two classes of men were never able to comprehend Lincoln: those who judged entirely by conventional standards of breeding and those who were poisoned by political hatred or blinded by egotism and worship of their one ideal. A combination of the two brought about the invectives of a Wendell Phillips. An absence of these factors in greater or lesser degree enabled Emerson, Lowell, Norton, Motley, and others to divine the ability of Lincoln accordingly. It is interesting to note in individual instances the cause of final capitulation. For Lowell and Emerson it was the realization of the harmony and wisdom of Lincoln's course of action and expression of purpose, which came to each of them only after study and careful weighing of evidence. For Norton it was the realization of a new kind of dignity of thought and expression, which seemed at first glance uncouth. For Motley it was an intuitive knowledge of the character and sagacity of the untried man that gave a firm faith in what he would become.

The conception of Lincoln as a man of very ordinary talents who became in five years of stress educated to a point of intellectual greatness cannot hold. It was inevitable that Lincoln should grow and change, but the essential elements of greatness which were generally recognized after his death and canonization were, if they existed at all, present in the Lincoln of 1860. As we have seen, these elements were occasionally recognized even at an early date, and as the months passed by, the careful observer who perceived them became more and more convinced of his opinion. That Lincoln educated his observers to his greatness seems as plausible as that he achieved it all within so brief a period of years.

THE LINCOLN LEGEND

The point has been often made that Lincoln was never in the largest sense a popular and recognized leader outside of Illinois before his election, and it has been further contended that during his Administration he was not so considered. John Brown was the spirit that inspired the Abolitionists, but he in no wise symbolized the spirit which brought volunteers who were unopposed to slavery. The least that can be claimed for Lincoln is that he was the hope of those who placed the Union above all other issues. A survey of public opinion from 1860 to 1865 reveals no figure that can challenge Lincoln's general popularity. The *Diary* of Adam Gurowski, a document which is generally typical of all dissatisfactions with public men of the time, criticizes and ridicules Lincoln unmercifully, but it is significant that, checking criticism for criticism, Lincoln is the only figure besides Grant who comes out of the ordeal with enough approbation to offset his condemnation.

From 1860 to 1865 Lincoln was the only man who can be said to have maintained from year to year the confidence of any great portion of the people in the North. Although he was certainly distrusted and hated, he enjoyed a larger degree of confidence than is generally admitted. If he was a genius, he was recognized as such within his brief period of elevation by the more perspicuous of his contemporaries. In many ways the Lincoln now known to the world is a mythical figure, but it must not be forgotten that even to his contemporaries he was more than an ordinary man.

III

Between Folklore and Fiction

In CONSIDERING the character of the young Lincoln and
that of his parents as portrayed in the varied, and often
contradictory, accounts given by both biographers and
fictionists, one is struck by the consistent emphasis in
practically every case on certain incidents which forecast
the later Lincoln. All but the best biographers are as intent as the fictionists in presenting a story that is worthy
of the later Lincoln. If they do not hesitate to paint what
they consider an accurate picture of the squalor of his
early life, it is only because that background enhances the
romance. If their conception of romance makes such a
background seem alien to the beautiful story, they consistently seize upon every opportunity to relieve the dark
picture. In critically examining the story of Lincoln's
early life, then, it is essential to keep in mind the later
figure.

By far the most important source of information on the
period of Lincoln's life from birth through his New Salem
days is Herndon. Lamon may be set aside, because what
he gives on the period is taken largely from Herndon's
manuscripts. Of the information which Herndon had, a
portion — how large is uncertain — was given by Lincoln himself in conversations which took place throughout
the years of their partnership and before Herndon had

established his purpose of writing a biography. These were recalled and related at first hand. But by far the larger portion of information was collected for the purpose of biography after Lincoln's assassination. The method of collection was very simple. Herndon visited the New Salem country and interviewed as many old settlers as remained; he visited and wrote to the surviving relatives of Lincoln and to the older inhabitants of the Kentucky and Indiana settlements where the family had lived. In the case of the Kentucky informants we must consider that it is in every case a memory of fifty years at the least; in that of Indiana, thirty-five years; New Salem, thirty years. Furthermore, much of the information came from the children of parents who had died. But these things are no obstacles to the memory of a great man; we may judge from the material that Herndon got. Later Ida M. Tarbell collected a considerable amount of similar material, but it is chiefly to Herndon that the writers of poetry and fiction have gone for their matter.

There is a vast difference between pure fiction and folklore, though it is often hard to detect. It is largely of these two species of material that the accounts of the early life of Lincoln are composed. The occasion for the two is, however, practically the same. Once Lincoln's fame had become established nationally, the facts of his early life as remembered came to have a generally new significance, and those persons who felt that because of a geographic proximity they should know something of the man, but did not, began to gather what they could and manufacture what they could not gather. Hence there came into existence a body of material between fact, fiction, and folklore that will never permit an entirely accurate evaluation. Toward this material a present-day biographer may take whatever attitude he chooses. He may use what seems best for his purpose; he may present much of it and leave the reader to draw his own conclusions; he may elaborate it yet more and interpret as he desires. The poet and fictionist are at even greater liberty.

In surveying the enormous amount of material in all three fields — biography, fiction, and poetry — it has been difficult to determine in many cases which is the more factless. In all three the material is colored not so much by the fact that the author is writing biography, fiction, or poetry as by his attitude and method. Hence a biography is often largely legend, and a novel is often quite commendable as biography. The better biographies, of course, are excepted, although even the best yet written show in particular instances a tendency to accept legend when facts are not obtainable. It is the purpose of this chapter to examine some of the popular and important phases of these early years as they are related in the literature of all three types, with an eye to the beginnings of each legend and to the general significance that each attains.

I

THE GENESIS OF THE HERO

The birth and parentage of Lincoln have come from the realms of uncertainty and speculation through an era of dispute to an established tradition based on a few facts. The cycle of stories which revolve about Thomas Lincoln and Nancy Hanks and the wondrous babe passes through many strange and contradictory phases. Nancy Hanks and the boy have become a pure legend. Thomas Lincoln has left with his unideal memory enough of uncertainty to permit the polishing which has made the most of what may be supposed.

In the earliest biographies the accounts of Nancy Hanks are brief and based largely upon the author's imagination. Of the campaign biographies only those by J. L. Scripps and W. D. Howells show much acquaintance with the simplest facts, and those were such as Lincoln himself gave in brief in the letter to J. W. Fell and the autobiography written for J. L. Scripps.[1]

Then came that great piece of fiction, *The Pioneer Boy*, by W. M. Thayer, which gave a considerable picture of the Lincolns, but which had little more basis than the author's imagination. Nancy Hanks was presented, quite naturally, as a kind and loving mother who was a continual inspiration to her family. She was a woman of extraordinary intelligence and great spiritual force. The author wrote these things without taking a great chance that they would be contrary to fact. In J. G. Holland's *Life* the number of facts is not much increased, and the picture given is highly colored with praise. These biographies, together with an early 'dime novel' biography by J. O. Victor and one by the worthy Horatio Alger, Jr., are in the 'Parson' Weems tradition. Lincoln furnished an ideal figure for the vindication of the honesty, industry, and grit that was 'bound to rise.' He was a model of purity and a stainless example. But during these years from 1860 to 1865 legends, gossip, and scandal had been gathering, and among them were disgraceful stories of Nancy Hanks's immorality and Abraham's illegitimacy. The first known references in print are in the campaign literature of 1864 satirizing and vilifying Lincoln.[2] But

[1] See Lincoln, *Complete Works*, 1, 596, 638–44.
[2] *Book of the Prophet Stephen* and *Abraham Africanus I*.

though the story had been growing apace for some time and had become well disseminated by gossip, the actual literature did not appear until after the biographies of Lamon and Herndon.

It is to Herndon that we owe the first collection of what information of importance there was available concerning Nancy Hanks, and from it there is little that can be extracted without question. Those who claimed to remember Nancy differed in their opinions even of her physical appearance. Dennis Hanks, who certainly knew her as well as anyone then living, first described her as 'spare Made thin Visage.... Lite hare and Blue Eyes,'[1] and later maintained that her 'hair was dark — eyes blueish green' that she was five feet eight inches tall and weighed 'one hundred and thirty pounds.'[2] The several other describers differed among themselves as much as Dennis Hanks did with himself. Of the conglomeration of evidence one may take the choice of physical attributes according to his own idea of what a heroine should be, and that seems to be what those who *knew* Nancy did.

In regard to her qualities of mind and character those who knew her are quite in agreement in essentials. She was uncommonly intelligent — intellectual, in fact. 'Her memory was strong, her judgment... accurate. She was spiritually and ideally inclined.'[3] She was, above all, kind and affectionate. It is interesting to note that these excellent qualities were assigned to her, before Herndon began collecting his material, by such biographers as W. M. Thayer, who had little information other than his own imagination.

[1] Hanks to Herndon, Weik MSS., quoted from Beveridge, I, 16.
[2] Second Chicago statement, quoted from Beveridge, I, 16.
[3] *Ibid.*, I, 16.

Lincoln himself revered the memory of his mother and attributed to her whatever ability he possessed. It would be difficult to estimate to just what extent one of Lincoln's statements, as recorded by Holland, has moulded the legendary figure of his mother, 'All that I am, or hope to be, I owe to my angel mother.' The statement was made to Herndon, who wrote a little less worshipfully, 'All that I am or ever hope to be I owe to her.' It is such an expression as any man is likely to make, but in this case it has been of great significance. It has furnished the keynote of the Nancy Hanks legend.

The matter of Nancy's education has never been and probably never will be definitely settled. The traditional account is that she was educated far above the average woman of her time and community. She is represented as teaching her husband what little he knew of reading and writing. To Abraham she devoted all of her spare time, reading the Bible and teaching him to write. In the face of this legend is the fact that she signed legal documents by making her mark. A. J. Beveridge has attacked this part of the legend by stating: 'She was absolutely illiterate. No signature of Nancy Hanks has yet been discovered.... There is no evidence whatever that she could read.'

The following sentences, taken from biographies by I. N. Arnold and J. G. Holland, are typical of the less exaggerated but fanciful accounts in biography:

She was unusually intelligent, reading all the books she could obtain. She taught her husband, as well as her son Abraham, to read and write. She was a woman of deep religious feeling, of the most exemplary character, and most tenderly and affectionately devoted to her family. Her home indicated a degree of taste and a love of beauty exceptional in the wild settlement in which she lived.... Hers was a strong, self-reliant spirit, which commanded the respect as well as the love of the rugged people among whom she lived.

Mrs. Lincoln, the mother, was evidently a woman out of place among those primitive surroundings. She was five feet, five inches high, a slender, pale, sad and sensitive woman, with much in her nature that was truly heroic, and much that shrank from the rude life around her. A great man never drew his infant life from a purer or more womanly bosom than her own; and Mr. Lincoln always looked back to her with an unspeakable affection.... His character was planted in this Christian mother's life. Its roots were fed by this Christian mother's love; and those who have wondered at the truthfulness and earnestness of his mature nature, have only to remember that the tree was true to the soil from which it sprang.

If the biographers, with the help of 'those who knew' Nancy, created a legendary figure, they created one which in essentials directly suited the taste of the poets and novelists. It only remained for the legend to be given its decorations. It was not enough that legend had said that Nancy was deeply religious, in the wild manner of religion on the frontier. Hezekiah Butterworth portrays her, *In the Boyhood of Lincoln*, as more of 'a visionary.' 'They say that she used to see things at camp meetin's and lose her strength, and have faraway visions. She might have seen fairies.' She was the mystic mother of a mystic son — to quote one of the epic poems, *A Man of Destiny*, by E. L. Staples —

> A life that hid a solemn mystery.

That Nancy Hanks was superstitious is quite likely. But superstition has become something far more significant to a novelist in the light of mystical interpretations of Lincoln's character. She, too, was a dreamer of dreams that were prophecies, and such dreams were the inspiration of her boy:

> 'I had such a wonderful dream — the same one I had before you were born, my Boy. God had answered my prayer and sent me a son. I watched him grow to be a strong, brave, patient, wise and gentle man. Thousands hung on his words and the great from the ends of the earth came to do him homage. With uncovered head he led me into a beautiful home with white pillars. And then he bowed and whispered in my ear. "This is yours, my angel mother. I bought it for you with my life. All that I am I owe to you"...'

Thus Thomas Dixon portrays her in his novel, *The Southerner*.

Further, her religion is a thing of poetic beauty, an odd combination of pantheism and Calvinism. And in her religion and philosophy of life she is quite incomprehensible to her husband and friends. Out of place, out of time, she is an exotic being, and from her Abraham Lincoln draws the qualities which make him a prophet and savior of men. This picture is typical of what the average fictionist has made of Nancy Hanks, and practically every phase is an idealization of a fanciful biographical reminiscence.

The poet has been freer in his conception. Consequently, Nancy is conceived as a Madonna of the Backwoods. For example, James Oppenheim's poem on the wondrous babe, 'The Lincoln Child':

> Frail Mother of the Wilderness,
> How strange the world shines in,
> And the cabin becomes a chapel
> And the babe lies secure —
> Sweet Mother of the Wilderness,
> New worlds for you begin,
> You have tasted of the apple
> That giveth wisdom sure....

BETWEEN FOLKLORE AND FICTION

The antecedents of Nancy Hanks have, ever since the publication of Lamon's *Life of Lincoln*, been a question on which the ink of many biographers and genealogists has been spilt. The illegitimacy of Nancy seems at last to be above suspicion. Although there are two genealogies [1] which prove her legitimate, there is Herndon's testimony as to what Lincoln believed,[2] and then there is the corroborating testimony given by W. E. Barton in *The Lineage of Lincoln*. Now, I am so little of a genealogist that I hesitate to comment even briefly on these works, but here, if anywhere, the legend-makers have been at work. Caroline H. Hitchcock in her *Nancy Hanks* traces the Hanks family back through centuries to derive the name from the Egyptian *Ankh*, but with the Hanks family of Kentucky she makes numerous mistakes. Her mistakes were made with the purpose of getting an unblemished sequence for Nancy's family. W. E. Barton, after upsetting Hitchcock, proceeded to produce a genealogy in which he makes the Hankses cousins of the Lees, and Lincoln and Robert E. Lee distant kinsmen.[3] Perhaps this is something to be thankful for. Genealogies are matters of great seriousness to a surprising number of people. For them Lincoln could never have been great with an undistinguished lineage. Certainly, however, the blue blood in the veins of the Hankses or the Lincolns did not alter the status of either Thomas or Nancy or Abraham. They

[1] C. H. Hitchcock, *Nancy Hanks*, and J. H. Lea and J. R. Hutchinson, *Ancestry of Abraham Lincoln*.

[2] That his mother was the natural child of Lucy Hanks and a well-bred Virginia planter (see Herndon, 1, 3).

[3] W. E. Barton, *The Lineage of Lincoln*. The life of Lincoln genealogy seems to be as vain and fleeting as the proverbial bliss of this world. An irate Virginian has, so he maintains, refuted Barton's attempt to make Lincoln a Lee, with considerable righteous indignation. See Lyon G. Tyler, *Barton and the Lineage of Lincoln*.

were poor folks, poor whites, if you will, and so they remained until Abraham Lincoln himself raised the family's social position. It would be difficult to find a family contemporary with the Hankses and Lincolns in Kentucky whose lineage, if traced diligently, could not boast of many good and sound people as well as an occasional aristocrat. If David Starr Jordan is reliable, most of us of English descent are descendants through Isabel de Vermandois of Charlemagne, and according to E. M. Best, 'Every one of us is descended from William the Conqueror, and Anglo-Saxons are, all of us, at least thirtieth cousins to each other.'[1]

Of all the pictures of Nancy Hanks there is none more highly idealized than that given by Maria T. Davies in her novel, *The Matrix*, although there are elements in the picture that are entirely out of keeping with the spirit of the legend. Nancy's family connections are quite regular. The Hankses are models of Virginia gentility, on whom the rough-and-tumble Lincolns desire to pattern their own children. The glorious lineage of both families is a topic for fireside conversation, and the famous ancestors are a source of pride to the children. Nancy is a superwoman. 'She was probably the first woman in Kentucky to enter trade and secure her own financial independence.' She is utterly fearless, an athletic amazon who breaks horses. She is tender, too, and the nurse and protectress of unfortunate girls. It is from her lack of prudishness that the gossipy legends begin. She is intellectual. And so on *ad infinitum*. She is a picture of what the author probably considers the ideal modern woman.

The legendary Nancy was frail and sad — sad with

---

[1] D. S. Jordan and S. L. Kimball, *Your Family Tree*, 13. The genealogy of Abraham Lincoln, as well as that of Calvin Coolidge, is traced to Charlemagne.

weight of ages past, and premonitions of the years to come. Amid the rough, perhaps squalid, environment of half-faced camps and frontier settlements her spirit dwelt in another world, where life was beautiful. For her there were mystic prayers in the winds of the wilderness, and the whippoorwill and the darkened moon were talismans of Providence. She was wise with age-old wisdoms of birth and death and the inly glowing fire of eternal truth. Hers was a chosen lot to bear the savior of a nation and a race. The sweetest spirit of the years, our lady of sorrows, she gave to the world a perfect soul. Even as Mary she was chosen, and her babe was a carpenter's son.[1] She did not die. Her spirit walked the earth with her son and was ever in his dreams, a comfort and inspiration in his hour of trial.

The figure of Thomas Lincoln has never attained the legendary significance that attaches itself to Nancy Hanks. In the first place he lived too long. His memory was fresh and vivid at the beginning of Lincoln's ascendancy, for he did not die until January 17, 1851. When biographers came to write of Abraham Lincoln's father, there were the plain facts of the ordinary man who had numerous shortcomings. Then, too, there was general knowledge that Abraham Lincoln had never had much respect or love for his father. Indeed, it would seem that he held not even the love of a friend for his own father. He would not visit him during the lengthy illness that terminated the old man's life, and he did not attend the funeral. The relationship of father and son is not without its mystery. Both were, according to the unanimous testimony of friends and rela-

[1] The Christ analogy is inescapable in the legend of Lincoln, whether of the child or the man. More must be said of that anon, but here it is well to note that few authors have failed either to hint the analogy or to develop it at length.

tives, good-natured and friendly in a marked degree. Yet when Abraham was a lad, there were blows in plenty; and when he became grown there were only the necessary relations between the two.

The entire life of Thomas Lincoln had been a succession of hard and easy times, during which he moved along without gaining much, or losing much. He was just such a man as were the majority of his neighbors. His life was rough and poor, but neither rougher nor poorer than were the lives of many others. Had not his son become great, he would never have been accused of being a failure. He had no great ambition, and there was no shortcoming of it. The worst that can be said of him is that he was always poor. As Abraham attributed whatever genius he had to his maternal ancestry,[1] so the world has been content to consider the father no great source of explanation for the son. Thomas is not, however, without his supporters. As an antidote to the many bitter pictures of a shiftless, neglectful husband and unkind father, his strength of moral character and principles have been emphasized time and again. In view of the fact that much of Abraham Lincoln's genius has been presented as predominantly moral rather than intellectual, this character in his father is not without significance.

Thomas Lincoln is not without his legendary aspects, however; one of the most persistent of which is that he was the first Abolitionist in Kentucky. This legend begins in two of the early campaign biographies in the form of statements to the effect that Thomas moved to Indiana because of the growth of slavery in Kentucky.[2] This

[1] Herndon, I, 3.
[2] J. H. Barrett, *Life of Abraham Lincoln*, and J. G. Howard, *Life of Abraham Lincoln*.

seems to have had no more basis than shrewd supposition. It fitted well into the biography of his son. It was consistently denied by Dennis Hanks.[1] Herndon in denying the story notes inaccurately that there were not over fifty slaves in Hardin County at the time. And the fact remains that an aversion to slavery did not keep Thomas from serving as slave 'patroller' in 1805. Yet the story has grown in the popular telling.

In the hands of the novelist this legend has been magnified into a story of emancipation paralleling on a small scale the act of Abraham Lincoln. In *The Matrix*, by M. T. Davies, young Thomas, having inherited a slave from his mother, becomes conscious of the great moral wrong involved in one man's owning another. He begins to express himself against slavery and frees the slave. Thereupon he becomes very unpopular. As the days go by he becomes more and more outspoken on the subject, and as a result he is ostracized, and in his trade as a carpenter suffers want of employment. Eventually he has to leave, a victim of his own righteousness, a martyr for freedom. He removes to Indiana that he may breathe the air of a free country.

Possibly the best character sketch of Thomas Lincoln in his younger days, up to the time of Nancy's death, in either biography or fiction is that given by Thomas Dixon in his novel *The Southerner*. The character is not without an uncertain element of sentimental legend, but it is consistent. The biographical facts about Thomas Lincoln are cold, and the attempts to make him intellectual and consistently industrious are patently false. Dixon does

---

[1] 'It is said in the Biographies that Mr. Lincoln left the State of Ky. because... slavery was there. This is untrue.' — Hanks's second Chicago statement quoted from Beveridge, 1, 33.

not attempt to remodel him. His Thomas Lincoln is a man who regards learning and professional employment as degrading to a real man who would 'ruther fight Injuns an' wil' cats or rob a bee tree any day.' He thinks that 'Dan'l Boone wuz about biggest man that ever lived.' He visions *work* as a frightful bogey. He is afraid that when he is dead his headstone will bear the inscription, 'Born a Man — and Died a Jackleg Carpenter.' 'Wouldn't that be awful?' To one who knows the philosophy of the male in certain of our backwoods sections today, the character is delightfully familiar. And just there lies at once a probably accurate estimate, and yet the truly heroic and poetic element of the entire frontier legend as it is given in the lives of such men as David Crockett, Daniel Boone, or Thomas Lincoln. If they were men who did not fit into the prosperity of an organized community, yet they were heroic in the wilderness.

In general the character of Thomas Lincoln is unattractive and has not been of importance in the growth of the mystic legend of Lincoln. As an epic summary of his shortcomings, *A Man of Destiny* may be quoted again:

> He was an ill-starred man, like Sisera,
> And in their course the stars against him fought!

On the many legends of Lincoln's illegitimacy it is necessary to comment, though briefly. W. E. Barton has dealt with them at length in *The Paternity of Lincoln* and has probably disposed of them with sufficient finality in spite of a few significant mistakes. The legend, or legends, as he deduces, probably did not begin before 1860, but certainly they were broadcast and generally known in political circles much earlier than he supposes. The statement that the story did not get into print until 1872, when it appeared in Lamon's *Life of Lincoln*, is disproved by very specific references in political satires of 1864.[1] The exact nature of these brief references would seem to indicate an early currency of the Kentucky scandal of Abraham Inlow. But, far from damaging Barton's thesis, these references rather uphold it by giving an earlier starting-point for the legends in the various localities. It is more probable that a legend could have got under way and developed in North Carolina and Virginia, if a few years of general currency preceded Lamon's *Life of Lincoln*. Eight or nine years can enshroud popular gossip in an antiquity that is well-nigh unapproachable.

The general source of the legend is in the matted thicket of uncertainty which all but obscures the early life of the Lincolns in Kentucky. In 1860 there was need of a Lincoln biography. The first material given to J. L. Scripps by Lincoln formed the basis of at least two of the campaign biographies.[2] A representative was sent to Springfield for a few days by William Dean Howells to collect the materials which were later woven into the brief biography by Howells and John L. Hayes. One of the campaign biographies shows practically no knowledge of Lincoln's early life and relies on fiction.[3] When LaRue County, Kentucky, became aware that the Republican presidential candidate had been born therein, its inhabitants began to talk and search for those who might have known the Lincolns. A few were found, and as time went on their mem-

[1] *Abraham Africanus I: His Secret Life as Revealed under the Mesmeric Influence.* Lincoln is referred to as 'Abe Hanks, likewise named Abe Lincoln' (p. 46). In the *Book of Prophet Stephen* the following passage, which refers to the Inlow stories, appears: 'Now it came to pass on the seventh day of the eighth month, the same being the fifth month of the reign of Abraham, the son of Inlow, whose mother was of the Ethiopian tribe of Hanks... etc.' (pp. 29–30).

[2] Those by J. L. Scripps and D. V. G. Bartlett.

[3] The 'Wigwam Edition.'

ories improved, until the stories became numerous and lengthy. The decidedly questionable authenticity, wholly or in part, of all these stories has been dealt with by L. A. Warren in *Lincoln's Parentage and Childhood*, but the stories are generally such as might have been told of any family. Reminiscences of old men concerning their childhood playmate are likely to be inaccurate, but it is significant that, although the stories may be questioned, they do not differ materially in spirit. The biographers have seen fit to use what of the material they wished and to omit what they wished, without a great deal of questioning.

While the inhabitants of LaRue were recalling their vague notions of the Lincolns, one man, Samuel Haycraft, clerk of the County Court at Elizabethtown, began searching the court records for facts of the family. To make a long story short, he found the record of the marriage of Thomas Lincoln and Mrs. Sarah Bush Johnston, but found no record of the marriage of Thomas Lincoln and Nancy Hanks. This failure became noised abroad, and from it grew suspicions and gossip, which by the inspiration of Abraham Lincoln's political enemies were woven into definite stories that gathered a new element in each telling. At a time when Lincoln was perhaps the best-hated as well as the best-loved man in the country, it is not strange that the stories traveled along the 'grapevine telegraph' until they had become well established in the border States. It is interesting to note that the most fruitful soil for the growth of the stories was in the States of Kentucky, Virginia, North Carolina, and South Carolina — to be more specific, the mountainous western parts of Virginia and the Carolinas and the mountainous eastern parts of Kentucky and Tennessee. The fierceness of partisan sentiment in these border sections without doubt assisted the dissemination of the stories, but the remarkable fact is that they were often perpetuated by avowed Unionists and admirers of Lincoln, until they were woven in with the facts and fictions of local history.

It would be useless to retell the many separate and yet closely connected stories of Lincoln's birth. Anyone who has not become acquainted with some or all of them may find a lengthy presentation in W. E. Barton's *Paternity of Lincoln*. It is worth while, however, to add to Barton's comments a note on the significance of these legends when taken as a part of the whole.

It would be hard to find another national hero the modern world over whose life has become as much the common property of each individual. It was so in these border sections, and to a large extent farther north, within a few months after his election. During that brief period as at no time since, the forces of legend-making were at work. There was at once a great popular hero and a great popular villain in the person of Abraham Lincoln. About this man's life there was little authoritative information that dated back of 1850, and very little of that was in print. There was, as a result, practically no check on the stories that began to weave themselves about his name. The situation, especially in the rural sections, was not unlike that in which the oral legends of King Arthur probably began. And just as the inoffensive legends, which have not been and probably never will be entirely disproved, grew up; so these scandalous seven fathers of Lincoln came into existence, each to the degradation of Nancy Hanks. If, however, the figure of Lincoln had remained purely that of a folk-hero for a hundred years, if his biographers had never had printing presses, the legends of Lincoln's birth would probably have been assimilated into the great legend as one of the supernatural evidences. What hero-myth is without its mystery of birth? If it was doubted that man could have fathered and mothered the gods of the ancients, it might be expected that there would be a mystery as to Lincoln's genesis; and the hiatus between the seven fathers and seven places of birth and the probability of a supernatural origin is but a step. A few years in a non-printing age would have sufficed for the mountaineers of the Appalachians to have completely assimilated the conflicting elements into some story of Lincoln's spiritual origin.[1]

II

THE MODEL BOY

The life of the young Lincoln as it was remembered in after years by his friends who had known him as a boy, or had known people who had known him, was inevitably remembered in the spiritual presence of the savior of the nation, the martyr and saint; and the veil of sadness was before their misty eyes. So what was remembered took on a new significance. Every act became in some respect hallowed; as the man was great, so was the child; as the man was sad, so was the child; as the man was infinitely tender, so was the child; as the man was a prophet, so was the child; as the man was champion of the weak and oppressed, so was the child. What was not remembered was invented, and so the legend grew. As years went by, there were those who remembered things not in keeping with

[1] In part four of D. J. Snider's 'Lincoln Tetralogy,' *Lincoln at Richmond*, the figure of Lincoln has attained such a spiritual magnitude that the author finally concludes that he was begotten, 'Not of Tom Lincoln, but of God the Father' (p. 17), which is not out of keeping with modern Christian doctrine.

the legend, but generally there was reason to believe that they were unreliable witnesses.

Thus it was recalled that he was never late to school. He was a model of neatness and 'noted for keeping his clothes clean.' He was 'very quiet during playtime; never was rude; seemed to have a liking for solitude; was the one chosen in almost every case to adjust difficulties between boys of his age and size, and when appealed to, his decision was an end of the trouble.' Again, 'No stimulant ever entered his lips, no profanity ever came forth from them.' What a model for mothers to point out to their sons! When this boy grew up, he must have forgotten some of the principles which guided his youth, for he was never noted in later life for being excessively particular about his appearance.

The stories of Lincoln's kindness to animals are legion, and certainly many are fiction. Some of the more famous are doubtless fact, especially those which Lincoln himself related in later life, but these are merely the suggestions of what were to be remembered a few years later. Terrapins, toads, fawns, dogs, hogs, pigeons — all were beholden to young 'Abe' for protection against the cruelties of mankind. The fact that he never cared for the one great sport of the frontier, hunting, gave rise to many sentimental and fantastic stories of his 'chicken-heartedness.' There are stories of boyhood speeches and essays against cruelty to animals which, in view of the practice of invoking the name of Lincoln in behalf of all and sundry reform movements, it is strange have not been utilized by the anti-vivisectionists.[1]

[1] In contrast with this traditional softness is a story of how Lincoln, John Hanks, and Denton Offutt sewed up the eyelids of a drove of hogs that refused to be driven onto the flatboat bound for New Orleans. The versions of the story, as usual, are at variance and the specific part played by Lincoln is doubtful. It

Once during his boyhood in Indiana Lincoln wrote as a penmanship specimen copy for a friend the following couplet:

> Good boys who to their books apply
> Will all be great men by and by.

This bit of schoolroom philosophy is the theme of a great portion of the popular presentations of the boyhood of Lincoln. The pictures of young Lincoln studying before the flickering fire, lying at full length in the forest with his head on a log or on the counter of Offutt's store, reading, or leaning against a shock of fodder with the ever-present book in hand — such pictures as adorn the children's books of Lincoln and decorate the classrooms on Lincoln's Birthday — the never absent reiteration of his constant reading which appears in all accounts of his childhood and young manhood: these have created a popular fable that can never be dispelled. The facts of the studiousness of Lincoln were so colored in the first telling that their true color will never be known. To John and Dennis Hanks, as well as to Lincoln's father and stepmother and many friends of meager education and generally lowly ambitions in regard to study, the reading of Lincoln probably appeared enormous. When they began relating their recollections of the boyhood of the great man, the inference was too clear. 'Abe' had been a voracious reader in their eyes; he had achieved a grand success; the philosophy of the classroom was established; and their impressions of Abe's reading grew and grew. Thus the picture was painted, and thus it has been

is humorous to note, however, that the best argument given against the authenticity of the story is the immense tradition of Lincoln's softness (see Beveridge, 1, 107).

reproduced. Yet Herndon said of Lincoln the man
that

> He read less and thought more than any man in his sphere
> in America. No man can put his finger on any great book
> written in the last or present century that he read thoroughly.
> When young he read the Bible, and when of age he read
> Shakespeare; but, though he often quoted both, he never read
> either one through.

Subsequent biographers and critics have not been able to
establish a much larger list of books read by Lincoln as a
youth than that given by Herndon. Lincoln was never a
consistent reader, and yet he must ever be an exalted example of the doggerel theme. That he read sufficiently
and with comprehension goes without saying.

III

'HONEST ABE' AND 'FATHER ABRAHAM'

Lincoln was a local hero long before the conventions of
1860. It would be futile to attempt to set a date or name
an incident which would mark the beginning of all the
phases of his traditional figure. His honesty had apparently been a byword for years, although the countless
anecdotes of his honesty did not flourish until the campaign of 1860 and after. This phase of his popular character was as far-reaching in its appeal as the rail-splitting
episode.[1] Anyone who frowns upon the Washington
cherry-tree episode must find many stories of 'Honest
Abe' too disgusting for words. Those which have the
least claim to fact seem to be the most popular. The two

[1] In a political satire of 1864, *Abraham Africanus I*, the devil is represented
as telling Lincoln: 'You owe all your present success to four things. First, my
nomination. Second, your sobriquet of "Honest." Third, those weak points
of the Constitution.... Fourth, doing things quietly' (p. 10).

most often told anecdotes are of ancient standing and have, so far as I have been able to discover, not even the usual authority of some old friend of New Salem. The one tells how he closed up shop and walked several miles to return an overcharge of a few cents; the other, how he gave a customer short weight to the extent of a quarter of a pound of tea and on discovering his mistake again closed the store and carried the balance due to the customer. These are the stories that are told and retold in the grammar-school readers and the children's books. Side by side with Washington's 'Father, I cannot tell a lie,' these homely bits of honest example are enshrined, and they are true — in the spirit of the folk-hero.

Lincoln was a county-seat oracle for many years before his fame as a speaker of parables became national. The popular conception of his wit and wisdom was, until a martyr's death had hallowed it along with other memories, that of crude, sometimes questionable, and always humorous and to-the-point stories. The Rabelaisian character was admitted and generally accepted by the public. Enterprising humorists capitalized his fame and issued 'joke-books' which bore titles that connected the contents with 'Old Abe,' and many of the stories were directly assigned to him, though not one in ten was authentic.[1] Everyone who interviewed Lincoln came away with a story, true or false. It is recorded in many places how the dignity and solemnity of great occasions were upset by the inevitable story. Secretary Chase is generally represented as entirely out of sympathy with Lincoln's crude humor, and he certainly did not hesitate to frown upon

---

[1] An interesting example of these humorous perpetrations bore the title, *Old Abe's Jokes, Fresh from Abraham's Bosom; Containing all his Issues, excepting the Greenbacks, to Call in some of Which this Work is Issued.*

and regret it very highly on occasions. One of his friends, however, has left a picture of Chase condemning Lincoln's stories and then using them himself to advantage in the proper company.[1] The point is that this phase of the folk-hero was not looked down upon by the élite so much in reality as in imagination. Even Emerson remarked that in a more remote period he would have become mythological 'like Aesop or Pilpay or one of the Seven Wise Masters, by his fables and proverbs.' The two phases of this popular conception which have been at death grips since Lincoln's martyrdom were not so hard for his associates to reconcile as they have since become. There was a homely wisdom in the story and there was humor which might or might not be questionable. In the process of apotheosis these stories have been made into parables of saintly purity. On the other hand, those who enjoy a vulgar hero have made them fitly vile. The chimerical folk-hero must have his goatish part. It is significant that the day of the Lincoln anecdote is passing. During the first decade of the twentieth century numerous collections of Lincoln's yarns and stories still flourished, and since have gradually passed as the folk-hero became of less interest.

A cycle of stories has grown up as the result of another phase of the folk-hero; namely, his gentleness. It is a legend of pardons, reprieves, and fatherly kindness to the soldiers — a close analogy to the stories of kindness to animals which have already been noted as one of the most appealing elements of the legend of the boy Lincoln. The conventional picture given by the builders of the gentle legend is that of Father Abraham, a kindly, pleasant old man with a humorous smile which often fades into a look

[1] J. T. Trowbridge, *My Own Story*, 372.

of sadness.[1] He is forever enshrined in popular memory dressed in black, with tall hat and black shawl. The touch of earthiness is never in the picture drawn with loving fancy. He is never thought of as having any personal interest or ambition. It is only as the guardian angel of his children that he overlooks the vast arena of war and sadly smiles as the blood sinks into the thirsty sand. He bears his own burden uncomplainingly and gladly seeks to lighten the burden of others. His sad, plain features are simply glorious in their reflection of benignity, devotion, and a wisdom passing that of earth. Riding the circuit in Illinois, he is the friend of widows and orphans. Like Sir Charles Grandison, he always turns up at the moment of greatest need, renders the required assistance, and bows off the scene until some other extreme exigency arises. One does not wonder that Lincoln never grew rich; the marvel is that he ever had time enough of his own to make a living. Directing the affairs of the nation in Washington, he spends a large part of his time consoling distracted widows and mothers, personally looking after the soldiers' welfare, and issuing reprieves and pardons.[2]

There is a familiarity in this picture of the hero that breeds contempt even with its affection. Like the vision of God as a deified Santa Claus which may appear to the mind of a small child as he listens to his Sunday School teacher, it possesses a personal element which is difficult to retain in a conception of greater sublimity.

In no other phase of the legend do we have a better ex-

---

[1] The sobriquet 'Father Abraham' was popularized by James Sloane Gibbons in his war song 'We Are Coming, Father Abraham, Three Hundred Thousand More.'

[2] This Lincoln appears in such fiction as the following: M. R. S. Andrews, *The Counsel Assigned*; K. H. Brown, *The Father*; I. M. Tarbell, *Father Abraham*; T. N. Page, *The Red Riders*; R. H. Little, *Better Angels*.

ample of fiction becoming recognized as fact than in the matter of Lincoln's pardons. How many pardons Lincoln actually gave in the case of death sentences is not known. Two of the cases which are so often cited and romanticized are now, thanks to the investigations of W. E. Barton, known to be myth. It is certain, however, that there were two hundred and sixty-seven soldiers executed by the United States military authorities, and that each of these cases was tacitly sanctioned by Lincoln.[1]

There were such acts as the sweeping order in February, 1862, which provided for the wholesale release of political prisoners, and the Amnesty Proclamation of December, 1863. But these are not the type of thing to be romanticized. They are too capable of more prosaic interpretation as convenient political moves. Donn Piatt in his essay, 'Lincoln the Man,' offered a similar explanation for Lincoln's pardon of death sentences.

> There was far more policy in this course than kind feeling. To assert the contrary is to detract from Lincoln's force of character, as well as intellect. Our war-president was not lost in his high admiration of brigadiers and major generals, and had a positive dislike for their methods and the despotism upon which an army is based. He knew that he was dependent upon volunteers for soldiers, and to force upon such men as those the stern discipline of the Regular Army was to render the service unpopular. And it pleased him to be the source of mercy, as well as the fountain of honor, in this direction.

The most celebrated case of Lincoln's executive pardons is that of William Scott. It has become one of the almost indispensable anecdotes of Lincoln's years as President and has been the favorite myth of the tenderness of Father

---

[1] J. G. Randall, *Constitutional Problems Under Lincoln*, 175. 'No death sentence could be enforced without reference to the President.'

Abraham. One of the earliest versions appeared in the *New York Commercial Appeal*, April 21, 1862. It was related how the private 'Green Mountain boy' was sentenced to death for sleeping on his post and was pardoned shortly before the day of execution.

> The time drew near; the stern necessity of war required that an example should be made of someone; his was an aggravated case. But the case reached the ears of the President; he resolved to save him; he signed a pardon and sent it out; the day came. 'Suppose,' thought the President, 'my pardon has not reached him.' The telegraph was called into requisition; an answer did not come promptly. 'Bring up my carriage,' he ordered. It came, and soon the important state papers were dropped, and through the hot, broiling sun and dusty roads he rode to the camp, about ten miles, and saw that the soldier was saved!

In its many forms the story was generally accepted until W. E. Barton in his *Life of Lincoln* revealed that it was, so far as Lincoln was concerned, highly embroidered. The upshot of Barton's investigation was that, although Lincoln knew of the case, McClellan issued the pardon. No one drove in the hot sun to save Scott's life, and Lincoln probably never saw him.

The incident was celebrated in verse within a year by Francis DeHaes Janvier. 'The Sleeping Sentinel' was the title of the ballad which was in essentials the same as the above account. James E. Murdoch, a famous elocutionist of the period, published the ballad in 1866, along with his other favorite war pieces, with the note that he 'had the pleasure of reading this beautiful and touching poem, for the first time, to Mr. and Mrs. Lincoln, and a select party of their friends, at the White House.' *If* Murdoch read the poem to Lincoln, how Lincoln must have laughed!

BETWEEN FOLKLORE AND FICTION

The folk-story became history when in 1891 L. E. Chittenden, Register of the Treasury under Lincoln, testified to the fact that he knew all about it because he had been the one responsible for the soldier's pardon. He proceeded to give the most elaborate and fanciful version that had appeared in any branch of literature. The memory of such men as Murdoch and Chittenden has helped to create the Lincoln of the American folk.

This myth is the basis of one of the finest scenes in Drinkwater's play. It is the substance of several narrative poems. It is an episode in numerous Lincoln epics and novels. It appears in most of the biographies and collections of Lincoln anecdotes.

In March, 1863, Emerson referred to the lack of dignity which Lincoln displayed in running about saving soldiers' lives. Such an act was in keeping with the man he believed Lincoln to be, and although he did not approve, he did not doubt. That such a story was popular and current without denial for so long, is very strange, unless we realize that by general consent it was taken as true in spirit to the memory of Father Abraham.

Oddly enough, what is possibly the best expression of this legend of tenderness and pity appears in the poem 'Lincoln's Grave' by a Confederate soldier, Maurice Thompson, who conceived Lincoln in after years as a deity of tenderness and justice and a symbol of suffering and woe:

> He was the Southern mother leaning forth
> At dead of night to hear the cannon roar,
> Beseeching God to turn the cruel North
> And break it that her son might come once more;
> He was New England's maiden pale and pure,
> Whose gallant lover fell on Shiloh's plain;
> He was the mangled body of the dead;

He writhing did endure
Wounds and disfigurement and racking pain,
Gangrene and amputation, all things dread.
. . . .

Oh, every bullet-shock went to his heart,
And every orphan's cry that followed it,
In every slave's wild hope he bore a part,
With every master's pang his face was lit;
But yet, unfaltering, he kept the faith,
Trusted the inner light and drove right on
Straight toward his golden purpose shining high
        Beyond the field of death,
Beyond the trumpets and the gonfalon,
Beyond the war-clouds and the blackened sky.

IV

THE FRONTIER HERO

That curious and forever uncertain phenomenon, mob psychology, as it was demonstrated in the Illinois Republican Convention held at Decatur and in the National Convention held at Chicago in 1860, was of much the same variety that has always prevailed at political gatherings. The dramatic and unexpected can produce amazing results, among which are presidents. It would be foolish to assert that Abraham Lincoln was elected because of the popular heroic figure that he came to be within a few days of his nomination. But the importance of the heroic legend which made him at once and forever the symbol of democracy cannot be overestimated.

The worship of an extravagant and heroic figure was nothing new in American politics. John C. Frémont had nothing to his credit so important as his popular conception as the 'Pathfinder.' 'Old Hickory' and 'Rough and Ready' were more significant of the popular esteem for

Andrew Jackson and Zachary Taylor than all the praise that political friends could heap upon them. There was an heroic element in the frontier candidate that appealed as well in the more civilized portions of the country as in the environment in which it was bred. David Crockett enjoyed a popular idolatry in the East which wavered between the sublime and the ridiculous, and he became a pathetic figure only when he took his popularity too seriously. Lincoln inherited the popular throne which had been established by a frontier precedent. As time went on, he came to symbolize all that the heroic frontier had meant in its heroes of the past. It was this clustering of significances about his figure that made him immortally *the* American. He was the self-made man, the type of honesty, perseverance and grit, the intrepid Indian fighter, etc.

Richard J. Oglesby, a resident of Decatur and a friend of Lincoln, conceived a dramatic episode which he wished to present at the Illinois State Convention of 1860 in behalf of his friend Lincoln. He sought out John Hanks who had worked with Lincoln splitting rails in 1830, shortly after the arrival of the Lincolns, Hankses, and Halls in Illinois. Together they drove to the site of Lincoln's first Illinois farm and found the old rail fence which Lincoln and John Hanks had built thirty years before. From it they carried away two rails.

At an opportune moment during the convention, Oglesby introduced John Hanks, who brought in the rails bearing the legend:

Abraham Lincoln

The Rail Candidate

For President in 1860

The rest of the story of the State Convention is one of uproar and the vociferous selection of Lincoln as the Illinois candidate for the Republican nomination. The punning legend was accepted all over the State, and Lincoln became nationally known as the rail-splitter. 'In the words of an ardent Lincoln delegate, "These rails were to represent the issue of the coming contest between labor free and labor slave; between democracy and aristocracy."' They were more — the beginning of a popular legend which before many years were gone had gathered about its central figure all of the heroic tradition of the frontier and all of the meaning of the romance of democracy. The fact that there were many men in Illinois who had split rails — many more rails than Lincoln ever split — only served to enhance the meaning of the symbol. Lincoln rails were at a premium, and when the Chicago Convention was over, the rail had become a symbol of the Republican campaign.[1]

With the symbol of the rail before them the campaign biographers were not blind to the major theme of the Lincoln story as it was presented in the brief autobiographical account given to J. W. Scripps and as it was collected in brief from Lincoln's acquaintances. William Dean Howells was commissioned, together with John L. Hayes, to write a campaign biography. Evidently the task did not impress Howells as of any great moment, for he did not feel the need for personal investigation. But years after

[1] On the authority of Noah Brooks, Honoré W. Morrow denies that Lincoln's rail-splitting was very extensive. She quotes Brooks's relation of a conversation with Lincoln in which Lincoln said that he had not authenticated the rails brought in by John Hanks, but that 'if I ever split any rails on the piece of ground that those rails came from (and I was not sure whether I had or not), I was sure that those were the rails.' (See H. W. Morrow, *Mary Todd Lincoln*, 217.) In his biography of Lincoln, Brooks mentions the introduction of the rail as a symbol, but does not attempt to mitigate Lincoln's rail-splitting.

he remembered that the materials collected by an agent inspired him with the 'wild poetry of its reality.' An anonymous campaign biography published in Chicago, which gave no evidence of any certain knowledge of Lincoln's early life, portrayed him as the great example of American genius, and in an introduction, which anticipated the first chapter of F. J. Turner's *The Frontier in American History* in many notable particulars, assigned to the influence of the frontier whatever of peculiarity there was in American society and genius.[1]

The few significant incidents which are included in these early biographies explain the emphasis on the heroic theme — there is the rail-splitting, already famous, the flatboat voyages to New Orleans, the Black Hawk War, and varied accounts of physical prowess. He is above all other things 'the big buck of the lick.' In this rôle he is the champion of the weak and oppressed. Thus, in one great story are combined the elements on which the heroic legend that had been growing for years was to center. The fame of the frontiersman — the rail-splitter, Indian fighter, flatboatman, rough-and-tumble champion —found in Lincoln its highest type, a hero to glorify all its phases, except one. Lincoln was never a hunter.

As the country in general awoke to the realization that Lincoln was a hero, his friends did him the service of expatiating on the several episodes in which the mighty man was revealed. It was not enough that he was the strong man of the community; he was made to perform unbelievable feats of strength. He could outrun, outjump, outwrestle all comers. Those who remembered his strength with more moderation were simply outdone.

As a matter of history, the Black Hawk War is a ridicu-

[1] The 'Wigwam Edition.'

lous, if somewhat shameful, episode. No one has made its true significance any more apparent than Lincoln himself in a speech before the House of Representatives.[1] Yet its significance in the Lincoln legend is considerable. Several of the most familiar stories of his New Salem days are anecdotes of the war. It was then that as chosen champion of his company he was for the only time in his life outwrestled. One of the earliest yarns on record relates how he defied the entire company and saved the life of an old Indian who had strayed into camp.

But the great significance of the Black Hawk War did not become a part of the story until the fact became known that Lieutenants Jefferson Davis and Robert Anderson, who was later to become famous as the commander of Fort Sumter, participated in the episode as well as Lincoln. Here were three young men who were later to play important rôles in the Civil War. Quite naturally the fictionists and poets who were especially inclined made the most of the simple fact, and the Black Hawk episode was raised to the dignity of an epic prelude.[2]

The two flatboat excursions to New Orleans were commonplace enough. It was the easiest method that the Mississippi Valley farmer had of getting his produce to a

[1] By the way, Mr. Speaker, did you know I am a military hero? Yes, sir; in the days of the Black Hawk War I fought, bled, and came away. Speaking of General Cass's career reminds me of my own. I was not at Stillman's defeat, but I was about as near it as Cass was to Hull's surrender; and, like him, I saw the place very soon afterward. It is quite certain I did not break my sword, for I had none to break; but I bent a musket pretty badly on one occasion. If Cass broke his sword, the idea is he broke it in desperation; I bent the musket by accident. If General Cass went in advance of me in picking huckleberries, I guess I surpassed him in charges upon the wild onions. If he saw any live, fighting Indians, it was more than I did; but I had a good many bloody struggles with the mosquitoes, and although I never fainted from the loss of blood, I can truly say I was often very hungry. (*Works*, I, 142.)

[2] The most extravagant treatment of the Black Hawk War appears in D. J. Snider's *Lincoln in the Black Hawk War*.

considerable market. The boats that performed the voyage were great rough masses of lumber capable of floating a huge cargo. The current was the chief means of motion, but long sweeps which were necessary in managing the course of the boat added a few miles to each day's journey. At night it was necessary to tie up on the bank. Commonplace though the trips might have been, they must have had a large element of romance for Lincoln. They were his first view of an outside world. He remembered them in after years with enough vividness to mention them in his *Autobiography* along with a very small number of other events as important happenings in his early life.

It was the second of these voyages which became of great importance in the legend of Lincoln the Emancipator. We shall have occasion later to comment generally on the popular conception of Lincoln's significance as the Emancipator, but this one of many stories of his early hatred of slavery — all of the others with much less foundation than this — must be considered here.

After Lincoln had become universally known as the Emancipator, it was natural that antislavery anecdotes should be interpolated somewhere in the story of his early life. In 1865 this was done by John Hanks in a conversation with Herndon. Lamon gave the story in his biography from Herndon's material. It was not given by any of the earlier biographers.

Lincoln himself never mentioned it in writing and did so in conversation only to Herndon. In view of the significance which it has attained, it is strange that Lincoln should have neglected to relate so important an experience of his life at some later date, though it is not strange that the *Autobiography* written for J. L. Scripps did not men-

tion it, considering that it was for campaign consumption.
Herndon relates that

In New Orleans, for the first time Lincoln beheld the true
horrors of human slavery. He saw 'negroes in chains — whipped
and scourged.' Against this inhumanity his sense of right and
justice rebelled, and his mind and conscience were awakened
to a realization of what he had often heard and read. No
doubt, as one of his companions has said, 'Slavery ran the
iron into him then and there.' One morning in their rambles
over the city the trio passed a slave auction. A vigorous and
comely mulatto girl was being sold. She underwent a thorough
examination at the hands of the bidders; they pinched her
flesh and made her trot up and down the room like a horse,
to show how she moved, and in order, as the auctioneer said,
that 'bidders might satisfy themselves' whether the article
they were offering to buy was sound or not. The whole thing
was so revolting that Lincoln moved away from the scene with
a deep feeling of 'unconquerable hate.' 'By God, boys, let's
get away from this. If I ever get a chance to hit that thing,
meaning slavery, I'll hit it hard.' This incident was furnished
me in 1865, by John Hanks. I have also heard Mr. Lincoln
refer to it himself.

That this story is fiction it is difficult to prove, as, indeed, are many of the unlikely tales of Lincoln that have
for authority the memory of a friend. To say that John
Hanks and William Herndon lied is too much unless some
concrete denial of Lincoln is unearthed. But along with
the fact that Lincoln never mentioned it except to Herndon goes the fact that the original narrator, John Hanks,
did not go to New Orleans with Lincoln — though he went
as far as St. Louis — and could not have observed what he
described.[1] Also, if Lincoln became greatly perturbed at

[1] In the *Autobiography* written for J. L. Scripps in 1860, Lincoln told of both
boat trips to New Orleans, and of the second, that 'Hanks had not gone to New
Orleans, but having a family, and being likely to be detained from home longer
than at first expected, had turned back from St. Louis.' (*Works*, 1, 641.)

this early date about the evils of slavery, he certainly did not manifest any great determination against it for some years. But in keeping with the legend of the Emancipator the spirit of the story is true, and even doubting the verbal accuracy of John Hanks, the later biographers conclude the incident possibly a fact. It is hard to give up an incident of so much significance in the light of the popular conception of Lincoln, because it is a splendid example of his prophetic power and of his early consecration to a life purpose.[1]

As a dramatic incident the slave market has meant much to the primarily literary half of the Lincoln legend, although the story as told by Herndon has needed little dressing up. It is a remarkable testimony to the imagination displayed by Herndon that those who work Lincoln material into verse or fiction have usually not found it necessary to do more than retell. In some instances the

---

[1] There is a decided contrast between this and the spirit of Lincoln's account of the slaves seen en route to St. Louis in 1841, given in a letter to Miss Mary Speed, which is his earliest authentic account of any impressions of slavery:

'By the way, a fine example was presented on board the boat for contemplating the effect of condition upon human happiness. A gentleman had purchased twelve negroes in different parts of Kentucky, and was taking them to a farm in the South. They were chained six and six together. A small iron clevis was around the left wrist of each, and this fastened to the main chain by a shorter one, at a convenient distance from the others, so that the negroes were strung together precisely like so many fish upon a trot-line. In this condition they were being separated forever from the scenes of their childhood, their friends, their fathers and mothers, and brothers and sisters, and many of them from their wives and children, and going into perpetual slavery, where the lash of the master is proverbially more ruthless and unrelenting than any other where; and yet amid all these distressing circumstances, as we would think them, they were the most cheerful and apparently happy creatures on board. One whose offense for which he had been sold was an over-fondness for his wife, played the fiddle almost continually, and the others danced, sang, cracked jokes, and played various games with cards from day to day. How true it is that "God tempers the wind to the shorn lamb," or in other words, that he renders the worst of human conditions tolerable, while he permits the best to be nothing better than tolerable.' (*Works*, I, 52–53.)

story monopolizes the entire significance of the flatboat voyages, the emphasis depending upon whether the author is writing in the religious or the heroic vein. Often the incidents of each trip are combined into one. In the poetic vein the river voyage is best portrayed by Carl Sandburg. Indeed, in most respects *Abraham Lincoln: The Prairie Years* is the only complete treatment of Lincoln's early life which realizes the heroic qualities of the material and presents it in an heroic manner.

Without entirely abandoning the realm of possibility, Sandburg portrays with imagination what the voyage might have meant to a raw frontier youth with eager sensibilities as well as a strong body. Lincoln is never an ordinary frontier roughneck to Sandburg, and whether we conceive that biography may be legitimately poetic or not, the fact remains that Sandburg has told this important episode with more appreciation of its latent epic qualities than is ordinarily found in Lincoln literature. This is the sort of thing that has brought Sandburg recognition as Lincoln's most understanding interpreter. One may judge for himself from the following passage, which is in spirit and style typical of Sandburg's work:

As the snow and ice began to melt, a little before the first frogs started shrilling, in that year of 1828, they landed the boat and pushed off.

In charge of the boat Mr. Gentry had placed his son Allen, and in charge of Allen he had placed Abe Lincoln, to hold his own against any half horse, half alligator bush-whackers who might try to take the boat or loot it, and leave the bones of those they took it from, at Cave-in-Rock on the Illinois shore, or other spots where the skeletons of flatboatmen had been found years after the looters sold the cargo down the river. The honesty of Abe, of course, had been the first point Mr. Gentry considered; and the next point had been whether he could handle the boat in the snags and sandbars. The two young men pushed off on their trip of a thousand miles to New Orleans, on a wide, winding waterway, where the flat-boats were tied up at night to the river-bank, and floated and poled by day amid changing currents, strings of other flatboats, and in the paths of the proud white steamboats.

Whitecaps rose and broke with their foam feathers, a mile, two miles, beyond the limit of eyesight, as fresh winds blew along the Ohio River. Cave-in-Rock was passed on the Illinois shore, with its sign 'Wilson's Liquor Vault and House of Entertainment,' with a doorway 25 feet high, 80 feet wide, and back of that entrance a cavern 200 feet deep, a 14-foot chimney leading to an upper room, where one time later were found 60 human skeletons, most of them rivermen lured and trapped by the Wilson gang that camped at Hurricane Island near-by.

Timber-covered river bluffs stood up overlooking the river like plowmen resting big shoulders between the plow-handles; twisted dumps and runs of clay banks were like squatters who had lost hope and found rheumatism and malaria; lone pine trees had silhouetted their dry arms of branches on reefs where they dissolved and reappeared in river-mist lights as if they struggled to tell some secret of water and sky before going under.

The nineteen-year-old husky from Indiana found the Missis-sippi River as tricky with cosmic twists as Aesop's fables, as mystical, boding, and promising as the family Bible. Sand-bars, shoals, and islands were scattered along with the look of arithmetic numbers. Sudden rains, shifting winds, meant new handling of oars. A rising roar and rumble of noise might be rough water ahead or some whimsical current tearing through fallen tree-branches at the river side. A black form seems to be floating up-river through a gray drizzle; the coming out of the sun shows it is an island point, standing still; the light and air play tricks with it.

The bends of the river ahead must be watched with ready oars and sweeps or the flatboat naturally heads in to shore. Strong winds crook the course of the boat, sometimes blowing it ashore; one of the crew must hustle off in a rowboat, tie a hawser to a tree or stump, while another man on the big boat has a rope at the check-post; and they slow her down. Warning signals must be given at night, by waving lantern or firewood, to other craft.

So the flatboat, 'the broadhorn,' went down the Father of Waters, four to six miles an hour, the crew frying their own pork and corn-meal cakes, washing their own shirts, sewing on their own buttons.

Below Baton Rouge, among the sugar plantations known as the 'Sugar Coast,' they tied up at the plantation of Madame Duquesne one evening, put their boat in order, spoke their good nights to any sweet stars in the sky, and dropped off to sleep. They woke to find seven negroes on board trying to steal the cargo and kill the crew; the long-armed Indiana husky swung a crab-tree club, knocked them galley-west, chased them into the woods, and came back to the boat and laid a bandanna on a gash over the right eye that left a scar for life as it healed. Then they cut loose the boat and moved down the river.

At New Orleans they traded, sold the rest of their cargo of potatoes, bacon, hams, flour, apples, jeans, in exchange for cotton, tobacco, and sugar, and sold the flatboat for what it would bring as lumber. And they lingered and loitered a few days, seeing New Orleans, before taking steamer north.

On the streets and by-streets of that town, which had floated the flags of French, British, and American dominion, young Abraham felt the pulses of a living humanity with far heart-beats in wide, alien circles over the earth: English sailors who sang 'Ranzo' and 'Boney,' 'Hangin' Johnny,' and 'O Fare-you-well, My Bonny Young Girls'; Dutchmen and French in jabber and exclamative; Swedes, Norwegians, and Russians with blond and reddish mustaches and whiskers; Spaniards and Italians with knives and red silk handkerchiefs; New York, Philadelphia, Boston, Rome, Amsterdam, become human facts; it was London those men came from, ejaculating, "'Ow can ye blime me?'

Women in summer weather wearing slippers and boots; creoles with dusks of eyes; quadroon and octaroons with elusive soft voices; streets lined with saloons where men drank with men or chose from the women sipping their French wine or Jamaica rum at tables, sending quiet signals with their eyes or openly slanging the sailors, teamsters, roustabouts, rivermen, timber cruisers, crapshooters, poker sharps, squatters, horse thieves, poor whites; bets were laid on steamboat races; talk ran fast about the construction, then going on, of the New Orleans & Pontchartrain Railroad, to be one of the first steam railroads in America and the world; slaves passed handcuffed into gangs headed for cotton fields of one, two, six thousand acres in size; and everywhere was talk about niggers, good and bad niggers, how to rawhide the bad ones with mule whips or bring 'em to N'Orleans and sell 'em and how you could trust your own children with a good nigger.

As young Abe Lincoln and Allen Gentry made their way back home to the clearings of Pigeon Creek, Indiana, the tall boy had his thoughts. He had crossed half the United States, it seemed, and was back home after three months' vacation with eight dollars a month pay in his pocket and a scar over the right eye.

Similar in spirit to Sandburg's treatment is S. W. Meader's *Longshanks*, a novel of some merit as a picture of river life, which gives an interesting version of the first voyage, replete with fights and trials of strength, in which Lincoln is the conqueror of all comers, including 'broadhorn' crews, river pirates, and negroes. An Olympian struggle between Lincoln and David Crockett is introduced to establish Lincoln's supremacy over all frontier heroes.

The heroic element of Lincoln's early life has been the stumbling-block for those who recognize it and yet have not the sympathetic understanding to make it real. Not one of the epic poems or dramatic attempts has succeeded in grasping the truly heroic element of the frontier. The chief difficulty in every case is the memory of how heroes have been portrayed in the past, and the author makes it

painfully evident that he has read Homer and Shakespeare. One of the earliest attempts to portray the heroic
element will provide a sufficient example of the general
failure.

The Tragedy of Abraham Lincoln (1876) by Hiram D.
Torrie was one of the first dramatic productions based on
the life of Lincoln. The author was an American, but not a
native of the frontier. He relates in the introduction that
he had visited Illinois in order to collect his material and
gain a comprehension of the setting. John Hanks was his
chief informant. Taking the story in all the legendary
glory that John Hanks could impart to it, the author proceeded to dramatize it *à la* Shakespeare, and produced a
Lincoln who puns every few lines, and frontiersmen who
talk a strange jargon of mingled Shakespearean and
Illinois-American idiom. The play opens on a prairie
where games are about to commence among the young men.

> *Lincoln.* Among the lists there's not a lad I see in all these sports I
>   have not beaten oft.   (*Trying to fix his mind on his book.*)
> It may turn out that what Hanks says is right;
> That these warm friends would have a little spree
> Before my duties at the store commence —
> This selling conscience, like my goods, so much per yard.
> They now should come, I hope they'll be in time;
> I never was too late — they're coming now.
> I'll put this 'Blackstone' up. (*Hiding his book.*) They'd laugh at me.
>   (*Enter Hunters, Wrestlers, Jumpers, Judges, Spectators, etc.*)
>   *1st Hunter.* Well, Abraham, as father of the tribe,
> 'Tis best, perhaps, to see you first on hand.
> (*Looking at the rails.*) Have split enough for all creation yet?
>   *Lin.* I've split enough to fence you fellows in,
> But don't intend to leave you any *stakes*!
>   *1st Hunter.* First rate; it's believed, I know that you'll take them.
>   *1st Runner.* If running tongues can win, you chaps stand well!
>   (*Judges, Umpires, coming forward.*)

Umpire. From this small store, and round to this here tree,
(*Pointing.*) Who passes first, can call this purse his own.
(Shows a purse.)

Lin. As I in innocence am like a lamb,
Like him you'd have me *gambol* with my legs.
Think'st thou upon a *bank* I'll make a run?

Lincoln as the culmination of all the heroism of the frontier is nowhere more intemperately idealized than in Fred Lewis Pattee's poem *The Man of the West.* Violently patriotic and metrically rampant, the poet holds up his gigantic hero of a gigantic race as the sum total of all that is good and grand in the world. The heroes of old are pygmies beside him. The civilization which he represents is worthy to surmount all others. There is a verve and grim gusto in the poem which is admirably adapted to the expression of what, were it otherwise told, would be worse than blatant.

> *Out of the West a Man —*
> *One man from all the West,*
> *In all the years, a myriad compressed;*
> *What lion breed, what sky, what potent earth*
> *Shall give him birth?*
> *What arms his cradle be,*
> *What scenes and men shall mould his infancy,*
> *This typal Man, this latest, strongest, best,*
> *This hero of the West?*
>
> Only the bravest came,
> The coward trembled at the two months' sea;
> Only the strongest came, —
> The weakling feared the storm's inclemency;
> Only the best survived, —
> The faint and weary sank beneath their load,
> Beneath the squalor of the winter woods,
> The grinding toil, the maddening solitudes;
> Only the fit and few,

THE LINCOLN LEGEND

The demigods alone, shall blaze the road
  In worlds unmanned and new;
Only the granite will,
Only the spark divine no force may kill;
  Only the doubly picked, the best from out the best,
  Those mighty ones who broke our mighty West.

Behold them fling the seed,
This Titan breed,
  Crashing the forest down,
  Razing with sweat the site for mead and town,
And pressing ever westward undismayed, —
  A century of forest and of toil,
  Of bare-hand battle for the naked soil,
As Jacob wrestled on the midnight sod,
As face to face with God.

   .   .   .   .

Behold this hero, gaunt and border born,
  A man with every shred of soul and heart
  Of our new soil a part.
  Behold him; this is he,
  This Jarl full-lunged, in every fibre free,
Unpolished and ungainly; honest youth
Is evermore uncouth, —
  And we are young. Thank God, these western lands
  Are still in swaddling bands;
No task completely done;
The mighty day is hardly yet begun.
  Behold him solid to the inner ring
  Like some gnarled forest king.
Behold him, self-reliant as a god,
Erect, clear-eyed, unawed;
  A man of bare-armed toil,
  Who want has known and all the fret and moil
And lonely heartache of the pioneer.
Behold him here,
  This sad-eyed, silent man,
And note the mighty power

BETWEEN FOLKLORE AND FICTION

Coiled in his soul and waiting for its hour,—
   The power to seize its day; to work and plan
And bide its time; and single out the best,—
The training of our Man-producing West.
   From out the West a Man.
Behold our hero, him we joy to hold
Before our sons to thrill and test and mould.
   No Bismarck he,
   No man of blood and iron and destiny;
No Philip void of conscience and of heart;
No self-awed Bonaparte;
   But one as gentle as a mother's soul;
As tender as a maiden, as a child
As pure of heart and undefiled;
   Yet strong withal and mighty to control
   And bend the kings of men to do his will;
A man of humble heart, yet strong to sway
A continent his way
   God's purpose to fulfil.

And they have called us small and craven-souled,
   Slaves of the dollar mark,
   Without a thought above the maddening cark
That makes for gold;
   And they have cast
   The taunt that we're a herd without a past.
Without a past! My God, and have they read
The roll-call of our dead?

   .   .   .   .

With him our model can we sordid be?
With him to mould us shall we not be free?
   And shall we not in every nerve be true,
   And shall we not for God our duty do?
And humble be,
And gentle as the Christ of Galilee?
   Yet fierce withal to right a brother's woe
   And fight and die if duty hold it so?

To guard our country's honest name
From every breath of calumny and shame?
   To die exulting with our latest breath,
   If but the dear land profit by our death,
To hold forever in our inmost breast
A mighty love for this, our mother West,
The land of all God's goodly land the best.

And this we learned of that strong, typal man
Who drew our plan,
   That final plan, the growth of our new soil,
   The culmination of three centuries' toil,
The plan of empire that shall dominate
The tyrant state,
   And sweep injustice from the ocean's brim,
And make us strong forever, having him.

Ah, deathless one, we see the hand of God
   And we are still.
He does not work in petty human ways,
   All glory to His will.
The mighty He casts down,
   And those of low degree,
   The pure in heart, His mighty ones shall be.
And this the message to our rising West:
There is no high or low, and truth is best.[1]

Thus we find several varieties of literature perpetuating the story of the frontier hero. Most of the literary works present a highly idealized character and a misconceived frontier, but in Sandburg's biography, which may be considered primarily literature, both the background and the character of Lincoln are more sincerely idealized than elsewhere.

The material which the novelist, poet, or playwright

[1] This poem, as well as the general subject matter of this chapter, should be compared with Chapter VI.

uses in his work is generally selected from the mass of popular biographical accounts. The variety of this material enables the author to produce almost any type of character he desires without inventing incidents, but not even this variety has sufficed in most cases.

In general the picture of Lincoln presented in the reminiscences of old friends of his youth is in keeping with the popular conception which, arising after his death, was legendary in a universal fashion; but there are elements of the story which never could become a part of the later legend, in that they were too obviously out of keeping with the spiritual picture. Thus the wilderness hero has remained somewhat a local legend confined to the Lincoln country. The drinking, cock-fighting, rough-and-tumble hero, 'the big buck of the lick' who dared anyone to 'come on and whet his horns,' the lover of broad humor — such a hero was worthy idolatry on the frontier, perhaps, but not in New England. Hence New England made its own Lincoln, which it was able to a certain extent to foist upon the Lincoln country. And as the spiritual picture grew, the reminiscences became more and more in keeping with it. What there is of the frontier hero in the great Lincoln of poetry and fiction, and the religious legend that they preserve, is spiritualized and hallowed by the simple process of omission, emphasis, and invention, which has so largely biased even the biographical accounts.

V

LINCOLN AND ANN RUTLEDGE

The sentimental aspects of the Lincoln legend are few, but in the Ann Rutledge romance there is sufficient concentration of sentimentalism to make up for any lack that might be noted elsewhere. It was inevitable that this sentimental aspect should come, because, if for no other reason, of the apparent lack of the very article in Lincoln himself. No one dared make Lincoln's courtship or married life with Mary Todd a sentimental affair. The domestic relationship was too well known to be, not merely matter-of-fact, but on occasions unbearably cross and common. Mrs. Lincoln was not a romantic figure during the years following Lincoln's death when she was berating Congress for not giving her a pension and making a national parade of her supposed destitution. She was a vain, extravagant, mentally unbalanced woman — a picture of great pathos that can inspire nothing but pity in the student of her misfortunes. But to her inconsiderate and not-too-tender contemporaries she was a disgrace to the memory of her sainted spouse. Mary Todd had been a very human woman in her early years also. She had her faults, though few that cannot be found in good women every day. She was, perhaps, too well known to be considered the love match for a sainted martyr.

Perhaps it would seem foolish to say that Lincoln needed a soul mate to complete his mythical figure, but what other conclusion is possible after a survey of the avidity with which the Ann Rutledge story was devoured and disgorged by a sentimentally inclined group of biographers, fictionists, and poets, who have probably succeeded in making it an everlasting part of the legend? Ann Rutledge suited the requirements for this sentimental aspect of Lincoln's life precisely in that there was little positive that could be said about her. This vagueness gave the legend-makers an ideal figure to work into the grand passion of the hero's life.

The story, in brief, tells how Ann Rutledge, the golden-haired belle of New Salem, died and forever ended the only earthly love of Lincoln. Ann was betrothed to a prosperous young farmer named McNeil. Suddenly McNeil decided to return to his home in the East. Before he left he swore faithfulness to Ann and revealed to her the fact that his real name was McNamar. He had been forced to change his name, he said, but not because he was guilty of misdeeds. Ann waited her lover's return, but he came not. Neither did he write. Ann sorrowed and grew doubtful. When her family learned McNeil's correct name, they did not doubt that he was a villain who had come West to escape punishment. Lincoln had long admired Ann, and, now that McNeil had seemingly deserted her, he began to court her favor. In time Ann agreed to marry Lincoln whenever he became financially able, but she could not forget that her vow to McNeil was unbroken and that he might return any day to claim her. She did not, according to Herndon, ever love Lincoln as she had loved McNeil. She gradually pined and eventually died of her sorrowful plight; those who remembered that her father died at the same time, however, said that it was chills and fever. Lincoln was distraught with grief. He became quite insane, and was cared for by a friend until he recovered. Forever after Lincoln was enshrouded in melancholy. This was his only true love. With her his heart was buried.

In the preface to Herndon's biography the following statement is given as the guiding principle of the author: 'If the story of his life is truthfully and courageously told — nothing colored or supposed; nothing false either written or suggested — the reader will see and feel the presence of the living man.' Herndon's biography has so often been designated as the height of the realistic biographies of Lincoln that to term it romantic is heresy. Yet romantic it is in spite of avowed intentions of realism. Even in the presentation of details unsavory to the Lincoln-worshiping public, Herndon was guided by a romantic principle. If the paternity of Lincoln was darkened by the shadow of illegitimacy and his early life a series of squalid and unbeautiful places and events, the ultimate greatness of the man was the more enhanced. If the soul of Lincoln was harassed by doubt and his religion unorthodox, the more romantic was his melancholy genius. So, when Herndon encountered the very brief facts of this early and quite inconsequential attachment, it was the romantic principle that imparted to the affair a great significance.

Possibly there were other motives which influenced Herndon in this instance. It has been charged that his hatred for Mrs. Lincoln was the inspiration of the story.[1] That Herndon had little love for Mary Lincoln and that she repaid him in kind is notorious; but to assume that Herndon's dislike would have prompted him to pillory the widow of a friend as an unloved woman, as a mate of convenience, and to seize upon so roundabout a way of doing it, is malignant and probably unjust. Herndon had sufficient to say of Mary Lincoln in his biography, but when he gave the Ann Rutledge legend to the world in 1865, it was probably a lack of perception of the implications involved and a sense of the fitness of things that permitted the untimely disclosure. He was callous and inconsiderate, but not vengeful, and his callousness may have been the result of blindness to all but the development of the romance of his hero.

On November 16, 1866, Herndon delivered in the old

[1] See W. E. Barton's account of Ann Rutledge in *The Women Lincoln Loved.*

Springfield Courthouse a lecture entitled 'Ann Rutledge, New Salem, Pioneering, and the Poem.' This lecture contained the first of many accounts of Lincoln's great romance and established the general tone and color which the legend has kept in its several forms. The material for this lecture had been gleaned a scant month before in a conversation with John McNamar. There is no record that would indicate any great interest in Ann's story on the part of Herndon earlier than this.

That he had known of the affair for some time seems evident, but how long he had been convinced of the great significance which he attached to it in his version published in November, 1866, is uncertain. Many of the manuscripts collected or written from conversation by Herndon, containing the testimony of surviving relatives of Ann and of old settlers around New Salem, are undated; many of these have only a year date; and a few have the day specified. An examination of these dated statements is significant.

One of the earliest accounts, and by an honest man apparently, is that of James Short to Herndon, dated July 7, 1865. James Short lived within half a mile of McNamar's farm while the Rutledge family lived there, and Lincoln came to see him 'every day or two'; and yet he knew nothing of love-making, much less of engagement.[1] James Short was intimate with the Rutledges, Mrs. Rutledge having kept house for him at one time. Later, when Herndon had delivered his lecture, James Short undertook to deny the far-fetched statement that Lincoln refused to eat on account of the death of Ann.

McNamar, in May, 1866, stated: 'I never heard any person say that Mr. Lincoln addressed Miss Ann Rutledge

[1] This and the succeeding statements are quoted from Beveridge.

in terms of courtship, neither her own family nor any acquaintances otherwise. I heard simply from two prominent Gentlemen of my acquaintance and Personal friends that Mr. Lincoln was Grieved very much at her death.' And yet, in October of the same year, this same McNamar was to give Herndon the account which is the basis of the first published version of the story.

But Herndon was persistent in his questions concerning Ann, and even before the October interview with McNamar he got brief remembrances to his liking. Herndon was a lawyer and as such a skilful questioner. If he had an idea that something might be true, he was adroit and relentless in trying to worm it out of his informant. There is no more complete example of this than his continual prodding of Dennis Hanks in regard to the father of Nancy Hanks. It is pitiful to observe Dennis, covered with wounds and confusion, valiantly trying and lying to cover the facts of Nancy's birth and give her an honest right to have been born. Using the same method, Herndon sought information concerning the relationship of Lincoln and Ann Rutledge. In this case his informants were many, and they had nothing to conceal. How much persistent questioning of old people who knew Lincoln and Ann could have suggested to them is uncertain. How many leading questions he was forced to use before he succeeded in refreshing old memories we can never know. But it seems reasonable to infer, from the general nature of the early accounts with little or no reference to the great attachment, and from the gradual increase and building up of a series of sentimental accounts, that the legend grew apace from the time he began stirring the soil.[1]

[1] In a series of articles which appeared in the *Atlantic Monthly*, December, 1928, to February, 1929, entitled 'Lincoln the Lover,' Wilma Francis Minor

There can be no doubt of some attachment on the part of Lincoln. Herndon must have had some knowledge to lead him on. He states, 'I knew Miss Rutledge myself, as well as her father and other members of the family.' [1] Then, too, it is quite natural that the fanciful superstructure had some foundation of fact. Here, as in other cases, it is the process of addition and exaggeration rather than of complete creation that gives the legendary element to the story.

Recent investigations, chiefly those of W. E. Barton, have reduced the entire episode to a few bare facts which are far removed in tenor from the melodramatic romance set afloat by Herndon. So far as Lincoln was concerned, it may be briefly summarized. Lincoln knew Ann and very probably loved her. She returned his affection. Possibly there may have been some sort of tentative engagement. When Ann died of typhoid fever, Lincoln was sad, but within a short while he was paying his respects to another young lady. There is no trustworthy evidence that Lincoln's love for Ann lasted long after her death, and his memory of her was not of any considerable efficacy in his later life.

At any rate, on November 16, 1866, Herndon delivered

added a considerable amount to the Ann Rutledge legend. Her sources were a series of forged letters supposedly written by Lincoln and Ann. If there is any significance in the material, it lies in the fact that the sentimentality of Herndon's story could not be improved upon even by supposedly intimate letters by Lincoln and Ann themselves. Evidently the author of the forgeries was well acquainted with and an admirer of Herndon's story and sought only to elaborate it.

[1] Herndon, I, 128. How much this statement may mean is uncertain. Barton states that 'The town New Salem had vanished long before he [Herndon] *ever* [the italics are mine] visited the spot.' (*The Soul of Abraham Lincoln*, 148.) Herndon would have had to visit New Salem before it vanished in order to have known Ann more than by reputation; for she died in 1835, and New Salem had not 'vanished long before' that time. Barton may mean, however, only that New Salem had vanished before Herndon began collecting his material.

a lecture which established a new and — in so far as the significance of the episode has been interpreted — entirely legendary phase of Lincoln's life. With the unrestrained fervor of a sentimental and romantic artist he described an element in the early life of Lincoln which he never knew to exist in the man of his own personal acquaintance. The inconsistencies of his story were not apparent to him because of the fullness of his rapture. Who does not love a lover? He was not the rational and analytic Herndon who also gave the cold and careful character analysis of Lincoln which has not yet been excelled. The heart of the portion of the lecture dealing with Ann Rutledge is as follows:

> Truth in history is my sole and only motive for making this sad story now public for the first time. History is sacred, and should be so held eternally by all men.
>
> . . . .
>
> No earthly blame can be attached to the girl, and none to the men in their fidelity and honor to her. It all so happened, or was decided by fate. It shall, in truth, be explained hereafter to the satisfaction of all. It is a sad, thrilling story. The young girl saw her condition. Her word of promise was out to two men at the same time, both of whom she loved, dearly loved. The consciousness of this, and the conflict of duties, love's promises, and womanly engagements, made her think, grow sad, become restless and nervous. She suffered, pined, ate not and slept not. Time and struggle, as supposed and believed by many, caused her to have a raging fever, of which she died on the 25th of August, A.D., 1835. She died on a farm seven miles north, bearing a little west of New Salem, and now lies buried in the Concord graveyard, six miles north, bearing a little west of New Salem, and four miles from Petersburg.
>
> On Sunday, the 14th day of October, A. D. 1866, I went to the well cultured and well stocked farm of Mr. [McNamar]. I went with book in hand, in search of facts. I have known

the gentleman whom I visited, for more than thirty years. He received and welcomed me into his house most cordially, and treated me most hospitably. He acted like a gentleman, and is one. He is the man who knows all the story so far as it relates to [*Lincoln*]. He knows it and has————————. He owns the [*farm*] on which the young girl died; and if I could risk a rapid and random *opinion*, I should say he purchased the [*farm*] in part, if not solely, because of the sad memories that cluster over and around it. The visit and my task were truly delicate. Without holding you longer in uneasy and unnecessary suspense, from what took place then and there, permit me to say, that I asked the gentleman this question: 'Did you know Miss Rutledge? If so, where did she die?' He sat by his open window, looking westerly, and pulling me closer to himself, looked through the window and said: 'There, by that ——' choking up with emotion, pointing his long forefinger, nervous and trembling, towards the spot — 'there, by *that* currant bush, she died. The old house in which she and her father died, is gone.'

I then, after some delay, asked the further question: 'In what month and year did she die?' He replied, 'In the month of August, 1835.' After further conversation, leaving the sadness to momentarily pass away, I asked this additional question: 'Where was she buried?' In reply to which he said, 'In Concord burying ground, one mile southeast from this place.' 'Can you tell me exactly where she lies buried?' I remarked. He said, 'No, I cannot. I left the country in 1832 or 1833. My mother soon after died, and she too, was buried in the same little sacred graveyard, and when I returned here in 1835 I could find neither grave. The Berrys, however, may know Ann's.'

Evidently it did not occur to Herndon that it was a very odd kind of grief for a loved one which prompted McNamar to purchase the Rutledge farm for memory's sake and yet did not prompt him to learn anything about her grave. If McNamar was choking with emotion as he pointed toward the currant bush, it was evidently with emotion that had been successfully pent up for more than thirty years.

It was when he came to relate the effect of Ann's death on Lincoln that Herndon really waxed eloquent. Lincoln was not merely sorrowful, he was mentally distracted. Within a few days his melancholia became a veritable insanity. Herndon proceeded dramatically:

Did this dread calamity, of which I have spoken, crush him and thus modify, if it did not change his nature? It must be expected that his expressions would follow truly his own rational thoughts in part only, not wholly so in logic, at least. His utterances and expressions would be necessarily disconnected and sharply contrasted. It is said, and I believe it, that he lost his logical faculty — power over cause and effect, and their legitimate relation — through the momentary loss of memory alone. Imagine him racked in heart and body, in mind and soul, not forgetting the immediate and proximate cause of his condition. He must naturally and necessarily speak and utter what is in his own mind; sharply and incoherently, sadly and wildly. Hear him: 'What a time for joy today in town; the men and women looked so happy all through the village. Ah! me. No. Not today; it's night. There's a trick in it, and where's the fallacy? Does nature deal unjustly? I thought not. I'll see and tell myself. 'Tis a rude wind that blows no man joy. Where am I? What strange woods are these. It seems that I've run my compass and dragged my chains along this path. Why, wherefore is all this? These hills I've never seen before, and the wild valleys at my feet now have no more familiar face for me. What? 'Tis strange. How is it? What's that? These hands I think I've seen before, and yet I know them not. The clouds are cold, and where's fire? There it is! No, 'tis not. How goes it out? Who cheats me? and for what? I am sad; and thou sweet bird of night, sing on thy tune of whippoorwill; ah! who's that? 'Tis her I love. This path and hill I know; yet 'tis strange, strange, uncommon strange. I know it here and there, in spots. Why, wherefore is this? Who am I and what, 'mid nature's profoundest uncertainties, that come and go like chance, whither, no one knows. There the cocks crow. Did I not read — but, stay, did I not read law beneath the shade of this tree, grinding 'round the sun? I love her. Oh! immensities above me, below me, and around me.

'The dogs, the very dogs bark at me. These limbs and legs, feet and hands, are mine; yet 'tis strange! and ah! thou mysterious state of things. Isn't fate, chance, Providence, God — that so unwinds the world's and all their life? Grief! What's that? I'm tired and weary. The clothes I've got on and wear, I know are mine, and yet they seem not to be. Ah! dead and gone from me thou sweet one; and shall this aching crushed heart of mine never die and feel the pangs of nature never more. This old mill I've seen before, and often heard it grind. The waters in the pond are filled with shining, floating stars. Why don't they go out and sink in water ten feet deep, or more? It's curious, curious, strange, wondrous strange. Why, wherefore is that? Some trick deludes me. I'll search and tell myself. Ah! dead and gone, thou sweet one; dead and buried forever, forevermore, in the grave. Mortal man! so it is, and must be. Our hopes forever blast and wither in their tender growth. What is hope? What is death? What is forever, evermore, forevermore? Come gentle winds and cool my aching head; or, thou hanging thunderbolt, swiftly strike and scorch me. What's that in the mill pond, going splash, splash? 'Twas a fish, I guess. Let's go and feed it, and make it joy, and be happy. I love her, and shall marry her on tomorrow's eve. So soul be content, and endless joy shall come. Heart of mine be still, for remember sweet tomorrow eve. Oh! thou calmest, most boisterous profoundest uncertainties of things, hold off, or take another path not coming here. What! did I dream? Think; what did I say? It cannot be. No, it cannot be. She's dead and gone — gone forever. Fare thee well, sweet girl! We'll meet again.'

Shades of Lear and Hamlet! This is the Lincoln that Herndon claimed to be portraying as an historical reality. It is no wonder that Nicolay and Hay, as well as most of the other early biographers, avoided the Ann Rutledge story. It was Herndon's tendency to romanticize that jeopardized his entire biography of Lincoln. Patent exaggerations placed true accounts in doubt, and the result was that careful biographers were afraid to credit some of the truth that Herndon told.

When Herndon came to treat the Ann Rutledge romance a second time in his biography, he told a story somewhat toned down but in all essentials the same. He had collected considerable material in the form of reminiscences which corroborated McNamar's story of October, 1866, and by the time his biography appeared there was a well-established oral legend in Sangamon County generally the same as that which he told. He was able to take up the cudgel against the biographers who had depreciated his legend. He had stories from relatives and friends of Ann, not without their conflicting elements, but agreeing enough to furnish documentary evidence on the whole convincing. What can be said further in disproof of the fantastic portions of these reminiscences?

Consider the situation. A man had become immortal within a few years. Those who knew him as a young man were eager to tell what they knew of him. If there was an opportunity of dilating and coloring their story without their becoming conscious liars, they remembered the man freely. The relatives of Ann were glad that Lincoln had admired her, and it was certainly no injury to her memory or their reputation to make a simple attachment the one great love of Lincoln's life. Their accurate recollections of Lincoln's melancholia, which was always a constitutional part of his being, needed little inference to be made at the particular period the result of Ann's death; and to carry the inference farther, to make the melancholia of his later years largely the result of this early 'saddest chapter.' Herndon distributed printed copies of his lecture freely, and by the end of the year 1866 the legend was firmly established as common property. Anyone who had known Lincoln might remember that he referred to this glorious but sad romance in whatever unlikely words seemed best. Thus it became known that Lincoln's heart was forever buried in the grave of Ann Rutledge, that he was driven to partial insanity by her death, that he prostrated himself on her grave, that he raved at the elements for beating upon her grave, that he never loved another woman, *et cetera ad nauseam*. All of this in the face of the fact that he carried on his regular affairs as postmaster and surveyor without a hitch, and that he was paying his attentions generously, and in somewhat high humor, to another young lady within a year.

So Ann Rutledge became the one great love of the hero's life. His heart was forever with her. To her fragrant memory his weary mind returned in solitary hours for inspiration. Her spirit was with him, his guiding star. Together with the spirit of Nancy Hanks the shade of Ann Rutledge furnished the spiritual inspiration which gave Lincoln his immediate contact with the larger aspects of life and his confidence in the realms into which no mortal can pass.

In pure fiction this romance is in essentials quite the same as the historical legend, though each author has managed to add something to its absurdity. Amidst a background of illiterate 'Hoosier'-speaking country folk young Abraham and Ann speak the language of poetry or the rhetoric of Bostonians in a dime novel. McNamar becomes the heartless villain that one would expect — and which the investigations of Barton have shown him not entirely unfitted for in spite of his original picture as given by Herndon [1] — or he is omitted from the idyllic picture entirely, being a difficult character to reckon with when presenting Ann's complete and spiritual devotion to Lincoln.

The story is always an idyl of love and springtime, but the idyllic possibilities are better realized in Eleanor Atkinson's *Lincoln's Love Story* than elsewhere. Sentimentality of a Dickensian variety, which is to be laid at Herndon's door, becomes insipid. Lincoln's devotion is one of sentimental reverence for a femininity too exalted and pure for the earthly touch. If Lincoln was anything, he was realistic and occasionally crude in his dealings with women. Certainly one cannot find anything sentimental in his correspondence with women. Yet, from Herndon on down, the writers of the Ann Rutledge episode would have it believed that Lincoln was sickly sentimental in at least this one affair. Ann is in fiction more devoted to Lincoln than Herndon could make her. She is a frail flower — the typical Victorian heroine — whose trust in men is blighted by the treatment of McNamar. Her death is the culmination of worry and wasting away brought about by fear of the return of her faithless betrothed. Delicate, fragile, ethereal, she dies, an exotic plant unable to exist in a cruel environment. Even her unbounded love for Lincoln cannot keep her, and she languishes daily in his presence. Her love is only for him, but its efficacy must be reserved for another world. [2]

Descriptions of Ann which Herndon collected varied

[1] See *The Life of Abraham Lincoln* and *The Women Lincoln Loved* by W. E. Barton.

[2] There are numerous literary treatments of this story which are generally not much different from the important ones here discussed. Babcock's *Soul of Ann Rutledge*, Catherwood's *Spanish Peggy*, and Wright's *Lincoln's First Love* are other novels of interest which develop the story at length.

somewhat according to whether the observer admired pale-gold hair or scoffed at red hair. But from them and subsequent descriptions an ideal heroine with golden hair, dark violet eyes, and a complexion now rose and now pearl, changing like the anemones, has been portrayed.

The immense influence of the memory of Ann in Lincoln's later life, which Herndon suggests, if he does not develop, is a theme of great import to fictionists. Some are content with its being simply a holy and inspiring memory, but others make it more. In the poem *Lincoln and Ann Rutledge*, by D. J. Snider, written in halting hexameters and attaining an epic length of sixteen books loaded with presagings of the glorious future of the hero, Ann fights her battle of love caught between a consuming passion for Lincoln and an abnormal sense of allegiance to her thoughtless betrothed. On her deathbed as Lincoln is alone with her she encourages him:

> Love thee below I dare not — but I may out of heaven.

Lincoln admires her extreme morality and cherishes her example:

> Thus the mourner has stamped on his heart the deed of Ann Rutledge,
> Imagining her in her love he can rise into love universal.
> She will spring out of air to him when he is harried by trouble,
> Or when hit by men's hate he is tempted in vengeance to hit back;
> She will haunt him ghost-like in his night till again he shall love her,
> If in the trials of time he forget her deed's benediction.

From this time forward Lincoln lives a dual existence; his soul is with the soul of Ann Rutledge. She is his means of contact with the upper world, whence come the divine prophecies which he dreams and utters. In Snider's *Lincoln at Richmond* an epic conversation between Lincoln's 'Upper' and 'Lower' selves, the 'Upper Self' explains the situation:

THE LINCOLN LEGEND

I came hither sundered from thee
By thy life's greatest sorrow,
Born of thy love for woman
From whom the soul would not separate,
Whose death made no parting
Through the presence of me, thy Double
Passing with her beyond.
Thus I breach thy wall of finitude
Which was also mine own.

In kind with this epic spiritualism is a drama, *Spirit of
Ann Rutledge* by H. W. Gammans, in which the spirit of
Ann is in regular communication with Lincoln and is his
solace and companion in his agony. When bruised and
broken under the titanic burden of the presidency, it is
her spirit that comforts and advises him. Quite naturally,
the picture of Lincoln's wife is such as Herndon would appreciate. She is an exceedingly earthly female, patroniz-
ing and flashy. A physical mate, perhaps, but certainly
not the beloved of the soul of Lincoln.

But in spite of the sentimental extravagance of the
romance as told to the world by Herndon, and in spite
of the general insipidity of the further elaborations, there
is, perhaps, an heroic and genuinely poetic kernel in the
episode. The most generally recognized attempt to treat
this theme of heroic pathos is a poem in the once heralded
Spoon River Anthology by Edgar Lee Masters.

ANN RUTLEDGE

Out of me unworthy and unknown
The vibrations of deathless music;
'With malice toward none, with charity for all.'
Out of me the forgiveness of millions toward millions,
And the beneficent face of a nation
Shining with justice and truth.

BETWEEN FOLKLORE AND FICTION

I am Ann Rutledge who sleep beneath these weeds,
Beloved in life of Abraham Lincoln,
Wedded to him, not through union,
But through separation.
Bloom forever, O Republic,
From the dust of my bosom!

IV

The Prophet, Savior, and Martyr

On the Good Friday night that John Wilkes Booth crept into the President's box at Ford's Theater and murdered President Lincoln, he accomplished what he thought was a just revenge upon the man who had become to his unbalanced mind a monster responsible for all the evil and disgrace which had befallen and would befall the beloved South. But he accomplished far more than he, or any man then living, could have imagined. He gave the world a martyr and saint where it had once had a man.

The time was ripe for the deed. Lee had surrendered at Appomattox five days before. It was only a matter of time until Johnston's army would surrender. The Thirteenth Amendment had passed both houses of Congress in January, and the ratification by the States was recognized as certain. Lincoln had done what it had been contended he could not do — preserved the Union and destroyed the legally recognized institution of slavery. In success he was as supremely the master of the public as in failure he was of himself. He had but a month before uttered the words which are most commonly cited as indicative of his character and associated with his name:

> With malice towards none; with charity for all; with firmness in the right, as God gives us to see the right, let us strive on to finish the work we are in; to bind up the nation's wounds; to care for him who shall have borne the battle, and for his

BORGLUM'S STATUE OF LINCOLN, AT TRENTON, NEW JERSEY

widow, and his orphan — to do all which may achieve and cherish a just and lasting peace among ourselves, and with all nations.

At twenty-two minutes past seven o'clock on Saturday morning, April 15, 1865, Abraham Lincoln died. There was silence in the chamber, broken by the sobs of men; and Stanton, weeping, spoke those memorable words, 'Now he belongs to the ages.'[1] The sentiment was echoed throughout the world, and only the mad have since dared believe otherwise. One might survey the dramatic deaths of history — Caesar's, Joan of Arc's, Thomas à Becket's, or even Christ's — without finding one more dramatic than Lincoln's. It was, said Walt Whitman, one of 'those climax-moments on the stage of universal Time, where the historic Muse at one entrance, and the tragic Muse at the other, suddenly ringing down the curtain, close an immense act in the long drama of creative thought, and give it radiation, tableau, stranger than fiction.'

The rail-splitter and flatboatman was forgotten, and the teller of smutty jokes. The kind, sad face and the soft eyes of love were remembered, and in the hearts of the people the web of a new legend was weaving. Lincoln was the Prophet and Martyr of a holy cause. How could reason or conscience include the death of Lincoln with any reasonable ideal of a moral universe? The question was in every heart, and for an answer there came a legend. It was his to atone, even as Christ, for the sin of a nation. Emerson spoke at the funeral service held in Concord: 'Heaven wishing to show the world a completed benefactor, shall make him serve his country even more by his death than by his life.'

[1] Stanton's comment is generally given thus, but the witnesses varied the account. 'He belongs to the ages now' is the version of Corporal James Tanner. 'He is with the ages' is an unauthenticated version.

I

There is a respectable library, so far as numbers are concerned, of books and pamphlets dealing entirely with Lincoln's religion. In addition to these there are the appropriate discussions in the biographies and reminiscences. No biographer of Lincoln has been able to avoid the question, and it is yet unanswered to the satisfaction of all concerned. The religion of the ordinary citizen is, more or less, a private affair, but the religion of a popular hero is everybody's business. Sectarians have seized upon him as their own. He was a Baptist, a Methodist, a Presbyterian, a Spiritualist, a Universalist, a Catholic, and an infidel; and there is evidence to support any one of these claims. It is, however, not known that Lincoln was ever a member of any religious organization.

The controversy began in 1872 when Ward H. Lamon published his biography. Until that time the popular conception of Lincoln as the man of God had become a sacred myth. It was with the best intentions that Lamon set about restoring, with Herndon's help, the Lincoln that he had known. If Lincoln had not been canonized, there would have been no difficulties for those who wished to believe him a religious man; but unfortunately several of Lincoln's admirers had remembered statements made by Lincoln as to what he believed which were in some things questionable. In their adoration they were not content with the simple facts, which were evidence enough that Lincoln was by nature religious, but they felt called upon to give him a specific belief, which in most cases corresponded to the belief of the particular worshiper. Lamon and Herndon had a special grievance against a fellow townsman, Newton Bateman by name, who had testified, in terms partly questionable, to Lincoln's specific belief that 'Christ is God.'

Lamon's biography was assailed on all hands by a zealous public. Herndon and others who prided themselves on their infidelity came to his assistance. Testimony was divided among those who had known Lincoln well. The most fair-minded said that they could never ascertain exactly what Lincoln's religion was. The zealous reported many statements which they had heard Lincoln make and ransacked his public utterances for every shred of religious expression. There was no lack of material, for Lincoln spoke often of God during the latter days of his Administration.

There would have been no furor if it had not been for one word, *infidel*. Lamon claimed that Lincoln was an infidel whose 'theological opinions were substantially those expounded by Theodore Parker.' Yet few people of intelligence would today call Theodore Parker an infidel. Herndon admitted that he was an infidel himself and contended that Lincoln was. Yet Herndon gave the following statement of his own religious belief: 'You know my Religion, my Philosophy: that the highest thoughts and acts of the human soul and its religious sphere are to think, love, obey, and worship God, by thinking freely, by loving, teaching, doing good to, and elevating mankind. My first duty is to God, then to mankind, and then to the individual man or woman.' Against this statement we have Herndon's admission that he was an infidel and the recognized fact that he was considered one by many of his associates. The situation is not difficult to explain. To the great mass of people today a man who entertains even a slightly 'advanced' opinion in matters of religion is an infidel, or possibly an atheist. Terms are never defined.

It might be expected that a careful definition of terms and a fair consideration of Lincoln's authentic statements would bring about some definite conclusion. W. E. Barton gave in *The Soul of Abraham Lincoln* (1920) a careful study of all the evidence. The result was generally fair and intelligent, but the conclusion that Lincoln was a Calvinist was not the certainty that Barton presented it as being. The meaning of Calvinism was the difficulty. As Lyman Abbot pointed out in his review of Barton's book, Lincoln was certainly not a John Calvin Calvinist.[1] For John Calvin held that man had lost his freedom in the fall; and Lincoln's whole understanding of life was based on his belief in the free will, and therefore the moral responsibility, of man. Although Barton settled the controversy in its larger questions, there was still room for argument. For one thing, the influence of the Methodists on Lincoln was slighted, and Lincoln's spiritualistic leanings were summarily dismissed. Champions came to the defense of Lincoln's conversion and creed, and those who wished could still claim Lincoln as their own.

John G. Nicolay, who was as well qualified as any other to speak of Lincoln's religious views, admitted that he could never ascertain just what they were, even though he never doubted that Lincoln was essentially of a religious nature. Without presuming to classify Lincoln, according to any sectarian creed, we may, as Nicolay did, take his utterances as general evidence of his faith in God.

Whatever was Lincoln's religion, the fact remains that he became recognized upon his death as an authentic prophet. Some of the popular epithets of the poets writing his eulogy within a few days of his death illustrate the immediate recognition of his ordination, once he was dead.

[1] *Outlook*, XXIV, 656, April 14, 1920.

THE PROPHET, SAVIOR, AND MARTYR

He was the 'Prophet of the West,' 'the Savior,' 'saint,' 'Freedom's martyr,' 'Philosopher, Saint, and Seer,' 'priest and savior,' 'hero, martyr, saint,' 'A Second Christ,' etc.[1] Similar epithets abound in the sermons and funeral orations preached throughout the land on the prophet's death.

It is incredible — taking into full account the hysteria of public grief, inspired patriotism, and, perhaps, hatred of the South as the supposed criminal hotbed which plotted the assassination — that even popular fancy should have thus completely 'beatified' Lincoln without something more than fancy to work with. It is the purpose of what follows to present an account of the elements which gave Lincoln, in the mind of the people, even before his death an alignment with the power of another world, and to present some of the circumstances which gave the immediate stature to his mythical figure.

II

Lincoln identified himself at an early date with the purpose of God. This fact is inescapable. The evidence is voluminous in his authentic public utterances as well as in the fervid accounts of those who later recorded conversations on the point with Lincoln. The Abolitionists had for years claimed divine assistance in their crusade. The slave oligarchy had claimed divine approval of slavery. It is not necessary to make theatrical or journalistic capital of Lincoln as a Jehovah Man or the Abolitionists as Hebraic-Puritan zealots in order to present an interesting picture of affairs as they stood at the time of Lincoln's election. The fact that men claimed that they

[1] Selected at random from *Poetical Tributes*, published in July, 1865.

were acting in accordance with the plan of God does not mean that they were monsters of fiendish hate who attempted to camouflage their hatred by calling upon the Supreme Being as their stay and citing abstract moral principles as their guide. The least that can be granted is that Lincoln, the Abolitionists, the slavocrats, and the compromisers were all sincere in their attempt to do what was right as it was given them to see the right. It may be wondered that such statements are deemed necessary before dealing with Lincoln's identification of himself with divine purposes. They are made in order that what follows may not be interpreted as an effort to impugn the motives of Lincoln in any way whatsoever.

A few examples will serve to illustrate the growth of Lincoln's conception of his divine mission. It is not necessary to go back of the year 1861, although there are evidences throughout the years which show Lincoln's belief that he was acting according to the will of God as he conceived it. There is nothing unusual in the fact. It is to be supposed that men who try to do what is right believe that what they reason to be right is right. A religious man when elevated to a position of supreme importance cannot, perhaps, avoid this inevitable strengthening of his own convictions, once they are reached.

In his 'Farewell Address' at Springfield, Lincoln expressed quite naturally his expectation that God would attend him in his responsibility: 'Without the assistance of that Divine Being... I cannot succeed. Trusting in Him who can go with me, and remain with you, and be everywhere for good, let us confidently hope that all will yet be well.'

Beginning with the 'First Inaugural,' there is not an important public address or major message to Congress which does not contain some reference to the Supreme Being, encouraging a trust in God, expressing the belief that the course of the loyal States is right and supported by God, or admitting his individual responsibility to God. In addition to these are the proclamations of fasting and prayer, and thanksgiving, and the letters to representatives of religious bodies, and numerous references in private and public letters. The constant reiteration of the righteousness of the Union's cause and of the purposes of its Chief Magistrate was in harmony with the doctrine which Abolitionists had been preaching for years, and once the cause of the Union seemed to be victorious, the conclusion that the cause of the Union and the purposes of Lincoln were the will of God was inevitable. Nowhere did Lincoln express his convictions better than in the two concluding paragraphs of the 'Second Inaugural,' and their grandeur remains possibly the best evidence that Lincoln must have been right.

The Almighty has his own purposes. 'Woe unto the world because of offences! For it must needs be that offences come; but woe to that man by whom the offence cometh.' If we shall suppose that American slavery is one of those offences, which, in the providence of God, must needs come, but which, having continued through His appointed time, He now wills to remove, and that He gives to both North and South this terrible war, as the woe due to those by whom the offence came, shall we discern therein any departure from those attributes which the believers in a living God always ascribe to Him? Fondly do we hope — fervently do we pray — that this mighty scourge of war may speedily pass away. Yet, if God wills that it continue until all the wealth piled by the bondman's two hundred and fifty years of unrequited toil shall be sunk, and until every drop of blood drawn with the lash shall be paid with another drawn with the sword, as was said three thousand years ago, so still it must be said, 'The judgments of the Lord are true and righteous alto-gether.'

With malice toward none; with charity for all; with firm-ness in the right, as God gives us to see the right, let us strive on to finish the work we are in; to bind up the nation's wounds; to care for him who shall have borne the battle, and for his widow, and his orphan — to do all which may achieve and cherish a just and lasting peace among ourselves, and with all nations.

In the diaries of Secretary Welles and Secretary Chase there is preserved a record of the special Cabinet meeting of September 22, 1862, at which Lincoln announced his determination to issue the 'Emancipation Proclamation.' Both relate the incident which follows in practically the same detail:

> He remarked that he had made a vow, a covenant, that if God gave us the victory in the approaching battle, he would consider it an indication of Divine will, and that it was his duty to move forward in the course of emancipation. It might be thought strange, he said, that he had in this way submitted the disposal of matters when the way was not clear to his mind what he should do. God had decided this question in favor of the slaves. He was satisfied it was right, was con-firmed and strengthened in his action by the vow and the results.[1]

If we may rely on the testimony of various men who conversed with Lincoln at widely separated intervals con-cerning his mission, we must conclude that Lincoln anti-cipated the legend-makers by several years in the matter of his divine guidance. It has been said before that the Christ analogy is inescapable in the life of Lincoln, and it may be that he realized even before his apostles the full-ness of his mission.

On an evening in January, 1861, Lincoln talked with an

[1] *Diary of Gideon Welles*, I, 143.

172

old friend, Judge Gillespie. It was one of the darkest periods of his life up to that time. Every day the dissolution of the Government became, apparently, more certain, and the President-elect was powerless to do anything to prevent it if it had been possible to prevent it. Each day brought its additional number of difficulties to an Administration which would not attempt to deal with them, and consequently the increasing tangle would devolve a few weeks later upon Lincoln. Furthermore, Lincoln was not at all sure that he would be able to handle the situation. Ida M. Tarbell tells how on this evening he spoke as follows to his old friend:

> I would willingly take out of my life a period of years equal to the two months which intervene between now and my inauguration to take the oath of office now. Because every hour adds to the difficulties I am called upon to meet, and the present administration does nothing to check the tendency toward dissolution. I, who have been called upon to meet this awful responsibility, am compelled to remain here, doing nothing to avert it or lessen its force when it comes to me. ... I see the duty devolving upon me. I have read, upon my knees, the story of Gethsemane, where the son of God prayed in vain that the cup of bitterness might pass from him. I am in the garden of Gethsemane now, and my cup of bitterness is full and overflowing.

Another instance is related by Father Charles Chiniquy in his book of marvelous revelations entitled *Fifty Years in the Church of Rome*. He had, he relates, learned through devious channels of a Jesuit plot to assassinate Lincoln. Papal sympathy was entirely with the Confederacy, and the agents of the Pope were determined to end the war of coercion by killing Lincoln. Whether we are willing to swallow his account or not, we may take it as an introduction to what follows. Lincoln thanked Chiniquy very kindly and then answered, 'I see no other safeguard against those murderers but to be always ready to die, as Christ advises it.'

Lincoln then took his Bible, opened it at the third chapter of Deuteronomy and read from the twenty-second to the twenty-eighth verse. Afterwards he commented:

My dear Father Chiniquy, let me tell you that I have read these strange and beautiful verses several times, these last five or six weeks. The more I read them, the more it seems to me that God has written them for me as well as for Moses.

Has he not taken me from my poor log cabin by the hand, as he did of Moses in the reeds of the Nile, to put me at the head of the greatest and the most blessed of modern nations, just as he put that prophet at the head of the most blessed nation of ancient times? Has not God granted me a privilege, which was not granted to any living man, when I broke the fetters of 4,000,000 of men and made them free? Has not our God given me the most glorious victories over our enemies? Are not the armies of the Confederacy so reduced, to a handful of men, when compared to what they were two years ago; that the day is fast approaching when they will have to surrender.

Now, I see the end of this terrible conflict, with the same joy of Moses, when at the end of his trying forty years in the wilderness; and I pray my God to grant me to see the days of peace, and untold prosperity, which will follow this cruel war, as Moses asked God to see the other side of Jordan and enter the Promised Land. But do you know that I hear in my soul, as the voice of God, giving me the rebuke which was given to Moses?

Yes! every time that my soul goes to God to ask the favor of seeing the other side of Jordan, and eating the fruits of that peace, after which I am longing with such an unspeakable desire, do you know that there is a still, but solemn voice, which tells me that I will see those things, only from a long distance, and that I will be among the dead, when the nation, which God granted me to lead through those awful trials, will cross the Jordan, and dwell in that Land of Promise, where peace, industry, happiness and liberty will make every one happy, and why so? Because he has already given me favors he never gave, I dare say, to any man, in these latter days.

Why did God Almighty refuse to Moses the favor of crossing the Jordan, and entering the Promised Land? It was on account of his own nation's sins! That law of divine retribution and justice, by which one must suffer for another, is surely a terrible mystery. But it is a fact which no man who has any intelligence and knowledge can deny. Moses, who knew that law, though he probably did not understand it better than we do, calmly says to his people: 'God was wroth with me for your sakes.'

But, though we do not understand that mysterious and terrible law, we find it written in letters of tears and blood wherever we go. We do not read a single page of history, without finding undeniable traces of its existence.

Where is the mother who has not shed tears and suffered real tortures, for her children's sake?

Who is the good king, the worthy emperor, the gifted chieftain, who have not suffered unspeakable mental agonies, or even death, for their people's sake?

Is not our Christian religion the highest expression of the wisdom, mercy and love of God! But what is Christianity if not the very incarnation of that eternal law of divine justice in our humanity?

When I look on Moses, alone, silently dying on the Mount Pisgah, I see that law, in one of its most sublime human manifestations, and I am filled with admiration and awe.

But when I consider that law of justice, and expiation in the death of the Just, the divine Son of Mary, on the mountain of Calvary, I remain mute in my adoration. The spectacle of that crucified one which is before my eyes, is more than sublime, it is divine! Moses died for his people's sake, but Christ died for the whole world's sake! Both died to fulfill the same eternal law of the divine justice, though in a different measure.

Now, would it not be the greatest of honors and privileges bestowed upon me, if God, in his infinite love, mercy and wisdom, would put me between his faithful servant, Moses, and his eternal Son, Jesus, that I might die as they did, for my nation's sake!

Of the many examples of Lincoln's use of the conviction that he was a direct agent of the Lord, one is exceptionally interesting as a skillful display of human psychology. There were many times when Lincoln, in spite of his position as Chief Executive, could not enforce his plans without offering something far stronger than his personal opinion. After all, what could the Cabinet do but agree when he in all seriousness told them that he had a covenant with God to issue the 'Emancipation Proclamation' after the first Union victory? A similar instance occurred in the appointment of Senator Fessenden as Secretary of the Treasury upon Chase's resignation. For various reasons Fessenden refused the appointment. Finally Lincoln told him: 'I believe that the suppression of the rebellion has been decreed by a higher power than any represented by us, and that the Almighty is using his own means to that end. You are one of them. It is as much your duty to accept as it is mine to appoint.' Fessenden accepted the appointment.

Yet one other example may be taken from the many as especially significant. Its significance lies in the fact that it was a direct answer to the question of how far he believed the Almighty actually directed him. The question was put by L. E. Chittenden, who represents Lincoln answering as follows:

That the Almighty does make use of human agencies, and directly intervenes in human affairs is one of the plainest statements of the Bible. I have had so many evidences of his direction, so many instances when I have been controlled by some other power than my own will, that I cannot doubt that this power comes from above. I frequently see my way clear to a decision when I am conscious that I have no sufficient facts upon which to found it. But I cannot recall one instance in which I have followed my own judgment, founded upon such a decision, where the results were unsatisfactory; whereas, in almost every instance where I have yielded to the views of others, I have had occasion to regret it. I am satisfied that when the Almighty wants me to do or not to do a particular thing, he finds a way of letting me know it.

It would be easy, observing how these reminiscences in general recall things in keeping with the legendary Lincoln, to assume that any or all such accounts are interpolations done in the spirit of the legend that had become established by the time they were written; but they cannot be disproved. Furthermore, they have as their support all the evidence of Lincoln's authentic writings and the testimony in many places of such diarists as Chase and Welles, whose accounts were written before there was any established legend. In either case they are evidence of what the men who wrote them conceived Lincoln to be. He was authentically an instrument of the Divine Will. Whether we admit that Lincoln intentionally used his belief in divine guidance to strengthen his hold upon not only the mass of the people, but also upon his closest associates, we cannot avoid the conclusion that he so indelibly impressed his own belief that in after years the retrospect offered only the conclusion that Lincoln was inspired. It may be inferred that in this aspect of the legend Lincoln was himself the first legend-maker, but that does not mean that he wilfully misled people as to his own position in order to establish his divine agency. Perhaps Lincoln *was* a prophet.

III

In all the history of the world there is no more remarkable conspiracy of circumstances than that which brought about the final conclusion that Lincoln was of divine origin. It is a notable fact that medieval saints' legends bear in many instances an undeniable analogy to the histories of the prophets and even, in some instances, to the story of Christ. Whether these analogies were deliberately drawn, or whether they merely occurred, is a matter of opinion. In the Lincoln legend there is possibly something close at hand which will give an insight into the psychology of hagiography in general. When all the circumstances are considered, it is no wonder that Lincoln has become a second Moses or a second Christ. The wonder would have been if the world had failed to comprehend that he was.

The fact that the Christ analogy was possibly in Lincoln's mind has already been noted. When he read the New Testament he could not fail to note some of the parallels between the life of Christ and his own. Lincoln was a carpenter's son. The conditions in which he was born were quantitatively and qualitatively similar to those in which Jesus was born. His youth was obscure. His mission was not begun until he had passed some years in the ordinary walks of life. He was called to be the savior of his people. If Lincoln did not see the analogy, it was because he was unaware of things which became very evident to his followers.

Another circumstance was of considerable influence in creating the impression that Lincoln was like the men of God of old. Abraham was his name. Is it silly to suppose that in the subconscious mind of many people this simple fact was significant? Perhaps it was even consciously conceded. When we find such a general application of the popular 'Father Abraham' by his contemporaries — men like Emerson, Holmes, and Lowell, and women like Harriet Beecher Stowe and Mrs. J. T. Fields — it is perhaps a passive recognition of the popular conception of Lincoln, but once Lincoln was dead it was fraught with deep significance.

It was in the figure of Moses that the early poets of Lincoln found the counterpart for Lincoln which was second only to that found in Jesus. In *Poetical Tributes*, a volume of poems written on Lincoln and published within a few months of his death, the most popular simile is 'like Moses.' Like David, like Cromwell, like Achilles, like Christ, but above all, Lincoln was like Moses.

> He was our Moses; through the sea
>   Red with fraternal blood,
> He led our nation, while our foe
>   Sank in the angry flood.
> Through this dark wilderness of war,
>   Light from his face has shone,
> As from some Sinai's burning top,
>   He came a prophet down.

In view of the Reconstruction, one poet had a prophetic vision:

> Our Moses he — whose faithful hand
> Led us so near the promised land:
> He saw its distant palm trees wave —
> We strew their branches o'er his grave!

As the Emancipator, Lincoln was again like Moses:

> The prayer of the bondman went up night and day,
> 'Lord, send us a Moses to show us the way.'
> Like Moses of old, thou didst lead them safe through,
> Till the fair land of Canaan each pilgrim could view.

But the greatest conspiracy of circumstances was that which determined that Lincoln should be assassinated at Easter-tide. It was meet that the martyrdom should occur on Good Friday. Christ died for the world; Abraham Lincoln died for his country. On Lincoln's lips, had he spoken, would have been, 'Father, forgive them.' It was not without reason that the poets and orators placed the words of Christ in Lincoln's mouth, which had spoken only a few weeks before: 'With malice toward none; with charity for all.' On Easter Sunday there were many who thought with Henry Ward Beecher that Lincoln was risen: 'Disenthralled of flesh, risen to the unobstructed sphere where passion never comes.'

Lincoln was

> Like him, whose cause he served, whose home he shares,
> It was his solemn work, his mission high,
> Through weary months to bear a nation's cares,—
> Then, for the holy truths he taught, *to die!*

Or, in the lines of another poet:

> ... Thou hadst no room for hate;
> And, like Christ, thy orb in ocean dips,
> Forgiveness dropping from thy loving lips.

Or yet again in Edmund Clarence Stedman's sonnet on the assassination:

> 'Forgive them, for they know not what they do!'
> He said, and so went shriven to his fate,
> Unknowing went, that generous heart and true.
> Even while he spoke the slayer lay in wait,
> And when the morning opened Heaven's gate
> There passed the whitest soul a nation knew.

The Christ analogy was not merely a passing fancy induced by the circumstances of the assassination, nor yet by what may be considered Lincoln's confidence in his divine mission. There was a deeper parallel in the very thought-processes which produced the respective teachings of Jesus and Lincoln. It has long been an accepted fact that Lincoln's literary style owed more to the Bible than to all other traceable sources. His illustrative anecdotes were in many ways as remarkable in effectiveness as the parables of Jesus. His liberal use of direct quotations, such as the famous 'a house divided against itself cannot stand,' served to strengthen the connection. But, above all, whether they existed or not, the similarities in character — the charity, mercy, forgiveness, democracy, and selflessness — which his admirers found in Lincoln as in Jesus, made the analogy inevitable. It is much harder to explain how so many intelligent men among his associates could have been wrong about these qualities than it is to accept them. Hence the analogy has grown with the very study which might have been expected to refute it. The elements in Lincoln's character which do not support the analogy are easily passed over because they are not any more demonstrable than those that do and are not by any means so agreeable to the popular taste. Whoever studies Lincoln with even a fair amount of appreciation cannot avoid a general analogy, and, unless he is critical, it is likely that he, too, will conclude with E. W. Thompson that

> In visions wild as ours he shared,
> Until — dear Christ — with Thine was blent
> The death transfigured President.
> Strange — *strange* — the crown of thorns he wore,
> His outspread hands were pierced sore
> And down his old black coat a tide
> Flowed from the javelin-wounded side;

. . . .

The blended vision there was sent
In sign that our beloved meant; —
Children who wrought so mild my will,
Plough the long furrow kindly still,
'Tis sweet the Father's work to see
Done for the memory of me.

IV

In his biography of Lincoln, John T. Morse, Jr., commented that 'Lincoln was like Shakespeare, in that he seemed to run through the whole gamut of human nature. From the superstition of the ignorant backwoodsman to that profoundest faith which is the surest measure of man's greatness, Lincoln passed along the whole distance.' Lincoln was superstitious, but his superstition borders on something sublimely poetic when it is considered along with events which conspired to lend it a tinge of the genuinely spiritual. Where is the line that divides superstition from mysticism?

There was an element in Lincoln that may be interpreted as either superstition or mysticism of profound import. It has been said that we cannot account for the meanest specimen of mankind without entering the laboratory of the mystic, and certainly we shall never explain this Abraham Lincoln by the historical method alone. Lincoln achieved greatness, but the genesis of the mystery can never be analyzed. There are two attitudes of the human mind which enable us to react to the same phenomena in entirely different ways. Given an extraordinary circumstance, the one interprets it as unauthentic or meaningless, while the other interprets it as an evidence of some supernatural power. One man may say that Lincoln was inspired as much as was a prophet of old, meaning that neither was inspired; another may say the same and convey a genuine belief in the supernatural origin of Lincoln's power. All men differ in the extent to which they are willing or able to rationalize.

Without going into tedious detail, a few of the commonly cited prophecies may be mentioned here. There were the prophecies of prohibition, woman's rights, and the end of slavery. These had all been prophesied for years before Lincoln made public utterance on them. There are a few specific instances of mere coincidence with ultimate fact; such as the hopeful prophecy of Grant's victory at Vicksburg, which was made to General Sickles, and the rhetorical flourish of 1855 that the Autocrat of all the Russias would proclaim his subjects free sooner than Americans would voluntarily give up their slaves,[1] and there are the several prophetic dreams. Much or little may be made of these according to one's predilection. To the mystical interpreters of Lincoln they are signs and portents.

By far the most entrancing interpretation of Lincoln as a mystic is that given by Francis Grierson in *The Valley of Shadows*. For him Lincoln is the result and chief spirit of a great spiritual awakening which took place among the early pioneers on the prairies of Illinois. Remembering the early life in Illinois as it was when he was a boy, Grierson perceives through the years the workings of a new religion in the lives of a strange people — the descendants of Puritans and the settlers of Maryland and Virginia who retained all the best characteristics of their ancestors with something strangely original and characteristic of the time and place, something Biblical applied to the circumstances of the hour:

[1] Letter to George Robertson, *Works*, I, 216. Alexander II did emancipate the serfs on the day before Lincoln's inauguration.

In the late fifties the people of Illinois were being prepared for the new era by a series of scenes and incidents which nothing but the term 'mystical' will fittingly describe.

Things came about not so much by preconceived methods as by an impelling impulse. The appearance of *Uncle Tom's Cabin* was not a reason, but an illumination; the founding of the Republican Party was not an act of political wire-pulling, but an inspiration; the great religious revivals and the appearance of two comets were not regarded as coincidences, but accepted as signs of divine preparation and warning.

Swiftly and silently came the mighty influences. Thousands laboured on in silence; thousands were acting under an imperative, spiritual impulse without knowing it; the whole country round about Springfield was being illuminated by the genius of one man, whose influence penetrated all hearts, creeds, parties, and institutions.

The prairie was an influence in itself mystical. The atmosphere, 'palpitating with the presence of the all-ruling Spirit, diffused a feeling of an inscrutable power reaching out from the starry depths, enveloping the whole world in mystery.' The heavens with the awe-inspiring comet were at night a 'phantasmagoria seen from the summit of some far and fabulous Eden, vibrating with a strange mysterious glow.' The wide expanse of rolling prairie passed before the eye in all directions a mystic symbol of eternity.

Born in such time and place, Abraham Lincoln became at once the recipient and the prophet of a spiritual rebirth, which was something new and unfathomable. Grierson's estimate of Lincoln is fairly presented in a paragraph from *Abraham Lincoln the Practical Mystic*:

Abraham Lincoln, the greatest practical mystic the world has known for nineteen hundred years, is the one man whose life and example ought to be clearly set before the English-speaking peoples.... The thoughts, incidents, manifestations, which the majority of historians glide over with a careless touch, or sidetrack because of the lack of moral courage, are the only things that count in the life of that great seer. His whole existence was controlled by influences beyond the ken of the most astute politicians of his time. His genius was superhuman.

The place of dreams in the legends of all times is considerable. From Joseph to Freud the interpreter of dreams has been an honored member of society. The literature of any age would be sadly lacking were the dreams discounted. The dreams of Lincoln have come to be among the most significant mysteries of his life. Like Hamlet, Lincoln was possessed of melancholy which foreshadowed death, and he was warned of his doom by strange signs. The testimony is all but unanimous to his belief in dreams. Herndon relates several instances of his superstition in general and adds: 'He always contended that he was doomed to a sad fate, and he repeatedly said to me when we were alone in our office: "I am sure I shall meet with some terrible end."'

There are three famous incidents of supernatural nature which have become in the legend of Lincoln what King Arthur's dream on the eve of the last battle is to the Arthurian legend, or what Calpurnia's dream and the prophecy of the soothsayer is to the legend of Caesar. It is natural to suppose in the case of an ancient legend that prophetic dreams may have been manufactured by the legend-makers, but what can be said of Lincoln's dreams and strange visions?

The first of the three most famous instances was related by Lincoln to John Hay, Noah Brooks, and a few others. Noah Brooks gave the story from memory in an article which appeared in *Harper's Monthly Magazine* for July, 1865. Lincoln had related the circumstances as follows:

'It was just after my election, in 1860,' said Mr. Lincoln, 'when the news had been coming in thick and fast all day, and there had been a great "hurrah boys!" so that I was well tired out, and went home to rest, throwing myself upon a lounge in my chamber. Opposite to where I lay, was a bureau with a swinging glass upon it; and looking in that glass, I saw myself reflected nearly at full length; but my face, I noticed, had two separate and distinct images, the tip of the nose of one being about three inches from the tip of the other. I was a little bothered, perhaps startled, and got up and looked in the glass, but the illusion vanished. On lying down again, I saw it the second time, plainer, if possible, than before; and then I noticed that one of the faces was a little paler — say five shades — than the other. I got up, and the thing melted away, and I went off, and, in the excitement of the hour, forgot all about it — nearly, but not quite — for the thing would once in a while come up and give me a pang, as though something uncomfortable had happened. When I went home, I told my wife about it, and a few days after, I tried the experiment again, when, sure enough, the thing came back again; but I never succeeded in bringing the ghost back after that, though I once tried very industriously to show it to my wife, who was worried about it somewhat. She thought it was a sign that I was to be elected to a second term of office, and that the paleness of one of the faces was an omen that I should not see life through the last term.'

The second circumstance occurred a few days before Lincoln's assassination. It was told by Ward Lamon as he recalled the account given by Lincoln to a small group, including Lamon and Mrs. Lincoln, in the following words:

'It seems strange how much there is in the Bible about dreams. There are, I think, some sixteen chapters in the Old Testament and four or five in the New in which dreams are mentioned; and there are many other passages scattered throughout the book which refer to visions. If we believe the Bible, we must accept the fact that in the old days God and His angels came to men in their sleep and made themselves known in dreams. Nowadays dreams are regarded as very foolish, and are seldom told, except by old women and by young men and maidens in love.'

Mrs. Lincoln here remarked: 'Why, you look dreadfully solemn; do *you* believe in dreams?'

'I can't say that I do,' returned Mr. Lincoln; 'but I had one the other night which has haunted me ever since. After it occurred, the first time I opened the Bible, strange as it may appear, it was at the twenty-eighth chapter of Genesis, which relates the wonderful dream Jacob had. I turned to other passages, and seemed to encounter a dream or a vision wherever I looked. I kept on turning the leaves of the old book, and everywhere my eye fell upon passages recording matters strangely in keeping with my own thoughts — supernatural visitations, dreams, visions, etc.'

He now looked so serious and disturbed that Mrs. Lincoln exclaimed: 'You frighten me! What is the matter?'

'I am afraid,' said Mr. Lincoln, observing the effect his words had upon his wife, 'that I have done wrong to mention the subject at all; but somehow the thing has got possession of me, and, like Banquo's ghost, it will not down.'

This only inflamed Mrs. Lincoln's curiosity the more, and while bravely disclaiming any belief in dreams, she strongly urged him to tell the dream which seemed to have such a hold upon him, being seconded in this by another listener. Mr. Lincoln hesitated, but at length commenced very deliberately, his brow overcast with a shade of melancholy.

'About ten days ago,' said he, 'I retired very late. I had been up waiting for important dispatches from the front. I could not have been long in bed when I fell into a slumber, for I was weary. I soon began to dream. There seemed to be a deathlike stillness about me. Then I heard subdued sobs, as if a number of people were weeping. I thought I left my bed and wandered downstairs. There the silence was broken by the same pitiful sobbing, but the mourners were invisible. I went from room to room; no living person was in sight, but the same mournful sounds of distress met me as I passed along. It was light in all the rooms; every object was familiar to me; but where were all the people who were grieving as if their hearts would break? I was puzzled and alarmed. What could be the meaning of all this? Determined to find the cause of a state of things so mysterious and so shocking, I kept on until I arrived at the East Room, which I entered. There I met with a sickening surprise. Before me was a catafalque, on which rested a corpse wrapped in funeral vestments. Around it were stationed soldiers who were acting as guards; and there was a throng of people, some gazing mournfully upon the corpse, whose face was covered, others weeping pitifully. "Who is dead in the White House?" I demanded of one of the soldiers. "The President," was his answer; "he was killed by an assassin!" Then came a loud burst of grief from the crowd which awoke me from my dream. I slept no more that night; and although it was only a dream, I have been strangely annoyed by it ever since.'

The third and most famous instance was related by Lincoln to his Cabinet on the day of his assassination. Gideon Welles jotted the account down in his diary three days later. Stanton related it to his friends. Within a few days the story was common property, and appeared in newspaper accounts and in at least one poem written on the assassination. In itself it is symbolic and poetic. In its various forms and uses in the hands of dramatists and poets, it becomes one of the most effective circumstances of the great tragedy. Until his death Charles Dickens told his version of the dream, which he had on the authority of Stanton, with a great deal of embroidery, as one of his favorite after-dinner stories.[1] Gideon Welles gave the story under the date, April 14, 1865, as follows:

Inquiry had been made as to army news on the first meeting of the Cabinet, and especially if any information had

---

[1] The best account of Dickens's fondness for the story is given in *George Eliot's Life as Related in her Letters and Journals*, edited by J. W. Cross, III, 82. The story is told as Dickens told it to a small company which included George Eliot.

been received from Sherman. None of the members had heard anything, and Stanton, who makes it a point to be late, and who has the telegraph in his Department, had not arrived. General Grant, who was present, said he was hourly expecting word. The President remarked it would, no doubt, come soon, and come favorable, for he had last night the usual dream which he had preceding nearly every great and important event of the War. Generally the news had been favorable which succeeded this dream, and the dream itself was always the same. I inquired what this remarkable dream could be. He said it related to your (my) element, the water; that he seemed to be in some singular, indescribable vessel, and that he was moving with great rapidity toward an indefinite shore; that he had this dream preceding Sumter, Bull Run, Antietam, Gettysburg, Stone River, Vicksburg, Wilmington, etc. General Grant said Stone River was certainly no victory, and he knew of no great results which followed from it. The President said however that might be, his dream preceded that fight.

'I had,' the President remarked, 'this strange dream again last night, and we shall, judging from the past, have great news very soon. I think it must be from Sherman. My thoughts are in that direction, as are most of yours.'

Whatever significance the dream had for Lincoln, it has come to symbolize the mystery of his power, the mystery of all beyond life; and the symbol of the Ship of State with Lincoln as pilot has become one of the most popular conceptions in the early Lincoln poetry. Whitman's 'O Captain! My Captain!' later gave the popular image its lasting poetic form. The first poet to make use of the dream was Benjamin Franklin Taylor, whose rather ordinary poem, 'The President's Dream,' established the interpretation which still holds:

> Athwart the troubled waters swiftly sailing
> Thou saw'st the phantom vessel cleave its way:

Around its path the wandering winds were wailing,
  And white around it flashed the angry spray.
Alas! it flitted o'er a troubled ocean
  Where withering winds swept wildly as it past,
And urged it onward with unquiet motion,
  Tossed by the tempest long — but moored at last.

'Twas but the emblem of the swiftly gliding
  And waning hours of thy imperilled life,
The briefness of thy glorious day betiding,
  Thou pilot on the sea of freedom's strife!
Thou too wert battling with the tempest's power:
  Thine too a pathway o'er a strong deep;
But now the port is gained, no storm clouds lower,
  The bark is safe — Oh! faithful pilot, sleep!

All of these strange instances may be explained without any supernatural significance. The double image was quite likely produced by an unusual discrepancy in the focus of the eyes. The dream of death was the result of the almost continuous consciousness of the danger of assassination. From the day of his election Lincoln regularly received hundreds of threatening letters. Many plots and supposed plots were uncovered from time to time by the secret service. Stanton, Lamon, Hay, and others who were close to Lincoln were continually warning him against taking avoidable chances. The dream of the ship sailing which preceded so many important events is on ordinary grounds the most unusual of the three. Both the strange symbolism and the repetition make it undeniably prophetic for those who believe in prophetic dreams.

It is not remarkable that a man should dream strange dreams, but it is infinitely remarkable to some people that their import should become fact. It is not remarkable that a man should, in Lincoln's position and with his superstitious — or mystical — nature, become convinced that some all-ruling spirit was guiding him and making him its agent; but it is remarkable that he was able to impress others with a similar belief. A few such instances in the life of a man could be overlooked; but when they are numerous, they must be examined, and the more they are examined, the greater the wonder becomes to the credible.

Was there ever in history another such conspiracy of events and circumstances to insure the deification of a man? Those that may even be said to approximate it have long since been relegated to the realms of legend and myth. Certainly there is no creation of a poet's brain which holds a wider range of supernatural — or, perhaps, preternatural — circumstances and events. In the story of Lincoln we return to Endor and Delphi, and yet remain in the age of Darwin and Huxley. Truly, Lincoln lived a legend.

V

It has been seen how the variety of circumstances and incidents combined to make inevitable the popular apotheosis of Lincoln. One result became apparent in the biographical literature. It was impossible for a biographer to present Lincoln without some aspect of the prophet and savior. It may be said that there are elements in the life of Lincoln which can be interpreted no other way. Undoubtedly it is true that Lincoln's personality as remembered after his death presented these elements, but by the processes of omission and exaggeration they were emphasized out of all proportion. For example, it was easy to perceive in retrospect that Lincoln's question which forced Douglas to utter the Freeport Heresy was the result of a grand self-abnegation and far-sighted

prophecy, but that Lincoln realized the ultimate significance of the question at the time may be poetry rather
than history.

The development of the prophetic theme has been in
poetry and fiction somewhat more free than in biography.
In some instances it has been the only side of Lincoln
portrayed. Once the poet has realized the possibilities
of this Lincoln, all other aspects are either thrown to one
side or are reinterpreted to fit the general theme.

The incongruity of a prophet who tells Rabelaisian
stories is solved by making the stories over into unim-
peachable parables. The Springfield Lincoln is interpreted in the light of the Martyr President.

In the novels which attempt to portray Lincoln the
Lawyer as well as Lincoln the President, there is a clear
dichotomy between the two men. This dichotomy is
evident in the biographical studies also. At the very least,
an author finds himself dealing with two men rather than
one, and in most cases the Lincolns which appear in the
work of one author are more than two. Even though the
author is drawn to one more than the other in order to
give his character unity, the conflict is unavoidable.

For example, Winston Churchill's *The Crisis* portrays
the Lincoln of the fifties with the later Lincoln in mind.
The Christ analogy is drawn. The ineffable sadness of
Lincoln is magnified into the sadness of 'Christ crucified
or of Stephen stoned.' The very presence of the man
produces a rebirth in spirit. Young Stephen Brice returns
to St. Louis after hearing the Freeport debate, 'born
again,' and old Judge Whipple tells him later, 'I sent you
to see Abraham Lincoln — that you might be born again
— in the West.... O God, would that his hands — Abraham Lincoln's hands — might be laid upon all who com-

THE LIFE MASK OF ABRAHAM LINCOLN

plain and cavil and criticize and think of the little things
in life! Would that his spirit might possess their spirit.'
Lincoln is a prophet whose wisdom 'almost divine' is
to heal the nation. But Churchill also presents the Lincoln of the debates — the crude, rough, ugly frontier
lawyer — with accuracy, if not with appreciation. But
at the end of the novel there is nothing of the early Lincoln except the prophet and savior, much glorified, sad-
dened, and spiritualized.

Other novelists avoid this difficulty by taking only the
later Lincoln. Thomas Dixon, in both *The Southerner*
and *The Clansman*, portrays only the selfless martyr and
savior with a brief prologue in *The Southerner* portraying
the child Lincoln. Honoré Willsie Morrow in her Lincoln
'Trilogy' confines the action to the time between the first
inauguration and the assassination. Similarly, Drinkwater's play has little of the early Lincoln.

Lincoln receives in the novels of Irving Bacheller an
odd treatment. In *A Man for the Ages*, the Lincoln of
New Salem days is interpreted with a general fidelity
to a frontier type, which is in some things transfigured;
but in *Father Abraham* there is little or nothing of the sublime. Bacheller succeeds in keeping Lincoln a man, but
fails to attain any conception of his grandeur. His later
Lincoln is first of all, and quite naturally, the homely
friend and father who is somewhat out of place in the
White House.

It may be a legitimate question whether Lincoln can
be portrayed in both phases well and yet be at all convincing. The fact remains that there has been no biographer who has succeeded in doing justice to both.

The poets who have attempted to portray Lincoln in
narrative verse, generally cast in epic form, have experi-

enced the same difficulty. In a few instances the poet realizes the hiatus between the early Lincoln and the prophet and, admitting it, explains the difference by claiming a gradual awakening to the divine purpose. For example, in *The Burden Bearer*, by F. H. Williams, it is an awakening to the curse of slavery which inspires Lincoln and regenerates him anew, so that

> ... Awkward at first,
> Ungainly in his mien, nor having care
> For outward accessories, when his soul
> Rose in the majesty of spiritual power
> To lift the banner of eternal right,
> He seemed the Avatar of Justice, crowned
> With her undying bays. His attitude
> Unconsciously took on a classic mold;
> The lines of that lean figure fell apace
> Into the forms of beauty. From his eyes,
> Those sentient pools wherein strange shadows lay,
> Flashed forth the lightnings of a noble wrath,
> And flamed the indignation of a god.
> .   .   .   .
>
> That homely visage, as at first it turned
> Full-featured on a half believing throng,
> Became transfigured until they who gazed
> Visioned a nimbus seeming to surround
> The dark dishevelled hair.

On the other hand, Lincoln is more often the Man of Destiny from birth to death; as in James Oppenheim's 'The Lincoln Child,' he is born of God —

> Is born out of love!
> Mother love, father love, love of Eternal God —
> Stars have pushed aside to let him through —
> Through heaven's sun-down deeps
> One sparkling ray of God
> Strikes the clod —
> (And while an angel-host through wood and clearing sweeps!)

THE PROPHET, SAVIOR, AND MARTYR

And in *A Man of Destiny* by E. L. Staples,

> Onward through the years
> Of preparation passed he consecrate,
> Anointed by the hand of Providence —
> To the great sacrifice, the martyrdom
> Of his dear self to free his fellow man.
>
> Into his honest heart there brightly shone
> A revelation of the Will Divine;
> Within his soul he heard the voice of God,
> Clairaudient to the Eternal word.

The most voluminous of Lincoln poets, Denton J. Snider, presents an epic in four great episodes which solves the mystery of Lincoln by making him two beings instead of one. This duality is apparent wherever his story is told, but in the 'Lincoln Tetralogy' it is dealt with deliberately and mystically. The early hero as portrayed in *Lincoln in the Black Hawk War* is only awakening in his spiritual half. In *Lincoln and Ann Rutledge* his love for Ann becomes for him, after her death, a mystical tie with another world. In *Lincoln in the White House* his supernaturalism becomes supremely mystical. Not only is he aware of the mystic guidance of the 'upper world' and in communion with the departed spirits of the country's great men, but he regularly converses with them in his lonely moods. His foreboding dreams are but a small part of his experience. He is aware of his tragic end from the beginning of his task, as it is revealed to him by his 'Upper Cabinet.' This 'Upper Cabinet' is the chief source of Lincoln's inspiration and wisdom. There, and not with the 'Lower Cabinet,' lies his real help and guidance. Partially true to fact, the 'Lower Cabinet' has no voice in settling his policies. In the last episode, *Lincoln at Richmond*, Lincoln comes to realize that the 'Lower Self' which has monopolized a share of his life too great in proportion, passes over more and more into the spiritual world. The culmination of the action takes place when at last he passes over entirely to his 'Upper Self.' Lincoln relates his experiences on the *River Queen* en route to Richmond:

> A company of spirits were abroad
> Besides my wife and other living people;
> The Lord of all the sprightly presences
> Who have been inmates of the White House with me
> Since I first came to dwell at Washington,
> As I have often told you secretly,
> Appeared to step when I did on the deck,
> Remaining at my side the entire way.
> Or rather let me say the strangest truth,
> We were somehow a One inseparate,
> Fixed to a singleness of intellect,
> Two persons, but one personality,
> And I was in control of both of us.
> How great the difference from former days
> When I was ruled by the same presences
> Obeying them whenever they might come
> And breathe me wordless impress of their will!
> Still they appear and give command supernal,
> But that command is mind and I am they.
> Then they would fly down from some other realm
> I knew not whence, yet it was off outside;
> But now I feel them mine, though still supreme
> They be with all their primal sovereignty.
> That one great Lord of all the Presences
> The ruler of the Upper World, for me,
> Director of events of History,
> Became so strangely twinned with this my Self
> That I felt mine the voice of what he would;
> The change environs me with a new order,
> I have gone over to another life,
> Which still is the right essence of myself.

THE PROPHET, SAVIOR, AND MARTYR

The final passage represents the passing of Lincoln. The 'Upper Self' speaks to the 'Lower Self':

> So, my Lincoln, thou must pass out of life,
> And live forever;
> When thou art gone from thy people
> Thou shalt be their lasting Presence;
> Death cannot touch thee there,
> Though thy master and slayer here;
> Thy deed makes thee omnipresent,
> Sovereign, spaceless and timeless
> Over the two worlds, outer and inner,
> God's true Double.
> In thy dying thou shalt undeath Death,
> Letting him do to himself his own deed;
> Come over to me, O Lincoln,
> And render thyself the arisen.

This jog-trot mysticism is only an example of the idleness of words when used in an attempt to solve the mystery of Lincoln by fantastic vaporings. The mystical approach is capable of good, and even excellent, poetry, but it is hardly satisfactory as a means of portraying Lincoln. After all, 'this dust was once a man.'

Another of the long mystical interpretations, *Abraham Lincoln: A Poetical Interpretation*, by G. W. Bell, attains in places the dignity of true poetry. The poem is divided into three parts. The first, 'The Shaping Current,' develops the theme of the advancement of mankind toward truth under the guidance of a Supreme Being up to the epoch of Lincoln. The second develops the theme of Lincoln's service to mankind in the advancement of truth during his life. His divine mission is stressed:

> His call was of the deep unto the deep,
>   With vision flashing out as Nature's torch,
> Saw prejudice, the spectre, then o'erleap
>   Man's reason and o'erthrow the national arch.

THE LINCOLN LEGEND

He mastered principles that gripped the age.
    He saw beneath the coating of all form
The monster slavery, our heritage
    From out the past, a curse presaging storm.

The third part is the interpretation of the spirit of Lincoln, or the significance of his memory to the ages, which lies in the character of the man as much as in his accomplished acts. The culmination of the whole is a sonnet:

THE NATION'S SEER

The tall and stately pine-tree rears aloft
    Its needle-pointed vestments, bears its sway,
As prophet o'er a wilderness, and oft
    Tells to the ear attuned, of storms that play.
So rose Lincoln to his lonely view
    Above the hill tops springing from the plain;
Then saw he far beyond, and through and through,
    As earth contact thrilled messages of pain.

A man, our very own, to earth so near,
    So simple in his heartfelt tenderness,
Yet with a vision, piercing heights, a seer,
    Tracing the storm clouds and the war's duress.
        Seems human life a vain and worthless thing
        Attuned by Lincoln to love's deathless spring?

There is no mystical interpretation of Lincoln's genius, however, which can lay claim to greatness as poetry. The material is there, but the poet has not arrived who can treat the prophet and savior in the story of the time as he must be treated. The only successful attempts to spiritualize Lincoln are those which are not concerned with supporting a mystical thesis from the facts of Lincoln's life, although the facts may be in the background. Vachel Lindsay's 'Abraham Lincoln Walks at Midnight' is an example. To Lindsay, Lincoln is as abstract an ideal as

truth or beauty, and hence the poem is practically flawless
in spirit and execution.

> It is portentous, and a thing of state
> That here at midnight, in our little town
> A mourning figure walks, and will not rest,
> Near the old court-house pacing up and down,
>
> Or, by his homestead, or in shadowed yards
> He lingers where his children used to play,
> Or through the market, on the well-worn stones
> He stalks until the dawn-stars burn away.
>
> A bronze, lank man! His suit of ancient black,
> A famous high top hat and a plain worn shawl
> Make him the quaint great figure that men love,
> The prairie-lawyer, master of us all.
>
> He cannot sleep upon his hillside now.
> He is among us — as in times before!
> And we who toss and lie awake for long
> Breathe deep, and start, to see him pass the door.
>
> His head is bowed. He thinks on men and kings.
> Yea, when the sick world cries, how can he sleep?
> Too many peasants fight, they know not why;
> Too many homesteads in black terror weep.
>
> The sins of all the war-lords burn his heart.
> He sees the dreadnaught scouring every main.
> He carries on his shawl wrapped shoulders now
> The bitterness, the folly and the pain.
>
> He cannot rest until a spirit-dawn
> Shall come; — the shining hope of Europe free:
> The league of sober folk, the Worker's Earth,
> Bringing long peace to Cornland, Alp and Sea.
>
> It breaks his heart that kings must murder still,
> That all his hours of travail here for men
> Seem yet in vain. And who will bring white peace
> That he may sleep upon his hill again?

THE LINCOLN LEGEND

This poem was written during the World War, at a time of national stress and world uncertainty. It is one of the few good poems which develop the popular conception of Lincoln as the national saint. In the heroic movement of its lines it is in a class with Edwin Arlington Robinson's 'The Master' and Edwin Markham's 'Lincoln, Man of the People,' which are, perhaps, the best Lincoln poems from the more modern group of poets.

Lincoln as he walks at midnight is the symbol of all ideals of democratic humanity, but he is also the tender memory in apparition of the beloved personal saint, the folk Father Abraham. It was thus, in the Middle Ages that saints were said to have appeared at times of extreme exigency to cool the torturing fire, turn aside the blow, or snatch the helpless out of trouble; but Lindsay does not need the miraculous to convey his conception of Lincoln as the American saint. How much the name of Lincoln was called upon during the war and how often his utterances were read and quoted to quiet bitter fears and hopeless doubts, we may not forget. So was Joan of Arc canonized. So the ancient Britons looked ever for the time when Arthur would come again to assist them in their dire need. Without carrying the comparison farther into Christian mythology, we may observe how the cult of Lincoln has rendered him, as far as possible in an enlightened age, the deity of America.

As a further illustration from the several more or less successful attempts to spiritualize Lincoln, Edwin Markham's 'Lincoln Triumphant' will suffice. It is a typical example of the 'resurrection' poems and is somewhat better done than many.

> Lincoln is not dead. He lives
> In all that pities and forgives.

THE PROPHET, SAVIOR, AND MARTYR

> He has arisen, and sheds a fire
> That makes America aspire.
>
> Even now, as when in life he led,
> He leads us onward from the dead;
> Yes, over the whole wide world he bends
> To make the world a world of friends.

Verily, Lincoln is America's saint, or, perhaps, even in the verse of M. F. Seymour —

> Our God, if god there be,
> To hearken and implore.

It is altogether fitting that the National Lincoln Memorial should be a temple, a new Parthenon, when it is considered that for more than half a century Lincoln has enjoyed a popular worship that borders on idolatry. And as time 'disperses the solid angularity of facts,' it is likely that Lincoln will come to be more and more a 'constellation to hang in heaven an immortal sign,' but whether the legend of the prophet and savior will continue to be, as it has been in the past, one of the most popular phases of the myth it is impossible to conjecture. No abatement is in evidence at the present. Such books as Edgar Lee Masters's *Lincoln the Man* fall impotent before the public, a nameless sacrilege, because there is in Lincoln a direct appeal to the heart of the people which cannot be denied. If all the conspiracy of circumstances and events which cast him at once into the sky becomes eventually naught, and the interpreters of Lincoln are found false; still, the 'Second Inaugural Address' will be prophecy and its author somewhat allied with God.

V

The Emancipator and Savior of the Union

IN THE collection of Lincoln verse compiled and published within a few months after his assassination under the title *Poetical Tributes*, two outstanding achievements are extolled above all others — emancipation and preservation of the Union. Simple computation shows sixty poems which were primarily inspired by emancipation and sixty which were inspired by preservation of the Union, while six poems weave together praise of both achievements. Although the exactness of balance in numbers is a coincidence, the general significance is that Lincoln's accomplishment had already been generally centered in these two facts. There is no apparent conflict between these two themes as they are celebrated by early Lincoln poets, but the preference of the individual poet foreshadows somewhat the conflict in interpretation which was to come in succeeding Lincoln literature. A balanced interpretation is rare. Lincoln is either 'the Emancipator' or 'the Savior of the Union.' In the general legend the two figures are blended, but in individual poems or novels the conception of Lincoln is most often such that the one or the other becomes subordinate. It may seem strange that what Lincoln claimed to be merely a war measure has become one of his two greatest achievements, and possibly for all time the one great act of his life. Greatly as his service as captain of the ship of state has been extolled, it seems that popularly 'the Emancipator' is the enduring symbol to all the world.

The legend of the emancipator is closely aligned with the legend of the prophet and martyr, and in many instances the two are inextricably woven together. The downfall of slavery was, after all, Lincoln's greatest prophecy. In that, at least, he was able to effect, to a certain extent, what he had prophesied. He was like Wordsworth's 'Happy Warrior,' who

> Through the heat of conflict keeps the law
> In calmness made, and sees what he foresaw.

As if that were not enough for mortal man, Fate decreed that he should become in addition the martyr to the cause and usurp, to a considerable extent, the shrine of John Brown.

Hence it is that in our own country praise of the emancipator popularly equals that of the savior of the Union. Abroad the emancipator overshadows all conceptions of Lincoln save one, the symbol of democracy, which must be considered later. In the Lincoln poetry written in England, France, Spain, and Italy in commemoration of Lincoln, the liberation of the slaves is by far the most popular theme. To John Drinkwater, Lincoln is above all other things 'the World Emancipator.' To Japanese school children, if we may judge from their essays on Lincoln published by the American-Japan Society, Lincoln is more than anything else the great liberator.

I

Although Lincoln was convinced throughout his early life that slavery was morally wrong, he did not feel any of the zeal for its abolition which was inspiring young men in

New England. All attempts to make Lincoln an early Abolitionist are futile. The New Orleans slave-market story has already been noticed. There are many other fictions of a similar nature which have never made any claim to biographical truth, but which have in some degree established the necessary theme in the legend of the early life of the emancipator. These will be dealt with in the proper place. There are, however, statements of Lincoln which show with fair certainty just how much he was concerned with slavery as a young man.

In 1837 proslavery sentiment was strong in Illinois. During this year it was that Elijah P. Lovejoy was killed by a mob at Alton, and the press of his little antislavery paper destroyed. Instead of making an official protest against mob violence, the State Legislature drew up a set of resolutions condemning Abolition societies and their doctrines and maintaining that slavery 'is sacred to the slaveholding States by the Federal Constitution.' Lincoln would not vote for the resolution, and together with one other member, Dan Stone, drew up a protest against the resolutions and also against the Abolitionists. Lincoln's position is evident from one sentence, which maintains that 'the institution of slavery is founded on both injustice and bad policy, but that the promulgation of abolition doctrines tends rather to increase than abate its evils.'

This gives at once Lincoln's conviction of the moral wrong and the economic fallacy of slavery and the lie to any claim that Lincoln was an Abolitionist. What did Lincoln propose to remedy the evil at this time? Nothing. He was content with expressing the conviction that slavery was wrong.

The letter of Lincoln to Miss Mary Speed, written in

1841, in which he describes his reaction to the scene presented by a group of slaves in irons, has already been quoted in another place. If any conclusion can be reached from the description, it is that Lincoln's personal hatred of slavery had not at that date become apparent even to himself. It was still wrong, but Lincoln was not inspired with hatred for it. Lincoln wrote of this instance again in 1855, this time to James Speed. The two attitudes toward the same event present a remarkable contrast. Something had brought about a change in Lincoln's personal feeling. He now wrote as follows:

> I confess I hate to see the poor creatures hunted down and caught and carried back to their unrequited toil; but I bite my lips and keep quiet. In 1841, you and I had a rather tedious low-water trip on the steamboat from Louisville to St. Louis. You may remember, as well as I do, that from Louisville to the mouth of the Ohio, there were on board ten or a dozen slaves shackled together with irons. That sight was a continual torment to me; and I see something like it every time I touch the Ohio or any slave border. It is not fair for you to assume that I have no interest in a thing which has, and continually exerts, the power of making me miserable. You ought rather to appreciate how much the great body of the Northern people do crucify their feelings in order to maintain their loyalty to the Constitution and to the Union. I do oppose the extension of slavery, because my judgment and feeling so prompt me; and I am under no obligations to the contrary. If for this you and I must differ, differ we must.

Lincoln wrote this in 1855; yet in 1847, he had been engaged by a slaveowner in an attempt to send a negro mother and her children back into slavery, and, apparently, he had no compunction in accepting a fee for a service which, according to his later statement, should have been torment to him. The torment which the sight of slaves in 1841 gave him does not appear in the letter written at the time, but it cannot be proved, therefore, that he did not feel it. It is only reasonable to conclude, however, that Lincoln came gradually to have, in addition to the conviction that slavery was unjust, a personal desire that it should be limited and eventually exterminated. Yet he was wary of Abolitionism, and, while he came to court its favor, he would not commit himself to its policies.

It is impossible to undertake here an examination of the various expressions on slavery which were made by Lincoln during the momentous period from 1854 to 1860. Lincoln's position has been attacked in many instances and supported in many others by more or less careful students. In so far as his personal opinion was concerned, there is no better expression of it than that given in the Peoria reply to Douglas on October 16, 1854. Lincoln never receded from this express statement of belief. A few passages will convey his general conception as then spoken:

> This declared indifference, but, as I must think, covert zeal for the spread of slavery, I cannot but hate. I hate it because of the monstrous injustice of slavery itself. I hate it because it deprives our republican example of its just influence in the world; enables the enemies of free institutions with plausibility to taunt us as hypocrites; causes the real friends of freedom to doubt our sincerity; and especially because it forces so many really good men among ourselves into an open war with the very fundamental principles of civil liberty, criticizing the Declaration of Independence and insisting that there is no right principle of action but self-interest.
>
> . . . .
>
> The doctrine of self-government is right — absolutely and eternally right — but it has no just application as here attempted. Or perhaps I should rather say that whether it has such just application, depends upon whether a negro is not,

or is, a man. If he is not a man, in that case he who is a man may as a matter of self-government do just what he pleases with him. But if the negro is a man, is it not to that extent a total destruction of self-government to say that he too shall not govern himself? When the white man governs himself, that is self-government; but when he governs himself and also governs another man, that is more than self-government — that is despotism.

. . . .

What I do say is, that no man is good enough to govern another man without that other's consent.

. . . .

The master not only governs the slave without his consent, but he governs him by a set of rules altogether different from those which he prescribes for himself. Allow all the governed an equal voice in the government; that, and that only, is self-government.

. . . .

Slavery is founded in the selfishness of man's nature — opposition to it in his love of justice. These principles are an eternal antagonism; and when brought into collision so fiercely as slavery extension brings them, shocks and throes and convulsions must ceaselessly follow. Repeal the Missouri Compromise — repeal all compromise — repeal the Declaration of Independence — repeal all past history — still you cannot repeal human nature.

It is not difficult to jump from such a statement to the conclusion that Lincoln was in favor of liberating all the slaves in the country, but nothing is farther from the truth. The only policy which he can be truthfully said to have advocated up until the time of his election was this: namely, recognition of the fact that slavery was wrong and its complete prohibition in all Territories subject to the Federal Government. He reasoned that such recognition of the evil and restriction of it would eventuate in a gradual process of liberation within the slave States themselves. He did not expect complete emancipation according to his policy to become a fact in less than a hundred years, but that it would occur 'in the best way for both races in God's own good time.' Lincoln never harbored any more immediate plan until circumstances forced him to consider emancipation as an executive act.

Lincoln's complete aversion to extreme Abolition policies is nowhere made more evident than in his disapproval of John Brown and of the sentiment which he expressed and acted on. In the 'Cooper Union Address' he thus characterized John Brown: 'An enthusiast broods over the oppression of a people till he fancies himself commissioned by Heaven to liberate them. He ventures the attempt which ends in little else than his own execution.'

Those biographers of Lincoln who perceive that the great crusade against slavery was the one sublime movement of the century cannot but lament Lincoln's coldness on the subject. It is difficult, after having always heard of Lincoln as the emancipator, to recognize the fact that he was never an exponent of immediate emancipation and became the author of the proclamation only after the very act had been urged upon him for months. Charnwood considers Lincoln's attitude toward John Brown a flaw in his common-sense judgment, and it is a flaw from the standpoint of one who conceives the antislavery agitation to be the spirit of the age.

At the beginning of his Administration, Lincoln was not by any means ready to consider immediate freedom for all slaves. He did nothing about the matter at all. For some reason the Abolitionists expected an official act of proclamation concerning slavery to be one of the earliest achievements of the newly inaugurated president. Perhaps they felt that Lincoln owed his election to them and would not dare refuse them. Week by week, however, it became more evident that Lincoln would not do anything toward emancipation in an immediate way. He vetoed Frémont's proclamation after Frémont had refused to withdraw it and later restrained General Hunter. There would be no forcing Lincoln in the matter, and the antislavery element in the North raised a din that grew in volume until the appearance of the preliminary proclamation in September, 1862.

But Lincoln did attempt to influence legislation in behalf of gradual emancipation and compensation for the slaveholders. His chief reason for avoiding immediate emancipation seems to have been the conviction that it would not be practical or of benefit either to the country or the slaves; in addition to this, Lincoln wished to avoid any move which would antagonize the border States. The solution to the problem lay with these States. If they could be brought to a policy of gradual emancipation with compensation, Lincoln thought the antislavery element would be quieted and a definite step taken toward practical achievement.

In April, 1862, Congress passed a bill to abolish slavery in the District of Columbia. Lincoln signed the bill, but did not approve of its provisions for immediate emancipation. Senator Browning tells in his *Diary* of a visit to Lincoln on April 14, during which Lincoln regretted that the bill had passed 'in its present form' and commented that it would have been much better had it provided gradual emancipation. Apparently the antislavery element was gaining strength in Congress, and the members from the border States were becoming restive.

On March 6, 1862, Lincoln sent a special message to Congress in which he proposed that the United States give pecuniary aid to any State that would provide for gradual emancipation with compensation to slaveholders. His position he explained as follows: 'In my judgment, gradual, and not sudden emancipation is better for all.' A few days later he held a conference with representatives of the border States for the purpose of urging this plan. This failed to bring about any practical result. Again in July Lincoln attempted to gain for his policy some attention from the representatives of the border States. He invited them to the White House and addressed them at length. All his efforts came to naught, and it became clear to him that an executive proclamation would be the only solution. On July 22, 1862, he read to his Cabinet a proclamation of emancipation which was the same in effect as that which he later issued. Seward objected to the inopportuneness of the occasion, and Lincoln accepted his proposal that it should be withheld until the Union army had won a victory.

Lincoln wrote a letter to A. G. Hodges on April 4, 1864, in which he described his decision of 1862 and the circumstances attending it, as follows:

> When in March, May and July, 1862, I made earnest and successive appeals to the border States in favor of compensated emancipation, I believed the indispensable necessity for military emancipation and arming of blacks would come, unless arrested by that measure. They declined the proposition, and I was, in my best judgment, driven to the alternative of either surrendering the Union, or issuing the emancipation proclamation.

In connection with his plans for gradual emancipation, and later, complete emancipation, Lincoln proposed colonization for the freed negroes. He never contemplated with any degree of satisfaction the prospect of a free negro race living in the same country with a free white race. It is not in place to discuss the projects here. Some measures were undertaken as a beginning; all of them failed. It was with considerable regret that Lincoln came to realize that emancipation could not be correlated by the removal of the negro race from America.

On August 22, 1862, Lincoln wrote a letter in reply to Greeley's 'Prayer of Twenty Million,' which, among other things, had complained of the policy of the Administration in upholding slavery. In this letter Lincoln defined his purpose as follows:

> I would save the Union. I would save it the shortest way under the Constitution. The sooner the National authority can be restored, the nearer the Union will be 'the Union as it was.' If there be those who would not save the Union unless they could at the same time save slavery, I do not agree with them. If there be those who would not save the Union unless they could at the same time destroy slavery, I do not agree with them. My paramount object in this struggle is to save the Union, and is not either to save or destroy slavery. If I could save the Union without freeing any slave, I would do it; and if I could save it by freeing all the slaves, I would do it; and if I could save it by freeing some and leaving others alone, I would also do that. What I do about slavery and the colored race, I do because I believe it helps to save the Union; and what I forbear, I forbear because I do not believe it would help to save the Union.

At the time Lincoln wrote this letter he had already determined that it must be by 'freeing some and leaving others alone.' On September 22, 1862, he called a Cabinet meeting at which he gave notice of his resolve to issue the proclamation immediately in preliminary form. The story of that meeting has been told in an earlier chapter. The reception accorded the proclamation was possibly not what Lincoln had expected. Many Abolitionists were disappointed at the restricted area in which the proclamation was effective. Many thought the move a piece of chicane, for, it was contended, the only places over which the United States maintained any authority were not included. The proslavery element was outraged. Yet this was the act which was to become 'the central act of Lincoln's Administration.'

In no less than half a dozen places Lincoln's letters reiterate the position which he took from the beginning; namely, that the proclamation was merely a war measure. What he did for the negro race, he did only because it benefited the cause of the Union.

Now, before the legend is considered in relation to this one act, it may be well to ask finally what Lincoln really considered to be his duty in regard to slavery, aside from the question of preserving the Union. It is futile to contemplate what might have been, but there is at least nothing on which to base any supposition that if there had been no secession Lincoln would have done more than contribute his support to any attempts to prevent the spread of slavery and to any attempts to procure gradual emancipation with compensation. The latter was the most radical view taken by Lincoln, even under the stress of war, until he saw that it would not be acceptable to the only slaveholding States in the Union. What he finally did was far-reaching in effect, and he was anxious that legislation should be passed which would make the freedom conveyed by his war measure more than a temporary matter. His support of the bill for the abolition of slavery by a constitutional amendment was strong and open. His chagrin at its first failure in June, 1864, was great. When the passage of the amendment was effected by Congress after Lincoln's election in 1864, he looked forward with satisfaction to the certainty of a Union without slavery.

Lincoln had enunciated his belief in regard to the evil of slavery in a passage long since famous: 'A house divided against itself cannot stand. I believe this government cannot endure permanently half slave and half free. I do not expect the house to fall — but I do expect it will cease to be divided. It will become all one thing, or all the other.'

With this belief as a key, Lincoln's policy becomes clear. From beginning to end, his purpose was to preserve the Union. The final abolition of slavery by constitutional amendment, Lincoln urged because it was his belief that the only hope of the Union was in the abolition of slavery.

How strange are the twists of reputation: Lincoln is 'the World Emancipator,' and yet his Emancipation Proclamation and, indeed, all that he did for the freedom of the slaves was done, not for them, but for the preservation of the Union. Alexander Stephens said that the Union with Lincoln, rose in sentiment 'to the sublimity of a religious mysticism.' Perhaps it did.

II

It has already been noted that in the volume of *Poetical Tributes* published shortly after Lincoln's death many of the poets seized upon either one or the other of Lincoln's great achievements as the theme of their eulogies. The underlying significance of this preference seems to have been in every case the author's conception of the final purpose and accomplishment of the war. To Bryant and

Whittier, the Civil War was fought to liberate the slaves.
Hence, to Bryant, Lincoln's greatest accomplishment was
that

> ... the bond are free;
> We bear thee to an honored grave,
> Whose proudest monument shall be
> The broken fetters of a slave.

Whittier's poem was inspired by the Emancipation Group
more than by Lincoln, and it is quite evident that the
Emancipation Proclamation meant far more to Whittier
than Lincoln did:

> Let man be free! The mighty word
> He spoke was not his own;
> An impulse from the Highest stirred
> These chiseled lips alone.

Neither poet has anything to say about the preservation
of the Union, and their poems are typical of the praise
that the Abolitionists meted out to Lincoln.

To Whitman, on the other hand, Lincoln was the Captain of the Ship of State. His real admiration of Lincoln,
as expressed in the poems added to *Drum Taps* after the
assassination, is of the man rather than of anything that
he did. The few expressions of admiration which Whitman
uttered before Lincoln's death, which have been considered
in an earlier chapter, show the same personal interest
rather than any recognition of public accomplishment.
But Whitman's most popular Lincoln poem owes much of
its popularity to the fact that it is the best expression of
appreciation for Lincoln's service in preserving the Union.
All in all, more people found a common ground of praise
and sorrow in 'O Captain! My Captain!' than in any
other poem. It has been said that Whitman owed a great

part of his popular recognition during his lifetime to this one poem. It is easily the best of the poems on this theme.

O Captain! my Captain! our fearful trip is done,
The ship has weather'd every rack, the prize we sought is won,
The port is near, the bells I hear, the people all exulting,
While follow eyes the steady keel, the vessel grim and daring;
   But O heart! heart! heart!
   O the bleeding drops of red,
    Where on the deck my Captain lies,
    Fallen cold and dead.

O Captain! my Captain! rise up and hear the bells;
Rise up — for you the flag is hung — for you the bugle trills,
For you bouquets and ribbon'd wreaths — for you the shores
 a-crowding,
For you they call, the swaying mass, their eager faces turning;
   Here Captain! dear Father!
   This arm beneath your head!
    It is some dream that on the deck
    You've fallen cold and dead.

My Captain does not answer, his lips are pale and still,
My father does not feel my arm, he has no pulse nor will,
The ship is anchor'd safe and sound, its voyage closed and done,
From fearful trip the victor ship comes in with object won;
   Exult O shores, and ring, O bells!
   But I with mournful tread,
    Walk the deck my Captain lies,
    Fallen cold and dead.

Before Lincoln's death there was a difference in artistic portrayals of Lincoln. Lowell's 'Two Scenes from the Life of Blondel' and John James Piatt's sonnet 'Stern Be the Pilot in the Dreadful Hour,' written in 1862, are the best examples of the early praise which anticipate the appreciation expressed by Whitman's 'O Captain! My Captain!' On the other hand, there are several nondescript poems which were written in praise of the Emancipator,

> Who now has done the greatest deed
> Which History has ever known.

Francis B. Carpenter chose the reading of the Emancipation Proclamation as the central act of Lincoln's Administration to be portrayed in the historical painting which now hangs in the Capitol. Generally, in these early pieces, one feels that the author chooses the one theme or the other without any deliberate desire to apotheosize Lincoln as the Emancipator, more than as the President, or *vice versa*, but later on, a sharper divergence appears in the two themes, until finally a novelist portrays the President in order to minimize the Emancipator, and a poetic scion of the Abolitionists writes an epic of Lincoln which is nothing more than the epic of Abolition.

It is impracticable to enumerate, much more to discuss, the many works which misinterpret Lincoln as the antislavery prophet. There are three epics and many short poems, short stories, and novels. The usual plan is to present Lincoln's early life as a period of preparation for the one divine event. The myth of the New Orleans slave market is utilized along with other fictitious incidents in which young Lincoln is either assisting slaves to escape from their masters or is chastising in righteous wrath the upstart Southern gentleman who has come to recapture the slaves. The underground railway is generally in full operation throughout the book or poem, and if the author hesitates to make Lincoln a direct participant, the implication is always that he is in sympathy with the project. Lincoln's associates are generally either Abolitionists or villains.

In the antislavery epics Lincoln's chief supporters in governing the country are, of course, the Abolitionists. One poet enumerates the 'great, godlike minds' who aided Lincoln as Sumner, Beecher, Frémont, Phillips, Lovejoy, and Garrison. It would be hard to find a group who were Unionists and yet helped him less. On the other hand, a novelist with a Border-State-Union bias chooses the Titans of the great struggle from the ranks of Westerners and Border-State men.

As examples of the literary presentations of Lincoln which take up these diverging themes, Lyman Whitney Allen's epic poem *The Emancipator* and Thomas Dixon's novel *The Southerner* and his play *A Man of the People* may be considered very good interpretations.

The Emancipator is the second part of 'An Epic Trilogy,' the first dealing with Washington and the third with Lee. Originally *The Emancipator* was a separate epic poem to which was awarded, in 1895, the *New York Herald* prize for the best poem on American history.

The poem opens with historic preludings which present the beginnings of the conflict of Liberty and Slavery. First of all there is the venerable theme of Puritan and Cavalier.

> The fragrant meadows of Runnymede
> Grow greener every succeeding year;
> The Ironside hoofs of the Puritan's steed
> Still crowd on the Cavalier.

Then comes the further development of the conflicting ideals as symbolized in the Mayflower and the slave ship:

> Fair Mayflower, breasting the wintry sea!
> Thou wert the promise of wakening spring;
> Embosoming Freedom's destiny
> And Liberty's issuing.

THE LINCOLN LEGEND

Dark Slaver, touching Virginia's shore!
 With captives laden from mast to keel;
 Thou wert the sign of the deepening sore...

Into the country oppressed by wrong comes the deliverer

 The champion of Liberty,
 The hope of a continent,
 God's answer to prayer.

He mounted to the People's Mystic throne,
 And counted, as he clomb, each step sublime;
He marked where its foundations, stone on stone,
 Sank deep into the crimsoned soil of time.
His tread became a kneeling as he rose
Transfigured by historic overflows.

 . . . .

So sat he on his high and sacred seat,
 He who knew God and God's perplexing ways —
Believing God patient with the feet
 Of the swift shod but loitering, with the praise
And blame commingled, waiting the clear word
Which God's true seers at last have ever heard.

 . . . .

The hour was come, and with it rose the man
 Ordained of God and fashioned for the hour;
  The saviour of a race;
For whom wrought ever, since the world began,
 The subtle energies of thought and power
  In lineal lines of grace.

Incarnate Conscience; Right's embodiment...
A master mind...
 He stood, the Nation's larger soul endowed
  With faith and hope sublime.

The hour was come, and in that hour he stood
 Responsive to the sacred voice that spoke
  From Heaven and earth and sea.
He heard the dusky toiling multitude
 Plaintively pleading that his hand should break
  Their bonds and make them free....

> And, lifting high o'er groaning multitude
> His sovereign scepter, smote with such a stroke
> The chains of centuries,
> That earth was shaken to its farthest rood;
> That millioned manacles asunder broke,
> And myriad properties
>
> Became, in one immortal moment — men.

Having accomplished this one great act, Lincoln sees the armies of the North become victorious. The Lord no longer holds them back because of the unremedied wrong of slavery. With victory, Lincoln's task is done, and from his lonely peak of perfection —

> Listening, he heard the sweet adagios
> Of quiring angels, and the morning song
> Of the redeemed and free; —
> And was not, for God took him; and he rose,
> Caught to the bosom of that martyr throng
> Who died for liberty.

Such is the legend of the Emancipator who, with the stroke of a pen, shattered the manacles of four millions of human souls in a state of servitude. It is of little import in the legend that men had campaigned for years against slavery and that many had done far more than Lincoln to bring about a sane view of the situation on the part of the general public, that Lincoln's dislike for slavery was never strong enough to make him an Abolitionist, and that the Emancipation Proclamation was itself only a promise of freedom. In this phase of the legend Lincoln functions again as a magnetic symbol around which all the ideal attributes, hopes, prayers, and achievements of a horde of crusading predecessors are clustered. It is a delicious bit of irony that Lincoln should be most completely apotheosized as the god of a sect which he at one time disapproved and whose members thought him a 'first-rate *second-rate* man.'

No one has understood better than the educated negroes that Lincoln was not, above all other things, the liberator of the colored race. They have honored his name in literature with sparing reference to their freedom. Perhaps they have not found the Emancipation Proclamation a sign to conjure with.[1] Easily the best Lincoln poem by a negro is that of Paul Laurence Dunbar, who writes, not of the Emancipator, but of

> The mighty Homer of the lyre of war!
> 'Twas he who bade the raging tempest cease,
> Wrenched from his harp the harmony of peace,
> Muted the strings that made the discord — Wrong,
> And gave his spirit up in thund'rous song.

Thomas Dixon's literary works undertake a portrayal of Lincoln which is in direct contrast with that of the anti-slavery legend and are to a certain extent an attempt to counteract it. The first of Dixon's works to portray Lincoln was *The Clansman*, published in 1905. In this novel Lincoln is primarily the folk-hero, Father Abraham, with certain obvious characteristics of the martyr. Although Lincoln appears only in the first pages of the book, the author's conception is made quite clear on certain points. First, Lincoln is not an Abolitionist; second, he is a Southerner; third, the North and not the South crucified Lincoln. It is probably not necessary to add that Dixon is a Southerner. Dixon's second novel, *The Southerner*, is entirely a novel of Lincoln, written with the purpose of showing that Lincoln was a Southerner. The only dif-

[1] The first biography of Lincoln by a negro, William E. Lilly's *Set My People Free* (1932), ends with Lincoln's inauguration but stresses the belief that his entire political career was moulded by his attitude toward slavery. As the title implies, it is a reminder and a plea.

ference between this and the Lincoln of *The Clansman* is emphasis, with possibly more adoration in the portrayal of the mysticism and altruism of the prophet. Lincoln is as much a prophet to Dixon as he is to the poets and novelists of the antislavery legend, but he is not the Emancipator. A goodly number of pages are devoted to scenes in which Lincoln's real attitude toward slavery is evolved with considerable historical fairness, but a much larger portion of the book is devoted to a portrayal of Lincoln's love for the Union. He bears the snubs and curses of his Cabinet for the sake of preserving the Union. He offers McClellan the presidency on condition that he uphold the Union. When Mrs. Lincoln points out the fact that his Cabinet members are trying to climb over him, he says, 'I've no right to think of my own ambitions.' It is due to the selfless, merciful President alone that the discordant elements are again woven into one nation.

The last of Dixon's portrayals of Lincoln is the play *A Man of the People* (1921). The one purpose of this play is to contrast the saving of the nation with the liberating of the slave. It was written, apparently, in answer to Drinkwater's play. Drinkwater's Lincoln entertains two devout purposes, to preserve the Union and to liberate the slave, both equally important. Neither may be said to supersede the other. Against such a conception Dixon in his preface evokes the spirit of history:

> While the popular conception of Lincoln as the Liberator of the slave is true historically, there is a deeper view of his life and character. He was the savior, if not the real creator of the American Union of free Democratic States. His proclamation of emancipation was purely an incident of the war. The first policy of his Administration was to save the Union. To this fact we owe a united Nation today. It is this truth of history which I try to make a living reality in my play.

The Lincoln of Drinkwater's play is the grander figure. All of the various legends are fused into one. Historical fact and legendary truth are united to produce a poetical conception which is vast and appealing.

A few comments further may be in keeping with Dixon's savior of the Union. Typical of all those who fictionize or poetize Lincoln, Dixon does not seem to question for a moment whether Lincoln really saved the Union. Without questioning the valuable service which Lincoln rendered as President, it is only fair to note that in this phase of the legend he has acquired, as in other phases, credit for the achievements of his entire Administration. Dixon's picture is typical in presenting the Cabinet as a group of self-seekers who labor for the Union only that their personal ambitions may be gratified. In a measure, it must be admitted, this was true. Chase, Stanton, and Seward — to a lesser degree — had the idea that they were individually the big men of the Government. But Lincoln has gathered unto himself the praise for what all did in bringing order out of chaos. In one phase of the legend Lincoln accomplishes this by his selflessness, by suffering the abuse of all comers if they are really working for the Union. In another phase he accomplishes the same end by his unquestioned mastery of men.

One of the most popular interpretations of Lincoln's genius is that given by Alonzo Rothschild in *Lincoln, Master of Men* (1900). With the title for a formula any example is grist to the author's mill. Lincoln's mastery of Frémont, Chase, and McClellan obviously never existed unless an odd definition be placed on the term. One might as well claim that Woodrow Wilson mastered William Jennings Bryan as that Lincoln mastered any one of these. Yet these men are cited and discussed at length as examples of Lincoln's power to procure results with men who had no personal allegiance to him. One cannot but admire Lincoln's treatment of these men, but admiration cannot suffice as proof for a thesis that makes Lincoln the master.

Nowhere is this tendency to subordinate a contemporary figure to an aggrandized Lincoln more apparent than in the story of the Great Debates. Even the best biographers have tended to give Lincoln a heavy verdict in the arguments, and the more idolatrous have pictured him as literally demolishing his great competitor. Nothing could be farther from the truth, except, perhaps, the view that Douglas routed Lincoln, which one finds occasionally in those bitter partisan diatribes that seek to make Lincoln at once the villain and the ignoramus. Of this stubborn myth George Fort Milton disposes fairly in *The Eve of Conflict* (1934). Subjecting it to proper tests, he concludes that

> the Lincoln of the debates stands revealed as a strong antagonist at grips with one quite as strong. At times both men seem political wrestlers crafty in verbal clutches, who spent much time in fumbling about for or escaping from effective holds. At times Lincoln was evasive and unresponsive; at times he indulged in unjustified personal aspersions, often he was candid — and occasionally not; occasionally Douglas met him on the same plane. There is no escaping the fact that Lincoln was an adroit and ambitious politician who never forgot that he was after Douglas's Senate seat.

But it seems to be the nature of the human mind to deal with history in some such manner. Great men are often contemporaries; it has been said that they most often come in groups. Some indefinable power transforms one of the number into the lodestar of the age. We think of Augustus Caesar and his contemporaries; we speak of

Shakespeare and other Elizabethans; or we admire Napoleon and his generals. It is not so simple a matter to conclude by saying that these were the true geniuses of the age; for Caesar has gathered the brilliance of his contemporaries unto himself, Napoleon enjoys the fame of his generals, and even Shakespeare's immortality is enhanced by the achievement of the Elizabethans, if not 'beautified with their feathers.'

In spite of the fact that the emancipation of the slave has been and probably will continue to be the one great act of Lincoln's life, the epic of Lincoln is not the epic of slavery alone. On the other hand, the emancipation theme cannot be minimized to the extent that Dixon would have it minimized. The correlation of the two themes in some fashion has produced the truly poetic conception. Drinkwater manages this in his play without lessening either theme. Stephen Vincent Benét follows the same plan in portraying Lincoln in *John Brown's Body*.

John Brown's Body is in many respects the most complete realization of the epic of the Civil War. Lincoln is the guiding hand in the struggle, but he is not the all-in-all of the period. He is the master, but John Brown is the spirit of the time. The Lincoln that gradually emerges is an heroic figure, gigantic, and sublime, but he is not the aureoled prophet. In the beginning he is

> The low clown out of the prairies, the ape-buffoon,
> The small-town lawyer, the crude small-time politician,
> State-character but comparative failure at forty
> In spite of ambition enough for twenty Cæsars.

But he alone rises above the tumult of the hour and maintains a spiritual poise and an iron resolve during the trying early months of the war:

> Only Lincoln, awkwardly enduring, confused by a thousand coun-

sels, is neither overwhelmed nor touched to folly by the madness that runs along the streets like a dog in August scared of itself, scaring everyone who crosses its path.

His huge, patient, laborious hands start kneading the stuff of the Union together again; he gathers up the scraps and puts them together; he sweeps the corners and the cracks and patches together the lost courage and the rags of belief.

He is a mystery as a man and yet a patent reality as the strong and dominating intellect of the period, and a ruler in fact:

> The parable-maker, humble in many things
> But seldom humble with his fortitude,
> The sorrowful man who cracked the sure-fire jokes,
> Roared over Artemus Ward and Orpheus C. Kerr
> And drove his six cross mules with a stubborn hand.

As the time goes on there is a notable growth in the man —

> A tempering of will in these trotting months
> Whose strong hoofs striking have scarred him again and again.
> He still rules more by the rein than by whip or spur,
> But the reins are fast in his hands and the horses know it.
> He no longer says 'I think,' but 'I have decided.'

As Benét reads Lincoln's thoughts and reveals them, the entire genius of the man resolves itself into one great faith that, above all, links his every act with heavenly guidance:

> ... If God reads
> The hearts of men as clearly as He must
> To be Himself, then He can read in mine
> And has, for twenty years, the old, scarred wish
> That the last slave should be forever free
> Here, in this country.
> I do not go back
> From that scarred wish and have not.
> But I put
> The Union, first and last, before the slave....

O Will of God,
I am a patient man, and I can wait
Like an old gunflint buried in the ground
While the slow years pile up like moldering leaves
Above me, underneath the rake of Time,
And turn, in time, to the dark, fruitful mold
That smells of Sangamon apples, till at last
There's no sleep left there, and the steel event
Descends to strike the live coal out of me
And light the powder that was always there.

But *John Brown's Body* is an epic of the war rather than
of Lincoln. Even this heroic portrait does not suffice. It
may well be wondered whether there is ever to be a poet
capable of fathoming Lincoln. There are too many Lincolns. When one is followed through carefully, others are
lost; and the result seems oddly unlike what was hoped
for. When several are combined, the artist must throw
up his hands, wondering whether the result is either
accurate or artistically true. Percy MacKaye in the
Lincoln Centenary Ode, having tried, laments:

The loving and the wise
May seek — but seek in vain — to analyze
The individual man, for having caught
The mystic clue of thought
Sudden they meet the controverting whim,
And fumbling with the enchanted key,
Lose it then utterly.

Perhaps the best poetic treatment in brief of the heroism
with which Lincoln accepted and accomplished his im-
measurable task is Richard Henry Stoddard's sonnet
'Abraham Lincoln.' In conception and execution it is
infinitely better than Stoddard's other Lincoln poem,
'Lincoln; an Horatian Ode.' The conception is fittingly
majestic, and the verse heaves with a rugged power that

matches strength with the titanic subject to express its awful grandeur, which all but jeopardizes the sonnet. Good heroic poetry is not too common among the Lincoln poems, and in sonnet form it is unusual anywhere.

> This man whose homely face you look upon
> Was one of Nature's masterful, great men;
> Born with strong arms, that unfought battles won,
> Direct of speech and cunning with the pen.
> Chosen for large designs, he had the art
> Of winning with his humor, and he went
> Straight to his mark, which was the human heart;
> Wise, too, for what he could not break he bent.
> Upon his back a more than Atlas-load,
> The burden of the Commonwealth was laid;
> He stooped and rose up to it, though the road
> Shot suddenly downward, not a whit dismayed:
> Patiently resolute, what the stern hour
> Demanded, that he was — that Man, that Power.

VI

The American

THE phases of the frontier legend which were gradually associated with the name of Lincoln from the time of his nomination are closely allied with another interesting phenomenon — the miracle of democracy which enabled a boy born in the dust to attain the highest place in the society of his country. The appeal of the selfmade hero is not yet dead, in spite of two generations of writers who have told the story over and over. It is not likely that it will die so long as there are lowly who aspire. Perhaps the widest appeal in the story of Lincoln lies in the fact that his life contains every step in the social ladder and that his rise was his own achievement.

There is an interesting series of essays on Lincoln by Japanese students in competition for prizes offered by the America-Japan Society which were published in special bulletins of the Society for February, 1927–29. These essays are interesting as indications of Lincoln's significance to young people whose cultural background is remote enough from that of Americans to give them an entirely different perspective from our own. Each essay has its particular theme. Yet the one dominating idea which is apparent in every essay is that Lincoln was a poor boy who became the greatest man in his country. He is the symbol of democratic achievement.

THE AMERICAN

It has been shown how Lincoln's popular fame was increased by a considerable amount of campaign literature which held him up as the veritable democrat, and how he came to symbolize democracy to such contemporaries as Emerson, Whitman, and Motley. It remains to be shown how Lincoln literature has enshrined this symbol and developed the theme of Lincoln's new and American type of genius.

Democracy and Americanism have become, to a certain extent, synonymous terms. In the praise of Lincoln this fact is evident. His democratic principles and his life connect him at once with the general ideal, equality of opportunity. It is a fit subject for the scoffer that there are thousands of lowly born who remain lowly in our republic, whose people still believe that men are for the most part created equal. It is, perhaps, a humorous matter that thousands of boys born in the dust expect some day to be the President of the United States. Yet the miracle does happen, and some one or two boys, regardless of birth, attain the cherished goal. It is not enough, very likely, that this possibility should be the limit of our attainment as a democratic people, but it is still of interest, not only to us, but to the world at large. It may be argued that as our society has changed, and will continue to change, the example of Lincoln becomes more and more inapplicable and less significant. If it is, it is so only in the false application; the principle which it illustrates will hold for any society. It is the principle of democracy which the poets have found forever vindicated in him. This they choose to represent as his most American significance. Their words are symbolic; their specific meanings are somewhat vague; but their spirit is unanimous.

For several years past the word 'frontier' has been the

magic key which unlocks every door in the devious labyrinth of history and literature. In 1893 F. J. Turner read to the American Historical Association a paper entitled 'The Significance of the Frontier in American History.' Later this paper grew into a book. The thesis which it developed was not new, but it had not, up to then, attained the dignity of historical interpretation. It will be observed in the present chapter how literary men advanced the same theory in interpreting Lincoln twenty years earlier. First of all, however, it may be well to examine this potent talisman and the effect of its introduction into the study of history and society.

Turner shows how the history of the United States was for more than a hundred years largely the history of westward expansion. The line of settlement moved with each generation as the oncoming tide spilled over the successive boundaries. The conditions of the frontier brought about a non-sectional type. All the immigrating nationalities lost their distinctiveness as they were thrown into the identical and primitive conditions. The frontier influenced not only its immediate society, but also the established society of the older Eastern country. The most important effect of the frontier was that it promoted democracy and individualism. Greatest development of all, however, was the intellectual traits which came from the conditions of the frontier:

> From the conditions of frontier life came intellectual traits of profound importance. The works of travelers along each frontier from colonial days onward describe certain common traits, and these traits have, while softening down, still persisted as survivals in the place of their origin, even when a higher social organization succeeded. The result is that to the frontier the American intellect owes its striking characteristics. That coarseness and strength combined with acuteness

and inquisitiveness; that practical, inventive turn of mind, quick to find expedients; that masterful grasp of material things, lacking in the artistic but powerful to effect great ends; that restless, nervous energy; that dominant individualism, working for good and for evil, and withal that buoyancy and exuberance which comes with freedom — these are the traits of the frontier, or traits called out elsewhere because of the existence of the frontier.

Turner saw that this interpretation implied, as it was carried back, similar influences in past history. Hence he noted that the Mediterranean Sea was to the Greeks what the frontier was to Americans. Similarly there was a frontier in the development of all Europe. Eventually the frontier becomes synonymous with progress in general, and by following all clues we arrive at the conclusion that the frontier has been the one great factor in the development of civilization. Therein lies the fallacy of interpreting the history of the United States too entirely by the frontier. We have in the frontier at once the cause and the effect of progress, democracy, individualism, acuteness, inquisitiveness, etc. Did the intellectual traits enumerated in the passage above come, as Turner contends, from the conditions of frontier life, or did the frontier come from the workings of these intellectual faculties in the pioneer? The individualism and democratic ideals which led the Puritan to wish freedom of worship were not the result of his settlement in New England, but the settlement was the result of these characteristics. Intellectual traits cannot be derived finally from environment. In fact, many varieties of intellect can be shown in any two isolated and different societies. We may hope that, as these characteristics existed before there was an American frontier, they will continue to exist now that it is gone. Or if we are infatuated with the symbol of the frontier, we may put it thus, in the words of Turner:

> In place of old frontiers of wilderness, there are new frontiers of unwon fields of science, fruitful for the needs of the race; there are frontiers of better social domains yet unexplored. Let us hold to our faith and courage, and creative zeal. Let us dream as our fathers dreamt and let us make our dreams come true.

Nothing will be gained by arguing whether the history of the frontier is the history of America, or whether the frontier society is the most American society, or whether the frontier hero is the type of American genius. Opinion is impregnable on its own ground. It is interesting, however, to note a few of the factors which have so impressed the importance of the frontier, particularly of a certain frontier, upon the American mind.

Before the Civil War the influence of that portion of the country which is roughly designated as the Middle West had gradually become a dominant factor in politics. The frontier had contributed presidents from both parties. It was in the Middle West that the real struggle between slavery and antislavery interests took place, and the political leaders of the Middle West were those who finally settled the struggle. Douglas was for the decade preceding the war the spokesman of the 'Young America' expansion doctrine which was largely the political doctrine of the section. The spirit of nationalism was a truly Middle Western element, and Lincoln later came to voice the general sentiment of the section in that regard.

In the Civil War the Middle West was the dominant factor in the North. Not only Lincoln, but the two great Northern generals, Grant and Sherman, were of the Middle West. It was the army composed of Middle Western soldiers that hacked its way down the Mississippi and burned its way through Georgia to break the back of the Confederacy. After the Civil War the Middle West may be said to have controlled politics for a quarter of a century. Beginning with Lincoln six presidents were chosen from the Middle West.

These are a few of the more potent facts which have strengthened the opinion that the Middle West is America and that the Middle Westerner is the American. The most extraordinary development of the idea comes, however, in the literature of Lincoln, which has made it a popular doctrine. Before historians took serious note of it, it was popular in literature, and now that historians are willing to let it rest, it continues in literature, having attained the dignity of a national legend.

I

An anonymous poem on the death of Lincoln, which appeared in the London *Fun* shortly after the assassination, expressed the significance of Lincoln's greatness to succeeding ages in two lines:

> Lincoln! thy fame shall sound through many an age,
> To prove that genius lives in humble birth.

Many of the poets writing at the time concurred in the sentiment. Lincoln's majesty was, as versified by R. H. Newell in *The Martyr President*, born of the spirit of democracy —

> The spirit to rise from the fetters of things
> And soar to a majesty higher than kings.

233

Richard Henry Stoddard developed this theme more at length in *Abraham Lincoln; an Horatian Ode* (1865):

> Ay! And his genius put to scorn
> The proudest in the purple born,
>   Whose wisdom never grew
>   To what, untaught, he knew —
>
> The people, of whom he was one.
> No gentleman like Washington, —
>   (Whose bones, methinks, make room,
>   To have him in their tomb!)
>
> A laboring man, with horny hands,
> Who swung the axe, who tilled his lands,
>   Who shrank from nothing new,
>   But did as poor men do!
>
> One of the people! Born to be
> Their curious epitome;
>   To share yet rise above
>   Their shifting hate and love.
>
> Common his mind (it seemed so then).
> His thoughts the thoughts of other men;
>   Plain were his words and poor —
>   But now they will endure!

James Russell Lowell developed the same theme in the passage on Lincoln added to the 'Harvard Commemoration Ode' after the poem was read on July 21, 1865. Lowell's treatment of the theme, however, adds an element of poetic ideality which is not evident in many poems of the same theme written at the time. Lincoln was a man of the people, but a new kind of man of the people, uncommon, strangely new. To symbolize democracy and at the same time render Lincoln extraordinary,

Lowell resorted to a mystical derivation of Lincoln's genius:

> Nature, they say, doth dote,
> And can not make a man
> Save on some worn-out plan,
> Repeating us by rote;
> For him her old world molds aside she threw,
> And, choosing sweet clay from the breast
> Of the unexhausted West,
> With stuff untainted, shaped a hero new,
> Wise, steadfast in the strength of God, and true.
> . . . .
>
> His was no lonely mountain peak of mind,
> Thrusting to thin air o'er our cloudy bars,
> A sea mark now, now lost in vapors blind;
> Broad prairie rather, genial, level lined,
> Fruitful and friendly for all human kind,
> Yet also nigh to heaven and loved of loftiest stars.
> Nothing of Europe here.
> Or, then, of Europe fronting mornward still,
> Ere any name of Serf or Peer
> Could Nature's equal scheme deface
> And thwart her genial will;
> . . . .
>
> Our children shall behold his fame,
> The kindly-earnest, brave foreseeing man,
> Sagacious, patient, dreading praise, not blame,
> New birth of our new soil, the first American.

This is great tribute, perhaps, but just what does it mean? Lincoln's Western nativity is stressed by several insignificant poems in the volume of *Poetical Tributes* published in 1865. Many of the funeral sermons and eulogies spoken at the time of his assassination stress the same fact. Something in the West seems to signify the typically American, it is true, but in Lincoln as elsewhere it is not easily set forth, without resorting to figures of speech. Certainly it is not the pioneer spirit of intellect; Lincoln was, if anything, intellectually conservative, without being, of course, hidebound. A comparison of Lincoln and Jackson does not reveal anything in Lincoln so Western as to make him above others the typical Westerner or pre-eminently the first American. There is no virtue in the poverty of his early life which makes Lincoln more representative than others originally of poor stock. It would be difficult to show, taking Lowell's figure literally, how the geography of Lincoln's Illinois or Kentucky had any peculiar significance in his life. Perhaps it is asking too much of a poem to get beyond the symbols, but is there something significant in them?

When Hawthorne said that Lincoln was 'essentially representative of all Yankees, and the veritable specimen, physically, of what the world seems determined to regard as our characteristic qualities,' he meant, evidently, that Lincoln typified the 'Sam Slick' or 'Uncle Sam' cartoon figure. When Hawthorne further admitted that Lincoln might easily be taken for a country schoolmaster, we can surmise that Ichabod Crane was in his mind. But even if we sense what Lowell means by his imagery, it is hard to put his meaning into words any less symbolic.

Working on the same principle, Emerson formulated in his remarks at the funeral services held in Concord, April 19, 1865, the American qualities of Lincoln. To Emerson the simple facts of his life were the most American things about him:

He was thoroughly American, had never crossed the sea, had never been spoiled by English insularity or French dissipation; a quite native, aboriginal man, as an acorn from the oak; no aping of foreigners, no frivolous accomplishments, Kentuckian born, working on a farm, a flatboatman, a captain

FRENCH'S STATUE OF LINCOLN
IN THE LINCOLN MEMORIAL AT WASHINGTON

in the Black Hawk War, a country lawyer, a representative in the rural legislature of Illinois; — on such modest foundations the broad structure of his fame was laid.

In external appearance and in the simple facts of his life, Lincoln seemed to Emerson a typical middle-class American, but the actual consideration of his genius brought the conclusion that he was not a typical middle-class man.

> This middle-class country had got a middle-class president, at last. Yes, in manners and sympathies, but not in powers, for his powers were superior....
>
> There, by his courage, his justice, his even temper, his fertile counsel, his humanity, he stood a heroic figure in the centre of a heroic epoch. He is the true history of the American people in his time. Step by step he walked before them; slow with their slowness, quickening his march by theirs, the true representative of this continent; an entirely public man; father of his country, the pulse of twenty millions throbbing in his heart, the thought of their minds articulated by his tongue.

The only complete attempt to express Lincoln's American genius is an allegory. Perhaps the author thought that allegory was more suitable than facts in developing the theme of genius. Rufus Blanchard's *Abraham Lincoln: the type of American Genius* (1882) is an ideal picture of the forces which moulded the genius of Lincoln. The characters that appear in the poem represent the waves of thought as they rolled over the body politic during the epoch. The poem is composed of fifteen cantos written in varied meter.

As an allegory the poem possesses the requisite vagueness. It is difficult to assign any character to any particular idea consistently, but Justice, Liberty or Freedom, Truth, Mercy, Democracy, the particular New England virtues and Southern virtues (whatever they each might be cannot be ascertained and seems to make little difference), and the frontier elements of Individuality and Self-Reliance — all glimmer faintly throughout the poem. Combined with the moral allegory is a political allegory of the conflicting spirits of New England and the South. Lincoln is the ideal product of all the traditions of the Old World coupled with the spirit of the New:

> A thought upon the stream of time is cast,
> And floating on along its mystic shore
> With gathering force as Centuries are past,
> It bears the fruit of ages gone before.

His coming is foreordained —

> According to the will of heaven's decree,
> Recorded when the angels first began
> To write the good and bad of fickle man.

As a lad in Kentucky he is often visited by spirits of New England, the Frontier, the Indian race; all leaving an impress upon his character and intellect, which makes him the type and genius of America that embodies the mental force, the conscience, and the destiny of the nation.

It is a question whether the poets have found in their subject those characteristics which are genuinely American, or whether they have chosen to celebrate Lincoln's qualities and characteristics as the ideal virtues of American genius, or whether they have merely made use of his popularity to preach their own ideal of American civilization. There is something of all three apparent, and in any one of the three there is worthy material. If there is something splendid in American civilization, it should be in Lincoln; if there is something grand in Lincoln, it should be a general American quality; if there is something extraneous to both which is worthy, it should be added to what is there. Such seems to be the theory on which the poets develop their hero. There is an impression of truth in this imaginative conception of Lincoln, but when an author becomes specific he is likely to come to grief.

II

The most ridiculous tendency in the legend of Lincoln the American is that which attempts to make him a Northerner in one case and a Southerner in another, a Yankee to a Yankee and a Virginian to a Virginian. There is a corresponding tendency in the literature of caste to present him as a common, ordinary man among men in one place and a genius among geniuses in another. After reading a mass of Lincoln literature, one is almost ready to throw up his hands and say with the darkey, 'Massa Linkum am eberywhere.'

Whitman, in his 'Death of Abraham Lincoln' lecture delivered first in 1879, questioned his audience: 'Have you never realized it, my friends, that Lincoln, though grafted on the West, is essentially, in personnel and character, a Southern contribution?' Although he did not attempt to explain just what he meant, it is likely that the South's chief claim to Lincoln was to Whitman based on the fact that he was born in Kentucky and that his ancestors had migrated from Virginia. Southern Indiana and Illinois were full of Southern settlers. Ancestry would make him a Massachusetts American if carried back a little farther.

Joel Chandler Harris published a volume of short stories in 1900 entitled *On the Wing of Occasions*, among which appeared 'The Kidnapping of President Lincoln.' Two Georgia rebels are involved in an attempt to kidnap Lincoln and immediately end the war. One of them is a sly old 'cracker,' Billy Sanders, 'who would have been placed in the illiterate class by a census-taker, though he had more real knowledge and native sagacity than one-half the people we meet every day.' The plot succeeds in so far that the rebels become acquainted with Lincoln, but there it ends. Sanders swaps stories with Lincoln. Lincoln is delighted with the old man; they are of a type. Sanders decides that it would be a shame to treat him so badly as they had planned and finally confesses the plot, asking pardon. His reason he explains to Lincoln: 'Down our way they say you're a Yankee, but if that's so, the woods is full of Yankees in Georgia, all born and raised right there.'

Thomas Dixon's novel *The Southerner* (1913) goes to considerable lengths to convey the idea that Lincoln was a Southerner in all things. On the title page appears the quotation from Whitman given above. The most preposterous example of the author's method is the following passage, spoken by Betty Winter, a Northern girl: 'He's a poet — a dreamer — and so typically Southern. I could easily picture him fighting a duel over a fine point of honor, as he once did.' The reference to a duel is to the Shields affair, which is one of the most ridiculous incidents of Lincoln's life and by no means chivalrous. Dixon's chief thesis is that Lincoln had the Southerner's attitude toward the negro and emancipated the slaves only in order to preserve the Union. Although there is some basis for the argument that Lincoln did not wish social and political equality for the negro, it cannot be argued that he held the typical Southern attitude, which considered slavery to be right.

Vachel Lindsay in *The Litany of Washington Street*

(1929) portrays Lincoln as the intellectual political scion of Virginia and admits, 'Lincoln is, to me, a typical Virginia man.'

A Northern novelist, Irving Bacheller, places Lincoln among Yankees who have migrated to Illinois and makes him so much like them that the inference is plain. In *A Man for the Ages* (1919) Lincoln is intellectually akin to New England. Even his wit is of a shrewd Yankee variety. Sampson Traylor, the chief Yankee character, is like him in his principal characteristics. Of Lincoln, Sampson says: 'He has spent his boyhood in the South and his young manhood in the North. He has studied the East and lived in the West. He is the people....'

The sectional jealousy which creeps into these biased works may be illustrated by a somewhat humorous circumstance. Winston Churchill in *The Crisis* presents his villain as a Yankee who bears the name of Eliphalet Hopper. The worst that can be said of Eliphalet is that he is an exaggeration of all the qualities which Southerners affected to despise in their Northern countrymen; namely, cold shrewdness, mercenariness, zealousness, and religiosity. Irving Bacheller, in retaliation, presents in *A Man for the Ages* Eliphalet Biggs, a Southern gentleman, as his villain. This Eliphalet is in turn an exaggeration of the qualities which New Englanders affected to despise in the Southerner; namely, hard drinking, flashiness, profanity, sneering and uneducated superiority, hot temper, and horrible cruelty to negroes. The Lincoln of *The Crisis* is favorably portrayed as a Westerner with a Southern background. The Lincoln of *A Man for the Ages* is favorably portrayed as a Westerner with Yankee characteristics and Yankee friends.

III

Not only are sectional characteristics combined in Lincoln, but also the characteristics of every level of society. He is at once 'Old Abe' and the eternal gentleman. In the facts of his early life an interpreter can find the authority for making him a poor white. In the facts of his achievement as President a poet perceives one of Nature's masterful, great men. Overlooking facts, another may find him the commonplace man of James Whitcomb Riley's 'Lincoln,' who cared for nothing but

> A peaceful life; — just toil and rest —
> All his desire.

This conception of Lincoln as an epitome of the people is in the nature of a folk-hero, and, indeed, it is difficult to distinguish in any one poem or novel how much the author is purposely recognizing a popular legend and how much he is delineating his own hero. It is safe to say that in most cases the poets and novelists of Lincoln are influenced as much by the folk-hero as by their own assessment of the historical facts of his life. In many Lincoln poems there is nothing more than an attempt to present the folk-hero. E. W. Thompson's 'We Talked of Lincoln' (1909) is one of the better poems of this type.

> We talked of Abraham Lincoln in the night,
> Ten fur-coat men on North Saskatchewan's plain —
> Pure zero cold and all the prairie white —
> Englishman, Scotchman, Scandinavian, Dane,
> Two Irish, four Canadians — all for gain
> Of food and raiment, children, parents, wives,
> Living the hardest life that man survives,
> And secret proud because it was so hard
> Exploring, camping, axing, faring lean. —
> .   .   .   .

THE AMERICAN

We talked of Abraham Lincoln in the night. —
Oh, sweet and strange to hear the hard-hand men
Old-Abeing him, like half the world of yore
In years when Grant's and Lee's young soldiers bore
Rifle and steel, and proud that heroes live
When folks their lives to Labor mostly give.
And strange and sweet to hear their voices call
Him 'Father Abraham,' though no man of all
Was born within the Nation of his birth,
It was as if they felt that all the Earth
Possess of right Earth's greatest common man,
Her sanest, wisest, simplest, steadiest son,
To whom the Father's children all were one,
And Pomp and Vanities as motes that danced
In the clear sunshine where his humor glanced.

We talked of Abraham Lincoln in the night
Until one spoke, 'We yet may see his face.'
Whereon the fire crackled loud through space
Of human silence, while eyes reverent
Toward the auroral miracle were bent
Till from the trancing Glory spirits came
Within our semicircle round the flame,
And drew up closer-ringed, until we could
Feel the kind touch of vital brotherhood
Which Father Abraham Lincoln thought so good.

A poem by Robertus Love entitled 'An Appreciation of
Lincoln' treats the same theme in the vernacular of the
people whom Lincoln is supposed to represent and whose
philosophy is supposed to be his:

Somewhar down thar round Hodgenville, Kaintucky,
    Or tharabouts, a hundred year ago,
Was born a boy ye wouldn' thought was lucky;
    Looked like he never wouldn' have a show.
    But... I don' know.
That boy was started middlin' well, I'm thinkin'.
His name? W'y, it was Abraham — Abe Lincoln.

THE LINCOLN LEGEND

Poor whites his folks yes? Yes, as pore as any.
 Them pioneers, they wa'n't no plutocrats;
Belonged right down among the humble many,
 And no more property than dogs or cats.
 But... maybe that's
As good a way as any for a startin'.
Abe Lincoln, he riz middlin' high, for sartin!

Somehow I've always had a sort o' sneakin'
 Idee that peddygrees is purty much
Like monkeys' tails — so long the're apt to weaken
 The yap that drags 'em round. No use for such!
 But... beats the Dutch
How now and then a little lad like Aby
Grows up a president — guvnor, maybe.

Abe Lincoln never had no reg'lar schoolin';
 He never quarterbacked nor pulled stroke oar,
Nor never spent his time and money foolin'
 With buried langwidges and ancient lore.
 But... Abe l'arned more
To set him forrerd in the human filin'
Than all the college fellers' kit and bilin'.

Abe Lincoln never did git hifalutin' —
 Not even that in Washington, D.C.
He jist kep' common, humble, ord'n'ry, suitin'
 His backwoods corn patch raisin' to a T.
 But... jiminy gee!
W'y, Abe was any statesman's peer and ekul
And wise as Solomon or Old Ezekul.

I reckon, I'm a bit too old-fashioned, maybe,
 But when I want a pattern for a man
I'm middlin' shore to measure Father Aby
 And cut to fit his homely human plan.
 And long's I can
I'm hootin' loud and rootin' proud, by hucky,
For that old boy from Hodgenville, Kaintucky

THE AMERICAN

Witter Bynner has written a poem in the same vein which will suffice as a last example of the type:

Lincoln? —
Well, I was in the old Second Maine,
The first regiment in Washington from the Pine Tree State.
Of course I didn't get the butt of the clip;
We was there for guardin' Washington —
We was all green.

I ain't never ben to the theayter in my life —
I didn't know how to behave.
I ain't never ben since.
I can see as plain as my hat the box where he sat in
When he was shot.
I can tell you, sir, there was a panic
When we found our President was in the shape he was in!
Never saw a soldier in the world but what liked him.

Yes, sir. His looks was kind o' hard to forget.
He was a spare man.
An old farmer.
Everything was all right, you know,
But he wasn't a smooth-appearin' man at all —
Not in no ways;
Thin-faced, long-necked,
And a swellin' kind of a thick lip like.

And he was a jolly old fellow — always cheerful;
He wasn't so high but the boys could talk to him their own ways.
While I was servin' at the Hospital
He'd come in and say, 'You look nice in here,'
Praise us up, you know.
And he'd bend over and talk to the boys —
And he'd talk so good to 'em — so close —
That's why I call him a farmer.
I don't mean that everything about him wasn't all right, you under-
    stand,
It's just — well, I was a farmer —
And he was my neighbor, anybody's neighbor.
I guess even you young folks would 'a' liked him.

Human nature is, perhaps, much the same all over the United States. Many supposed differences between the natives of various sections are imaginary. Within a national unit there may be many varieties of society, and yet a member of any one of them when transplanted in youth quite easily loses the most evident characteristics of his own group. There may be deeper characteristics which do not change, but when they are analyzed they may not be group characteristics at all. Chivalry was by no means so Southern as we have come to consider it. A Yankee monopoly of shrewdness is pretty much a popular fallacy. The whole process of making Lincoln our national type which embodies the characteristics of all sections and classes is fallacious, because it assumes that certain superficial characteristics are the correct index to sectional and social differences.

On the other hand, it is questionable if Lincoln's deeper qualities of mind and nature are typically American in any tangible way. We hear a great deal about the Celtic temperament and the Teutonic temperament, and yet, when these vaporous notions pass into the alembic, their individual qualities do not easily distil. And certainly in a polyglot nation it seems even less sensible to speak of a national temperament, much less a national genius. A few lines of poetry convey an idea as truth in a general way which, unless we are willing to admit them to be merely an attempt to express an intangible but ideal truth, are misleading. Thus, when we read in Maurice Thompson's 'At Lincoln's Grave' that

> He was the North, the South, the East, the West,
> The thrall, the master, all of us in one.

— we must remember that this Lincoln is an idealized symbol.

IV

Following in the tradition established by Lowell, who wrote of the sweet clay of the West out of which Nature had fashioned Lincoln, Edwin Markham more completely symbolized in 'Lincoln, the Man of the People' (1901), the heroic substance from which the American was moulded. The folk-hero is in the background, but is not emphasized in the poem. There is no flaw in the cast of the heroic figure. Lincoln is not so much the type of democracy as he is an abstract embodiment of the ancient and cosmic forces of genius and wisdom. Markham has several other Lincoln poems, none of which is comparable to this, his best.

> When the Norn Mother saw the Whirlwind Hour
> Greatening and darkening as it hurried on,
> She left the Heaven of Heroes and came down
> To make a man to meet the mortal need.
> She took the tried clay of the common road —
> Clay warm yet with the genial heat of Earth,
> Dashed through it all a strain of prophecy;
> Tempered the heap with thrill of human tears;
> Then mixed a laughter with the serious stuff.
> Into the shape she breathed a flame to light
> That tender, tragic, ever-changing face;
> And laid on him a sense of the Mystic Powers,
> Moving — all hushed — behind the mortal veil.
> Here was a man to hold against the world,
> A man to match the mountains and the sea.
>
> The color of the ground was in him, the red earth;
> The smack and tang of elemental things:
> The rectitude and patience of the cliff;
> The good-will of the rain that loves all leaves;
> The friendly welcome of the wayside well;
> The courage of the bird that dares the sea;

THE LINCOLN LEGEND

The gladness of the wind that shakes the corn;
The pity of the snow that hides all scars;
The secrecy of streams that make their way
Under the mountain to the rifted rock;
The tolerance and equity of light
That gives as freely to the shrinking flower
As to the great oak flaring to the wind —
To the grave's low hill as to the Matterhorn
That shoulders out the sky. Sprung from the West,
He drank the valorous youth of a new world.
The strength of virgin forests braced his mind,
The hush of spacious prairies stilled his soul.
His words were oaks in acorns; and his thoughts
Were roots that firmly gripped the granite truth.

Up from log cabin to the Capitol,
One fire was on his spirit, one resolve —
To send the keen ax to the root of wrong,
Clearing a free way for the feet of God,
The eyes of conscience testing every stroke,
To make his deed the measure of a man.
He built the rail-pile as he built the State,
Pouring his splendid strength through every blow:
The grip that swung the ax in Illinois
Was on the pen that set a people free.

So came the Captain with the mighty heart;
And when the judgment thunders split the house,
Wrenching the rafters from their ancient rest,
He held the ridgepole up, and spiked again
The rafters of the Home. He held his place —
Held the long purpose like a growing tree —
Held on through blame and faltered not at praise.
And when he fell in whirlwind, he went down
As when a lordly cedar, green with boughs,
Goes down with a great shout upon the hills,
And leaves a lonesome place against the sky.

In the hands of the larger American poets of the last
twenty-five years, this American legend of the nineteenth

century has been moulded into new and larger figures. Gradually the essence of heroism has been distilled from the chimeric folk-hero and from the amorphous mass of stories clustered about the Civil War President. Percy MacKaye's 'Lincoln Centenary Ode' may be considered a mark of transition. There are elements of the old conception with an occasional lapse from the traditional folklore into the vein of intellectual hero-worship which marks the better Lincoln poems of the twentieth century. There are good passages which give a better account of themselves taken alone. The poem is decidedly drawn out and marred by many of the weaknesses which are the bane of occasional pieces.

I

No ceremonial
Of pealèd chime was there, or blarèd horn,
Such as hath blazoned births of lesser kings,
When he — the elder brother of us all,
Lincoln — was born.
At his nativity
Want stood as sponsor, stark Obscurity
Was midwife, and all lonely things
Of nature were unconscious ministers
To endow his spirit meek
With their own melancholy. So when he —
An infant king of commoners —
Lay in his mother's arm, of all the earth
(Which now his fame wears for a diadem)
None heeded of his birth;
Only a star burned over Bethlehem
More bright, and, big with prophecy,
A secret gust from that far February
Fills now the organ-reeds that peal his centenary.

THE LINCOLN LEGEND

II

Who shall distil in song those epic years?
Only the Sibyl of simplicity,
Touched by the light and dew of common tears,
Might chant that homely native Odyssey.

For there are lives too large in simple truth
For art to limn or elegy to gauge,
And there are men so near to God's own ruth
They are the better angels of their age,
And such was he: beyond the pale of song
His grandeur looms in truth, with awful grace;
He lives where beauty's origins belong
Deep in the primal raptures of his race.

Yet may we strive to trace
His Shadow — where it pulses vast
Upon imagination, cast
By the oft-handtrimm'd lamp of history —
In carved breath, or bronze, that we might scan
The imagined child and man
Whose life and death are looms of our own destiny.

III

. . . .

How like a saga of the northern sea
Our own Kentucky hero-tale begins!
    Once on a time, far in a wintry wood,
    A lone hut stood;
    There lived a poor man's son that was to be
  A master man of earth.
And so for us,
Like children in the great hall of his spirit,
The homebred fairy-story spins
Annals whose grace the after-times inherit.

THE AMERICAN

The uncouth homestead by the trail of Boone,
The untitled grant, the needy exodus,
The ox-cart on the Indiana heath,
The log shack by the Sangamon, and soon
The fever'd mother and the forest death —
From these the lonely epic wanders on.
The longshank boy, with visage creased by toil
The laughter of the soil,
Cribbing his book of statutes from his chore,
Erelong his nooning fellows of the field
Hail their scrub-orator, or at sundown —
Slouching his gaunt and sallow six-foot-four —
Their native Touchstone of the village store.
Or from the turf, where he has matched his build
To throw the country champion in the loam,
Idly he saunters home
To rock some mother's cradle in the town;
Or, stretched on counter calico, with Clay
And organ-sounding Webster, dream the night away.

But time begins
Slowly to sift the substance from the slag.
And now along the county pike's last lap,
With giant shins
Shut knifewise in his wabbling rattletrap,
The circuit lawyer trots his tired nag
Toward the noon tavern, reins up, and unrolls
His awkward length of wrinkled bombazine,
Clutching his tattered green
Umbrella and thin carpetsack,
And flings a joke that makes the rafters roar:
As if, uplooming from of yore,
Some quaint-accoutered king of trolls,
Out-elbowing a sexton's suit of black
In Christmas glee,
Should sudden crack
His shrilly jest of shrewd hilarity,
And shake the clambering urchins from his back.

.   .   .   .   , ...

IX

The loving and the wise
May seek — but seek in vain — to analyze
The individual man, for having caught
The mystic clue of thought,
Sudden they meet the controverting whim,
And fumbling with the enchanted key,
Lose it then utterly.
Aesop and old Isaiah held in him
Strange sessions, winked at by Artemus Ward,
Till sudden in their midst bright Seraphim
Stood, summoned by a sad, primeval bard
Who, bearing still no name, has ever borne
Within his heart the music of mankind:
Sometime a lonely singer blind
Beside the Ionian sea:
Sometime, between two thieves in scorn,
A face in Calvary.
That was his master soul —
The mystic demi-god of common man —
Who, templed in the steadfast mind,
Hid his shy gold of genius in the bran
Of Hoosier speech and garb, softening the wan
Strong face of shrewdness with strange aureole.

He was the madstone to his country's ire,
Drawing the rancorous blood of envious quarrel
Alike from foe and friend; his pity, stirr'd,
Restored to its bough the storm-unnested bird,
Or raised the wallow'd pig from out the mire.
And he who sowed in sweat his boyhood's crop,
And tackled Euclid with a wooden spade,
And excavated Blackstone from a barrel
To hold moot trials in the gloaming, made
By lighted shavings in a cooper's shop,
He is the people's still — their Railsplitter,
Himself a rail, clean-grained, of character
Self-hewn in the dark glades of Circumstance

THE AMERICAN

From that deep-hearted tree
Democracy,
Which, by our race's heritage,
Reforests age on age,
Perpetual in strong fecundity.

. . . .

XI

But he is more than ours, as we are more
Than yet the world dares dream. His stature grows
With that illimitable state
Whose sovereignty ordains no tribute shore
And borderland of hate,
But grounds its justice in the joy it sows.
His spirit is still a power to emancipate
Bondage — more base, being more insidious,
Than serfdom — that cried out in the midst of us
For virtue, born of opportunity,
And manhood, weighed in honest human worth,
And freedom, based in labor. He stands forth
'Mongst nations old — a new-world Abraham,
The patriarch of peoples still to be,
Blending all visions of the promised land
In one Apocalypse.

His voice is heard —
Thrilling the molder'd lintels of the past —
In Asia; old Thibet is stirred
With warm imaginings;
Ancestral China, 'midst her mysteries,
Unmasks, and flings
Her veils wide to the Occident; the wand
Of hope awakes prone Hierapolis;
Even by the straits of old that Io swam,
The immemorial sultan, scepterless,
Stands awed; and heartened by that bold success,
Pale Russia rises from her holocaust.
And still the emancipating influence,

The secret power, the increasing truth, are his,
For they are ours: ours by the potencies
Poured in our nation from the founts of time,
Blending in us the mystic seeds of men,
To sow them forth again
For harvests more sublime
Throughout the world.

XII

Leave, then, that wonted grief
Which honorably mourns its martyred dead,
And newly hail instead
The birth of him, our hardy shepherd chief,
Who by green paths of old democracy
Leads still his tribes to uplands of glad peace.

As long as — out of blood and passion blind —
Springs the pure justice of the reasoning mind,
And justice, bending, scorns not to obey
Pity, that once in a poor manger lay,
As long as, thrall'd by time's imperious will,
Brother hath bitter need of brother, still
His presence shall not cease
To lift the ages toward his human excellence,
And races yet to be
Shall in a rude hut do him reverence
And solemnize a simple man's nativity.

Edwin Arlington Robinson's poem 'The Master' (1910)
is one of the best Lincoln poems. As an accurate interpretation of Lincoln it may want biographical fact to sustain
the general conception, but therein, perhaps, lies its
strength. Lincoln is stripped of all but the elemental
qualities of epic heroism and masterful genius. The folk-
hero is in the background, but the Olympian majesty of a
ruler ideally wise, all-seeing and all-comprehending, and

infinitely just, moves, we feel, among the heroes of an ancient world, the perfection of what they never dared to dream. Lincoln's humor, his one genuinely American element, becomes to Robinson a 'cryptic mirth' with which the laconic sage met the blind rage and sullen ignorance of his spoiled children. Robinson's poem stands as a point of departure for a new Lincoln legend designed to appeal to a new age.

THE MASTER

A flying word from here and there
Had sown the name at which we sneered,
But soon the name was everywhere,
To be reviled and then revered:
A presence to be loved and feared,
We cannot hide it, or deny
That we, the gentlemen who jeered,
May be forgotten by and by.

He came when days were perilous
And hearts of men were sore beguiled;
And having made his note of us,
He pondered and was reconciled.
Was ever master yet so mild
As he, and so untamable?
We doubted, even when he smiled,
Not knowing what he knew so well.

He knew that undeceiving fate
Would shame us whom he served unsought;
He knew that he must wince and wait —
The jest of those for whom he fought;
He knew devoutly what he thought
Of us and of our ridicule;
He knew that we must all be taught
Like little children in a school.

THE LINCOLN LEGEND

We gave a glamour to the task
That he encountered and saw through,
But little of us did he ask,
And little did we ever do.
And what appears if we review
The season when we railed and chaffed?
It is the face of one who knew
That we were learning while we laughed.

The face that in our vision feels
Again the venom that we flung,
Transfigured to the world reveals
The vigilance to which we clung.
Shrewd, hallowed, harassed, and among
The mysteries that are untold,
The face we see was never young,
Nor could it ever have been old.

For he to whom we had applied
Our shopman's test of age and worth,
Was elemental when he died,
As he was ancient at his birth:
The saddest among kings of earth,
Bowed with a galling crown, this man
Met rancor with a cryptic mirth,
Laconic — and Olympian.

The love, the grandeur, and the fame
Are bounded by the world alone;
The calm, the smouldering, and the flame
Of awful patience were his own:
With him they are forever flown
Past all our fond self-shadowings,
Wherewith we cumber the Unknown
As with inept Icarian wings.

For we were not as other men:
'Twas ours to soar and his to see.
But we are coming down again,
And we shall come down pleasantly;

Nor shall we longer disagree
On what it is to be sublime,
But flourish in our perigee
And have one Titan at a time.

Of Robinson's poem Louis Untermeyer says in *American Poetry Since 1900*:

Of all the tributes to the great emancipator, this is one of the few that maintains a genuine nobility and practically the only one that does not try to show the man's intimate humanity by some reference to rail-splitting and the use of 'Honest Abe.' Without descending from his austere level, Robinson actually comes nearer Lincoln than any of his compatriots.

This is a good appreciation, but not a fair one. Robinson is not the only poet to avoid the folk-hero; we may observe the same tendency in the poems of Fletcher and Markham. Further, there is a grave doubt whether Robinson really comes as near Lincoln as Untermeyer maintains. Here we have the same difficulty that appears in evaluating any item of Lincoln literature; namely, which Lincoln is to be the criterion? In getting away from the folk-hero something of exaltation is gained, but with the gain there is a loss. For example, there is no untruer note in any Lincoln poem than the transformation of Lincoln's humor into a 'cryptic mirth.' It is also a question whether the removal of the dross leaves, after all, the best conception of grandeur possible. There are poetic elements in Lincoln's very weaknesses. In *Tendencies in Modern American Poetry* Amy Lowell calls the poem 'strong, reticent, and noble,' but does not think it so good as Fletcher's poem. She later adds that the Lincoln in Robinson's poem, 'is part symbol, part man, slightly conventionalized, and a little remote and cold withal.' Whether it is as good as Fletcher's, there may be quite different

257

opinions, but the charge of conventionality, if by this is meant a conventional hero as opposed to the conventional picture of the unconventional Lincoln, is certainly just, and the coldness and remoteness may be likewise lamentable. Lincoln loses much of his appeal when he is cast according to the conventional mould of heroes. We may admire Robinson's Olympian Lincoln, however, as the best expression of the heroic symbol since Richard Henry Stoddard's Homeric sonnet.

Maintaining at once the ideal abstraction and cosmic symbolism of Markham's Lincoln and the Promethean heroism of Robinson's poem, John Gould Fletcher portrays Lincoln as a gaunt, scraggly pine tree, deep-rooted in the very soil of humanity. Beneath its branches a nation of men may find shelter and rest. Lincoln is here at once the symbol of national unity, the patron saint of Americanism, who guides his people from beyond and a remote, mystic spirit of all humanity. This 'Lincoln' was written in 1916.

I

Like a gaunt, scraggly pine
Which lifts its head above the mournful sandhills;
And patiently, through dull years of bitter silence,
Untended and uncared for, starts to grow.

Ungainly, labouring, huge,
The wind of the north has twisted and gnarled its branches;
Yet in the heat of midsummer days, when thunderclouds ring the
    horizon,
A nation of men shall rest beneath its shade.

And it shall protect them all,
Hold every one safe there, watching aloof in silence;
Until at last one mad stray bolt from the zenith
Shall strike it in an instant down to earth.

THE AMERICAN

II

There was a darkness in this man; an immense and hollow darkness,
Of which we may not speak, nor share with him, nor enter;
A darkness through which strong roots stretched downwards into the
  earth
Towards old things.

Towards the herdman-kings who walked the earth and spoke with God,
Towards the wanderers who sought for they knew not what, and found
  their goal at last;
Towards the men who waited, only waited patiently when all seemed
  lost
Many bitter winters of defeat;

Down to the granite of patience
These roots swept, knotted, fibrous roots, prying, piercing, seeking,
And drew from the living rock and the living waters about it
The red sap to carry upwards to the sun.

Not proud, but humble,
Only to serve and pass on, to endure to the end through service;
For the axe is laid at the roots of the trees, and all that bring not forth
  good fruit
Shall be cut down on the day to come and cast into the fire.

III

There is a silence abroad in the land today,
And in the hearts of men, a deep and anxious silence;
And, because we are still at last, those bronze lips slowly open,
Those hollow and weary eyes take on a gleam of light.

Slowly a patient, firm-syllabled voice cuts through the endless silence
Like labouring oxen that drag a plough through the chaos of rude clay-
  fields:
I went forward as the light goes forward in early spring.
But there were also many things which I left behind.

Tombs that were quiet;
One, of a mother, whose brief light went out in the darkness,
One, of a loved one, the snow on whose grave is long falling,
One, only of a child, but it was mine.

Have you forgot your graves? Go, question them in anguish,
Listen long to their unstirred lips. From your hostages to silence,
Learn there is no life without death, no dawn without sunsetting,
No victory but to him who has given all.[1]

The first two divisions are the superior passages. The fourth has been omitted. It is little more than an echo of Whitman's 'When Lilacs Last in the Dooryard Bloom'd.'

With her predilection for the Imagist poet in general, Amy Lowell considers this 'the finest poem on Lincoln which has been written.... Lincoln stands before us, at once a man and an aspiration, a recollection and a goal. He is the symbol of our possibilities, the reason for our courage.' In comparing it with Robinson's poem she considers Fletcher's poem the better because Lincoln 'is raised almost to the rank of pure symbol, as elusive and pervading as a brooding god.'

The poem is all that Amy Lowell says it is, and yet it is not therefore a better poem than Robinson's. It may gain something from its symbolism, but it loses contact with Lincoln. Robinson's poem is better as a poem than as an interpretation, but it never loses sight of the flesh-and-blood Lincoln, even while it transcends him. Fletcher's poem can only be assessed as a mystical yearning after something abstract and ultimate in this strange, heroic god.

Strangely like Fletcher's poem in the mystic conception of Lincoln is a poem already noted in another place, Vachel Lindsay's 'Abraham Lincoln Walks at Midnight.' There,

[1] Compare G. W. Bell's sonnet, Chapter IV.

too, Lincoln is the symbol of national unity and humanity's patron saint. Like Fletcher's poem it was written during the World War and looks to Lincoln as the guiding spirit of the democracy during the trials and tangles of a period of world unrest. How much our hero has taken on the functions of a medieval saint!

> The sins of the war-lords burn his heart.
> He sees the dreadnaughts scouring every main.
> He carries on his shawl-wrapped shoulders now
> The bitterness, the folly and the pain.
>
> He cannot rest until a spirit dawn
> Shall come; — the shining hope of Europe free:
> The league of sober folk, the Workers' Earth,
> Bringing long peace to Cornland, Alp and Sea.
>
> It breaks his heart that kings must murder still,
> That all his hours of travail here for men
> Seem yet in vain. And who will bring white peace
> That he may sleep upon his hill again.

Without multiplying examples further, we may observe from the poems already quoted that Lincoln has ceased to be merely an historical character, or even a folk-hero. He has founded a religious cult. There is a direct personal worship combined with an apostolic dissemination of his social philosophy, which every poet conceives to be in some obvious or subtle manner typically American. Like the master of every cult, Lincoln lives and speaks on the tongues of his followers. He embodies to some modern poets the entire hope of future America. Vachel Lindsay in a minor poem, 'The Litany of Heroes,' voices the sentiment thus:

> Would I might inspire the Lincoln in you all.

THE LINCOLN LEGEND

James Oppenheim develops in 'The Lincoln Child' a
theme of world brotherhood with Lincoln as master:

And lo, as he grew, ugly, gaunt,
And gnarled his way into a man,
What wisdom came to feed his want,
What worlds came near to let him scan —
And as he fathomed through and through
Our dark and sorry human scheme,
He knew what Shakespeare never knew,
What Dante never dared to dream —
That Men are one
Beneath the sun,
And one in life are equal souls —
This truth was his,
And this it is
That round him such a glory rolls —
For not alone he knew it was a truth,
He made it of his blood and of his brain —
He crowned it on the day when piteous Booth
Sent a whole land to weeping with world-pain —
When a black cloud blotted the sun
And men stopped in the streets to sob,
To think Old Abe was dead —
Dead, and the day's work still undone,
Dead, and war's ruining heart athrob,
And earth with fields of carnage freshly spread —
Millions died fighting,
But in this man we mourned
Those millions, and one other —
And the States today uniting,
North and South,
East and West,
Speak with a people's mouth
A rhapsody of rest
To him our beloved best,
Our big, gaunt, homely brother —
Our huge Atlantic coast-storm in a shawl,
Our cyclone in a smile — our President,

Who knew and loved us all
With love more eloquent
Than his own words — with Love that in real deeds was spent.

Shelley's was a world of Love,
Carlyle's was a world of Work,
But Lincoln's was a world above
That of a dreamer or a clerk —
Lincoln wed the one to the other —
Made his a world where love gets into deeds —
Where man was more than merely brother,
Where the high love was meeting human needs!
And lo, he made this plan
Memorably American!
Through all his life this mighty Faith unfurled!
Oh, let us see, and let us know
That if our hearts could catch his glow
A faith like Lincoln's would transform the world!
Oh, to pour love through deeds —
To be as Lincoln was!
That all the land might fill its daily needs
Glorified by a human Cause!
Then were America a vast World-Torch
Flaming a faith across the dying Earth,
Proclaiming from the Atlantic's rocky porch
That a New World was struggling at the Birth!

There is an intense nationalism in all Lincoln poetry, in fact in all of what has been termed 'the new poetry' in general. It has been customary to trace this nationalism from Whitman. Certainly there is a sweeping influence which, emanating from the inclusive spirit of Whitman's poetry, has not yet ceased to be felt in American literature, but nationalism is a subtle spirit in its workings and an intangible factor in its manifestations. To seize upon the spirit of Whitman's poetry and hold it up as American is easy, but is it, after all, the touchstone by which all Americanism is to be tested? National character and spirit change from one age to another. If there is to be any real significance in what is meant by such terms, it must be admitted that they denote something different in different connections. We cannot bodily bounce Longfellow and Holmes out of the national picture because they do not correspond in spirit with what we are now told is American. It is just as logical to eliminate Poe, and for similar reasons; but there is in great genius something which we wish to keep, and hence critics have been at some pains to place Poe in the picture along with Whitman. There seems to be a predilection for interpreting genius as national. Discussing Whitman's Americanism in *American Poetry Since 1900*, Untermeyer says:

> It was Whitman's use of the rich verbal material that flowered in the street rather than in libraries that gave him such potency. That large spirit was set free and made common to all men, not so much because of his form and philosophy, but because of his words. And it was this love and sublimation of what was racy that made him so great an artistic influence, an influence that was not only liberal but liberating. With his elemental dynamism, his desire to strike off chains rather than put up bars, he might be called — if rhetoric were permitted — the Lincoln of our literature.

This is tantamount to saying that genius is American, and yet how much of it is as true of Chaucer and Shakespeare! Are they too American?

Amy Lowell in speaking of the fact that Lincoln has become the symbol of Americanism says:

> Washington and Lincoln are the two great symbols of American life. But to deal adequately with Washington needs a historical sense, a knowledge of the eighteenth century, which few of our poets yet possess.... It is therefore to Lincoln that our poets turn as an embodiment of the highest

form of the typical American, the fine flower and culmination of our life as a separate nation.

There is some truth in this. There is, however, something further. Lincoln and Whitman have left an influence which for several decades has dictated the criticism and evaluation of things American. Not only are we closer to Lincoln than to Washington, but we are living in his very shadow. Also, there are fewer obvious elements in Washington to attract the poet. Having observed the many uses made of Lincoln, we might ask, indeed, where there is any other character who can offer the poet such varied matter. But, above all, there is the genius of Lincoln, exaggerated, perhaps, but yet without equal in American history, which must be enshrined as American.

There has always been among poets a belief that the land of one's birth, particularly the immediate locality, imparts something of its natural elements to its people. Wordsworth's 'Three Years She Grew' is but an odd development of the general sentiment which derives the Spartan from his rugged hills or Clym Yeobright from his native Egdon Heath. Lincoln is thus the product of level-lined prairie and the sweet clay of the West, or he possesses the smack and tang of elemental things, of the tried clay of the common road, the ruggedness of the cliff; he is our Atlantic coast storm in a shawl or a rugged pine whose roots stretch out through all the land. So he is elementally American. There is no question that can be put to such symbolism.

When he is made the epitome of the American people, however, we may wonder. Truly, his life portrays an American epoch and runs the gamut of Western society of the time, but it does not encompass New England or the South and cannot be made to. He was not representative of the America of Washington's day or our own, and with the passing of the frontier civilization which he truly represents during its middle period, he cannot be said to represent American society. There is no basis for making the frontier type which he represents more American than any other. It may be questioned whether the democracy which he taught is really the guide in present-day politics, and certainly the democracy which he lived has been abandoned, even in the Middle West, for a caste system which becomes more deeply delineated with each generation.

His genius is at once American and universal. He is infinitely capable of reinterpretation, and hence, unlike Washington, he is the symbol which succeeding epochs can glance back to for inspiration, regardless of the changing ages. The elemental matter remains for the future poet to employ in any way he desires, just as the several poets — only a few in reality — who have been considered here have employed it to their taste. Indeed, the possibilities of Lincoln as matter for literature have barely been realized.

VII

Whitman and Drinkwater

I

WHEN Whitman wrote the threnody on Lincoln, 'When Lilacs Last in the Dooryard Bloom'd,' he wrote first of all, perhaps, his own personal feelings; but he succeeded in capturing the spirit of national sorrow better than any other poet who wrote in memory of the martyred President. Elevated, poetic, ideally abstract as the poem is, its theme is a universal sorrow for the death of a man — not a myth. When others were eulogizing the prophet, emancipator, saint, martyr, and so on, Whitman could think of Lincoln only as a man whom he had admired and loved. The only phase of the popular legend which Whitman expressed was that of the savior of the Union, which is, perhaps, still the most historical of all conceptions.

Whitman in reality wrote four poems on the death of Lincoln. All four were published in a 'Sequel to Drum-Taps,' which was printed and inserted in the volume *Drum-Taps*, already in press at the time of Lincoln's death. Whatever Whitman had thought of Lincoln before the assassination, he had not published a line in his praise. The absence of fulsome eulogy in the poems written afterwards is significant. There is not even an appraisal of Lincoln's character which gives any idea that

Whitman really conceived him to be more than the man —

> This dust was once the man,
> Gentle, plain, just and resolute, under whose cautious hand,
> Against the foulest crime in history known in any land or age,
> Was saved the Union of these States.

This short poem, and another less significant. 'Hush'd Be the Camps Today,' are, together with those already mentioned, the only tributes from Whitman's pen until several years later, when he began interpreting Lincoln in lectures.

The remarkable thing about these poems is that Whitman seems to take Lincoln for granted. There is no attempt to fathom his genius. Richard Henry Stoddard was turning Lincoln over and over in his mind, wondering just what the man was, and concluding that at best he could be summarized as an epitome of the people, a symbol of democracy. Similar thoughts were revolving in Emerson's mind. Lowell was somewhat more comprehensive in deriving Lincoln from elemental and cosmic sources, rather than from the level of humanity above which Lincoln eventually rose. Neither Lincoln's modest origin nor his highest pinnacle of achievement interested Whitman profoundly. Later Whitman said of Lincoln:

> Lincoln is particularly my man — particularly belongs to me; yes, and by the same token, I am Lincoln's man: I guess I particularly belong to him; we are afloat on the same stream — we are rooted in the same ground.

How like Whitman this sounds, and how like us to accept his statement! It was something of this assurance that enabled Whitman to write of Lincoln as no other poet has written of him since, and to express the intimate grief of a great American poet for the great American leader, the gentle, plain, just, resolute; the sweetest, wisest soul.

James Oppenheim has caught, in his 'Memories of Whitman and Lincoln,' something of the feeling which has so closely knitted our memories of these two men together —

> These two great shadows in the spacious night,
> Shadows folding America close between them,
> Close to the heart.

They are kindred spirits, brothers, twined with the song of democracy in the heart of the poet.

Something is hidden deep — strange memories — strange memories —
Of him that brought a sprig of the purple cluster
To him that was mourned by all....
And so they are linked together
While yet America lives....

While yet America lives, my heart,
Lilacs shall bloom for Walt Whitman
And lilacs for Abraham Lincoln.

As we perceive that Whitman was closer to Lincoln in understanding than was any other poet of the time, so we feel when we read 'When Lilacs Last in the Dooryard Bloom'd' that Whitman better felt the pulse of the national heart. There is nowhere in literature, to my knowledge, such a vivid re-creation of a national mood and sentiment. All of the books, pamphlets, and articles that have been written in description of those dark days of Black Easter are as nothing compared with the few lines, poetically somewhat weaker perhaps than other parts, of the second division of the poem.

O powerful western fallen star!
O shades of night — O moody tearful night!
O great star disappeared — O the black murk that hides the star!

O cruel hands that hold me powerless — O helpless soul of me!
O harsh surrounding cloud that will not free my soul.

It is all the hysteria of sorrow, the sense of futility, the gloom of doubt, and the helpless indignation against unjust fate that seized a people when cast suddenly from a peak of attainment and joyous relief into the depths of uncertainty, despair, and fear.

The poem is uneven. The finest passages are those which describe the winding funeral train as it passed through the States on its westward journey. These passages merit the comment made by Swinburne in comparing the poem with Lowell's 'Harvard Commemoration Ode': 'The most sonorous anthem ever chanted in the church of the world.'[1]

Coffin that passes through lanes and streets,
Through day and night with the great cloud darkening the land,
With the pomp of the inlooped flags with the cities draped in black,
With the show of the States themselves as of crepe-veil'd women standing,
With processions long and winding and the flambeaus of the night,
With the countless torches lit, with the silent sea of faces and the unbared heads,
With the waiting depot, the arriving coffin, and the somber faces,
With dirges through the night, with the thousand voices rising strong and solemn,
With all the mournful voices; of the dirges pour'd around the coffin,
The dim-lit churches and the shuddering organs — where amid these you journey
With the tolling tolling bells' perpetual clang,
Here, coffin that slowly passes,
I give you my sprig of lilac.

[1] *Under the Microscope*, quoted from C. H. Page's *The Chief American Poets*, 681. I have not been able to verify this quotation as given here in the Bonchurch edition of Swinburne, but his other comments on the poem are no less final in the epithets 'perfect and grand' and 'a superb piece of music and color.'

Fit hymn for the funeral of a god, but written of a man, this polyphonic music swells through a grand exulting diapason of hope in grief and birth in death, fading at last into the beautiful simplicity of the four concluding lines of tribute.

> Comrades mine and I in the midst, and their memory ever to keep, for the dead I loved so well,
> For the sweetest, wisest soul of all my days and lands — and this for his dear sake,
> Lilac and star and bird twined with the chant of my soul,
> There in the fragrant pines and the cedars dusk and dim.

Thus Whitman, aside from all questions of opportunism, political chicanery, elements of genius, and relative merits, came closer to a human Lincoln than anyone else since. Biographers are only building up the solid stone of a reputation, while casting aside the scraps of untruth. Whitman seized upon the man as his own, and whoever reads this poem may come nearer to realizing intuitively what Lincoln was than he can ever realize reasonably from the mass of biographical facts.

The most remarkable piece of literature inspired by Lincoln since Whitman, it is generally agreed, is John Drinkwater's play *Abraham Lincoln* (1919). It is significant that, like Whitman and like the better biographers, Drinkwater is not concerned with proving a thesis. His interest is in Lincoln the man, whose character holds so profoundly dramatic interest.

It is perhaps not until one has read or seen Drinkwater's play that he fully realizes how much Lincoln means beyond the trivialities with which popular fancy has dressed him. One can hardly recognize the character as American, and yet it is as singularly Lincoln as any interpretation yet endeavored. Even the popular legends which are kept, take on a different significance as Drinkwater handles them, and we feel that, as Lord Charnwood says of the William Scott myth, 'If the story is not true... still it is a remarkable man of whom people spin yarns of that kind.'

This play is based on Charnwood's biography, and the sympathy and admiration which enabled the biographer to present Lincoln fairly and grandly are traceable throughout the play. By no means, however, does Drinkwater reproduce the identical Lincoln of Charnwood. It would be, of course, impossible to present an absolutely complete historical Lincoln within the confines of a drama, but aside from selecting important events and striking words spoken by Lincoln, Drinkwater with the touch of an artist weaves a unified character from the more dramatically significant phases of the hero. No biography can attain the same unity of character that the play attains. So much of the lesser Lincoln cannot be omitted in biography. Significantly, much of the success of the play depends on the fact that there is none of Lincoln before his nomination. Consequently there are fewer incongruities apparent in the whole man. I am personally not yet convinced that any biographer or literary artist can successfully weave the entire Lincoln into a wholly coherent account. There is a gap between the early Lincoln and the Lincoln of 1865 — although it may not be so wide as it often seems — which all but prohibits a united character, and naturally so.

From the opening scene until the last we see a character unfold in all its common simplicity, and yet we perceive its mystic depths. Lincoln is handled nobly and with as much imagination as the author perceives to have been inherent in Lincoln himself.

The first scene is in the parlor of Lincoln's home in Springfield at the time of his nomination in 1860. Lincoln among his fellow townsmen is presented in all simplicity and unassuming candor. With Cuffney and Stone he is neighborly and humanly ordinary as they indulge in apparently insignificant small talk and compliments. With the committee who come to announce his nomination he is at once humble and self-possessed. The few moments alone with Mrs. Lincoln show him quite in touch with the commonplaces of life. This scene is the only connection in which the early, undistinguished Lincoln is apparent. He has not yet emerged, but in his firmness, his certain faith in what must be done, and his frank, democratic honesty of purpose, the outlines of all that he later becomes are sketched. The remarks made by the committee when Lincoln leaves the room in order that they may discuss him privately are significant of what the reader may have concluded by this time.

Tucker: Well, we might have chosen a handsomer article, but I doubt whether we could have chosen a better.

Hind: He would make a great judge — if you weren't prosecuting.

Price: I'd tell most people, but I'd ask that man.

In the second scene we begin to perceive how this ordinary man will deal with the vast problems that confront him. Representatives of the Confederate States, White and Jennings, are in conference with Secretary Seward, who, complimented that he is considered by them the real head of the Government, is dallying with the prospect of abandoning Fort Sumter as a means of palliating the South. Lincoln comes in unexpectedly, realizes the situation offhand, and immediately quashes the entire project. Seeing through the petty diplomacy and dissimulation of both Seward and the representatives, he outlines the issue, not as a question of secession, but of slavery.

Jennings: ... We believe that the South does not want secession. It wants to establish the right to decide for itself.

Lincoln: The South wants the stamp of approval upon slavery. It can't have it.

When the representatives are gone, Lincoln checks Seward up, kindly but firmly, and Seward realizes how little he has comprehended the real problems.

Lincoln: ... Seward, you may think I'm simple, but I can see your mind working as plainly as you might see the innards of a clock. You can bring great gifts to this government, with your zeal, and your administrative experience, and your love of men. Don't spoil it by thinking I've got a dull brain.

Seward (slowly): Yes, I see. I've not been thinking quite clearly about it all.

Lincoln presents the problem of Fort Sumter to the Cabinet, asking their opinions. They are divided, the opposition against Lincoln's plan to provision the fort being led by Hook. In the end Lincoln takes the entire responsibility into his own hands by overriding the vote of the Cabinet and issuing orders for the provisioning of the fort. His position is briefly stated.

Lincoln: ... To temporize now, cannot, in my opinion, avert war. To speak plainly to the world in standing by our resolution to hold Fort Sumter with all our means, and in a plain declaration that the Union must be preserved, will leave us with a clean cause, simply and loyally supported. I tremble at the thought of war. But we have in our hands a sacred trust.

Nearly two years elapse between scenes two and three. In scene three Lincoln is presented informally as the kind, merciful President who suffers and sympathizes with his people. We are prepared for this phase when we learn from the maid Susan that the 'people call him Father Abraham now.' Two women are calling at the White House for tea, Mrs. Otherly and Mrs. Blow. Mrs. Otherly's boy has been killed in the Union army, and she expresses her horror of war with the request in the name of humanity that Lincoln stop the war. Lincoln realizes her sorrow and deals with her kindly, replying that he, too, realizes the horror of war, but that where humanity is jealous and aggressive, force can only be met with force. Mrs. Blow, whose husband Goliath Blow is too busy selling supplies to the Government to accept a commission, is vindictive against the shameful rebels. Lincoln dismisses Mrs. Blow summarily.

Lincoln: Good afternoon, madam. And I'd like to offer ye a word of advice. That poor mother told me what she thought. I don't agree with her, but I honour her. She's wrong, but she is noble. You've told me what you think. I don't agree with you, and I'm ashamed of you and your like. You, who have sacrificed nothing, babble about destroying the South while other people conquer it. I accepted this war with a sick heart, and I've a heart that's near to breaking every day. I accepted it in the name of humanity, and just and merciful dealing, and the hope of love and charity on earth. And you come to me, talking of revenge and destruction, and malice, and enduring hate. These gentle people are mistaken, but they are mistaken cleanly, and in a great name. It is you that dishonour the cause for which we stand — it is you who would make it a mean and little thing. Good afternoon.

The next visitor is a negro William Custis. It is remarkable that in spite of the incongruity of the negro's language and actions, the scene leaves a satisfactory impression. We are so steeped in this Lincoln that we are willing to overlook deficiencies in local color where it is almost indispensable or better entirely avoided. This is one part that might have been better. The same qualities that are emphasized in the early part of the scene are here emphasized with, in addition, Lincoln's natural equality of manners in dealing with a negro. This is one of the most difficult accomplishments of the entire play. Lincoln is frankly friendly without any false *camaraderie*, as he talks to the old negro, one old man to another.

The dramatic interest is well sustained in this scene where there is no movement in plot. The story stands still while we learn about Lincoln, and somehow we do not object. What he does is important only as it enables us to understand him.

Scene four is the climax, if the play can be said to have one. Lincoln has called the Cabinet in order to lay before them the Emancipation Proclamation. He begins by reading Artemus Ward's latest, 'High-Handed Outrage at Utica,' much to the irritation of Hook. He then becomes at once serious and after some general discussion of the Proclamation states his position.

Lincoln:... My duty, it has seemed to me, has been to be loyal to a principle, and not to betray it by expressing it in action at the wrong time. That is what I conceive statesmanship to be. For long now I have had two fixed resolves. To preserve the Union, and to abolish slavery. How to preserve the Union I was always clear, and more than two years of bitterness have not dulled my vision. We have fought for the Union, and we are now winning for the Union. When and how to proclaim abolition I have all this time been uncertain. I am uncertain no longer. A few weeks ago I saw that, too, clearly. So soon, I said to myself, as the rebel army shall be driven out of Maryland, and it becomes plain to the world that victory is assured to us in the end, the time will have come to announce that with that victory and a vindicated Union will come abolition. I made the promise to myself and to my Maker.

Several of the Cabinet object to the Proclamation on various grounds and Lincoln silences them.

Lincoln: Gentlemen, we cannot escape history. We of this administration will be remembered in spite of ourselves. No personal significance or insignificance can spare one or another of us. In giving freedom to the slave we assure freedom to the free. We shall nobly save or meanly lose the last, best hope on earth.

He places the proclamation in front of him.

'Shall be thenceforward and forever free.' Gentlemen, I pray for your support. *He signs it.*

When the meeting disperses, Lincoln calls Hook back. He remonstrates with him for his intrigues and jealousy. Hook, however, is unmoved either by pleading or firmness and retires still hostile. When Hook is gone, Hay comes in, and Lincoln asks him to read a little from *The Tempest*. Hay reads the passage beginning —

Our revels now are ended,

and the curtain falls as Lincoln musingly repeats —

We are such stuff
As dreams are made on, and our little life
Is rounded with a sleep.[1]

Scene five takes place in a farmhouse near Appomattox in April, 1865. There are two divisions of the scene, the first presenting the pardoning of William Scott in the

[1] Lincoln's fondness for Shakespeare is amply set forth by several biographers. The significance of the passage used by Drinkwater is consistent with a story told by Charles Sumner of the last days of Lincoln. It is in substance that on the way back to Washington from City Point, after the surrender of Lee, Lincoln read parts of *Macbeth* to his party. When he came to the passage —

Duncan is in his grave;
After life's fitful fever he sleeps well;
Treason has done his worst; nor steel, nor poison,
Malice domestic, foreign levy, nothing
Can touch him further.

—he paused after the first reading, and then re-read the lines with feeling. Sumner was deeply impressed and after the assassination recollected the significance of the passage. See E. L. Pierce, *Memoir and Letters of Charles Sumner,* IV, 235.

evening and the second the surrender of Lee on the following day. The pardoning of Scott follows Chittenden's account except for a change in time and place. The pathos of the scene is well-nigh unbearable, though the simplicity with which it is handled removes it entirely from the sentimental clack in which the story is generally told. Lincoln is not present at the surrender of Lee, but he has been with Grant up until the appointed time. The feeling is left that the spirit of Lincoln dominates the entire proceedings. The old tradition that Lincoln was responsible for the terms of surrender is not followed, but an equivalent is substituted.

> *Lincoln:* Where will Lee wait?
> *Grant:* There's a room ready for him. Will you receive him, sir?
> *Lincoln:* No, no, Grant. That's your affair. You are to mention no political matters. Be generous. But I needn't say that.
> *Grant* (*taking a paper from his pocket*): Those are the terms I suggest.
> *Lincoln* (*reading*): Yes, yes. They do you honour.

Scene six, the last, takes place in Ford's Theater. In answer to the cry from the audience, Lincoln speaks from his box. The speech is made up largely from Lincoln's addresses and closes with the concluding paragraph of the 'Second Inaugural.' When the cheering subsides, the play within the play proceeds, and after a few moments Booth slips into the box. It is over, and Stanton comes from the box to pronounce, 'Now he belongs to the ages.'

It is a tendency among biographers, and even among historians, to record the history of the Civil War in such a way that the reader feels the spirit of Lincoln presiding over all, but Drinkwater's play imposes better than any other work, literary or biographical, an artistic unity on the material through the character of Lincoln. In the

words of the 'Chronicler' who speaks after the curtain
falls on the last scene, it is as if

> presiding everywhere
> Jpon event was one man's character.
> And that endures; it is the token sent
> Always to man for man's own government.

The plan of the play is episodic; it is composed of six
scenes taken at wide intervals and united only by the
spirit and development of the character of Lincoln. There
is an attempt to present characters who serve as the conventional 'opposition' against which the protagonist
struggles, but the internal conflict of doubt and misgiving
is practically untouched. Burnet Hook is admitted, according to the author, 'to the historical company of Lincoln's Cabinet for the purpose of embodying certain forces
that were antagonistic to the President. This was a
dramatic necessity, and I chose rather to invent a character for the purpose than to invest any single personage
with sinister qualities about which there might be dispute.' In addition, each of the occasionally antagonistic
Cabinet members is presented in some conflict with Lincoln. It is in the scenes with Hook and Seward that we
are shown Lincoln's power. His gentleness, justice, and
humanity are revealed in his relations with his friends
Stone and Cuffney, visitors at the White House, Mrs.
Otherly and the negro Custis, and later with the soldier
William Scott. His iron-handed firmness in dealing with
insincerity and vindictiveness is shown in his treatment
of White and Jennings and in his rebuke to Mrs. Goliath
Blow. His humor is hardly realized, but his mystic faith
and melancholy are vaguely underlying every scene.

However much we realize that this Lincoln was a common man, we are most impressed by the fact that his com-

mon humanity is a guide to his statesmanship. It is by this statesman that Drinkwater is enthralled. Although he does not, as some of our own poets of the World War period do, call directly that the world look to Lincoln for inspiration in settling its problems, he places Lincoln before us as a noble example of the statesman risen to unusual heights through his firm faith in democracy and humanity. In the back-wash of the World War we were glad to forget that we once thought we were fighting to make the world safe for democracy, but if out of that struggle there survive some ideals which may be as true guides for the future as those set forth in the character of Lincoln by Drinkwater, we may consider it was not all in vain. In so far as Lincoln influenced the course of these United States, he influenced it nobly.

VIII

The Sculptors and Painters of Lincoln

THE legend of Lincoln has not been limited to literature and folklore. Once Lincoln was elected, artists began painting and sculpturing him as the hero. There remain several studies which were done before his death, none of which are particularly remarkable as works of art. The life masks cast by Leonard W. Volk and Clark Mills are still the most interesting reproductions of Lincoln's features, and they are not, of course, art. Like the mass of conflicting and often vaguely significant historical facts, these life masks are inanimate signs of a real Lincoln and hold at once all of the enigma, all of the certainty, all of the common, and all of the sublime that so many artists have attempted to portray in oil, marble, or bronze. As the literary artist has succeeded in grasping some aspect of Lincoln and weaving it into verse or prose, so have the sculptors and painters succeeded with their different themes.

One who is acquainted with any of the collections of Lincoln photographs realizes very likely that Lincoln was an uncommonly ugly man. In spite of all the sentimental testimony to his beauty, the photographs and life masks scarcely corroborate it. Many of the former have been retouched so considerably as to render them all but valueless as reproductions of his features. The life masks, however, do not lie. The testimony of all those who wrote of

Lincoln's appearance before his death agrees generally in the fact that he was extraordinarily homely, to say the least, but even the less observing noted something in his features which defied reproduction. There was in his deep-lined features a rugged, worn strength, and something ineffably melancholy, which struck all who saw him. But almost universally his observers commented on the striking impression of his eyes. Deep, luminous, and enigmatical, they were the most extraordinary portion of his strange features.

Truman H. Bartlett — himself an artist — in an essay on the portraits of Lincoln, which was published together with Carl Schurz's essay on Lincoln in a memorial volume in 1907, credits French sculptors with being the first to see the beauty of the life mask of Lincoln.

> Here in substance is what they said: 'It is unusual in general construction, it has a new and interesting character, and its planes are remarkably beautiful and subtle. If it belongs to any type, and we know of none such, it must be a wonderful specimen of that type.' Like things were said of it by other French artists, as I took pains to show it for examination. I lent the mask and a number of Lincoln photographs to the best French genre sculptor of modern times, for several months, for him to see what he could get out of it in making a face in clay. When he got through he made these observations: 'I can do nothing with that head, and I doubt if anyone in these times can. The more I studied it, the more difficulties I found. The subtle character of its form is beyond belief. There is no face like it.'
>
> Frémiet was particularly interested. He said, among other things: 'It seems impossible that a new country like yours should produce such a face. It is unique.'

Bartlett further relates of a Lincoln photograph that 'in the opinion of the three greatest sculptors of modern times — Frémiet, Rodin, and Aubé — "It is a new man; he has tremendous character."'

Although one cannot find fault with the artist's use of the term *beauty* to describe Lincoln's features, one may incline to one's own impression of homeliness. Character, tremendous character, Lincoln's face certainly does show, but is one to assume that the revelation of character is beauty? It is possible that the sculptors are more certain of what they mean by beauty than is the average man, who, although he often applies it indiscriminately to the merely symmetrical, reserves it in definition for the vaguely ideal. Hence it is that most men have judged Lincoln homely, in spite of the fact that they recognized the power, pathos, and humanity of his features. One may defer to the artists, for, as will be observed later, artists like doctors sometimes disagree.

Walt Whitman commented often on the failure of all photographs to comprehend the immensity and oddity of Lincoln's face. He said:

> Probably the reader has seen physiognomies (often old farmers, sea-captains, and such) that, behind their homeliness, or even ugliness, held superior points so subtle, yet so palpable, making the real life of their faces almost as impossible to depict as a wild perfume or fruit-taste, or a passionate tone of the living voice — and such was Lincoln's face, the peculiar color, the lines of it, the eyes, the mouth, expression. Of technical beauty it had nothing — but to the eye of a great artist it furnished a rare study, a feast and fascination. The current portraits are all failures — most of them caricatures.

In another place he noted:

> None of the artists or pictures has caught the deep, though subtle and indirect expression of this man's face. There is something else there. One of the great portrait painters of two or three centuries ago is needed.

283

It may be well to keep Whitman's opinion in mind while discussing some of the several more famous statues and portraits, for, after all, without setting oneself up as a critic of art, it is apparent that Lincoln has remained a mystery to the artists, most of whom, no doubt, prefer him so.

Of several early productions, the two which are today the most famous are the historical painting, 'The First Reading of the Emancipation Proclamation,' by Francis Carpenter, and the 'Emancipation Group' in bronze by Thomas Ball. Carpenter's painting now hangs in the Capitol, and Ball's statue stands in Lincoln Park, Washington. It is interesting that these two early productions should develop the same theme.

Carpenter's painting was begun in February, 1864, although the plan had been conceived much earlier. During the time the work was in progress, the artist was practically a part of the executive family and spent a period of six months at the White House. The account of these months Carpenter later published with the title *The Inner Life of Abraham Lincoln: Six Months at the White House* (1867). The following passages are those in which Carpenter explained his early inspiration and the patriotic fervor which eventually found expression on the canvas:

In common with many others, I had from the beginning of the war believed that the government would not be successful in putting down a rebellion based upon slavery as its avowed corner-stone, without striking a death-blow at the institution itself. As the months went on, and disappointment and disaster succeeded one another, this conviction deepened into certainty. When at length, in obedience to what seemed the very voice of God, the thunderbolt was launched, and like the first gun at Concord, 'was heard around the world,' all the enthusiasm of my nature was kindled. The 'beast' Secession, offspring of the 'dragon' Slavery, drawing in his train a third part of our national stars, was pierced with the deadly wound which could not be healed. It was the combat between Michael and Satan of Apocalyptic vision re-enacted before the eyes of the nineteenth century.

To paint a picture which should commemorate this new epoch in the history of Liberty, was a dream which took form and shape in my mind towards the close of the year 1863 — the year made memorable in its dawn by the issue of the final decree. With little experience to adapt me for the execution of such a work, there had nevertheless come to me at times glowing conceptions of the true purpose and character of Art, and an intense desire to do something expressive of appreciation of the great issues involved in the war. The painters of old had delighted in representations of the birth from the ocean of Venus, the goddess of love. Ninety years ago upon this Western continent had been witnessed — no dream of fable, but a substantial fact — the immaculate conception of Constitutional Liberty; and at length through great travail its consummation had been reached. The long-prayed-for year of jubilee had come; the bonds of the oppressed were loosed; the prison doors were opened. 'Behold,' said a voice, 'how a Man may be exalted to a dignity and glory almost divine, and give freedom to a race.' Surely Art should unite with Eloquence and Poetry to celebrate such a theme.

I have always felt that the last few lines of the above express Carpenter's Lincoln perfectly. The Cabinet members are portrayed with historical accuracy except for some idealization in a Victorian manner, but the face of Lincoln lacks only the halo and the dimness which will be contributed by years to make it at once medieval and Victorian in sanctity. In spite of the incongruity of the mantelpiece and chandelier, not to mention other objects, there is something about the picture which has always made it to my eye a Victorian 'Last Supper,' although not even Carpenter could paint from life and give Lincoln entirely an anaemic face.[1]

Thomas Ball's 'Emancipation Group' was unveiled on April 14, 1876. The seventeen thousand dollars which purchased the monument were entirely paid by sub-scriptions of negroes. The first contribution of five dollars was made by Charlotte Scott, of Marietta, Ohio, the morn-ing after the assassination.

The 'Emancipation Group' has never been as impressive to me as it has to others. Even at a time when Lincoln meant little to me except as a remote hero who had freed the slaves, the statue was made ridiculous by a chance reference which dubbed it 'Shine, Sir?' Whoever was the wit who coined the phrase, he may have had at least an innate sense of the artistic, as well as a sense of humor, for there is something ridiculously wrong with the entire effect of the statue. Perhaps it is the ever-kneeling negro.

The statue of Lincoln which has had more influence than any other in moulding the popular conception of the hero is the one by Augustus Saint-Gaudens which stands in Lincoln Park, Chicago. It was executed at the request of Eli Bates, who donated forty thousand dollars for the project. It was unveiled on October 22, 1887. Lincoln is represented as an orator, just risen from his chair, which is shown behind him, and waiting for the audience to be-come quiet before beginning his address. The attitude is

[1] The Carpenter painting is the only one which I have studied except the Thorpe portrait in the Capitol. Both are spiritualized. Prints which I have seen of the etching by J. P. Nuyttens, the Belgian-American painter and etcher, the painting by J. Reading Kelly, and the Schneider sketch show definitely the same spiritualization. The painting by Douglas Volk, of which I have also seen only a print, is a combination of realism and idealism. The face is rugged, heavy-lined, even grotesque, but about the eyes there is the spiritual expression which characterizes the other studies. These paintings are, in general, more spiritual than the statuary.

BALL'S 'EMANCIPATION GROUP'
IN LINCOLN PARK, CHICAGO

the one traditionally assigned to Lincoln at the beginning of an address — one hand behind him, the other grasping the lapel of his coat. His head is bent. The worn face is filled with a sense of power and the sadness of responsibility, sympathy, and love. The entire figure is marked by grace and an heroic manner.

Characteristic of the art of Saint-Gaudens, the statue is not an attempt to portray Lincoln accurately, but to represent an ideal hero with some of Lincoln's characteristics. In the reminiscences of Saint-Gaudens edited by his son, Homer Saint-Gaudens, there are quoted the two 'pet phrases' of the artist which may be considered the philosophy of art which produced the Lincoln statue. They are: 'After all, you can model anything. It all depends on the *way* it is done'; and, 'You cannot reproduce things absolutely; so, since you must err, err only on the side of beauty.'

In an address on Saint-Gaudens, delivered before the Brooklyn Institute of Arts and Sciences on February 22, 1908, Kenyon Cox attributed the greatness of Saint-Gaudens to the fact that he was free from the besetting sins of naturalism and the scientific temper. He said, 'I know no work of his to which raw nature has been admitted, in which a piece of study has been allowed to remain as such without the moulding touch of art to subdue it to its place.'

The characteristics which commend the Saint-Gaudens statue to the public are chiefly its imaginative presentation of Lincoln's character, its heroic breadth of treatment, and its nobility of feeling. Lincoln retains little of his personality. He is exalted to the dignity of a type and endowed with the majesty and grace of a Daniel Webster, which had so filled the public eye of his age that the living

Lincoln, awkward and ungainly, was thought to be sadly lacking in the desirable qualities of a statesman and orator. Saint-Gaudens's Lincoln is the same Lincoln that Edwin Arlington Robinson interprets in his poem 'The Master' — an heroic abstraction of elemental nobility and wisdom. This Lincoln is the incarnation of the master, the savior, the emancipator, the prophet, the man of sorrows; but it is not the rail-splitter, the circuit lawyer, or the rough joker. It is predominantly in the grand style, and the greatest praise can claim no more than that it is successfully done. Among statues of American statesmen, most of which give the impression of having been ordered and executed by the dozen, it stands solitary and aloof in conception.

Gutzon Borglum's seated statue of Lincoln, at Trenton, New Jersey, is one of the most interesting interpretations. It possesses power and nobility, but these qualities are softened by something infinitely human in spirit which no other statue attains in a similar degree. The attitude is informal, almost weary. The face is strong, kindly, and wistful rather than traditionally melancholy. If it could be named significantly, 'Father Abraham' would probably come nearer than any other of Lincoln's folk-names to expressing the character portrayed. Indeed, whether or not Borglum intended this Lincoln primarily to represent the folk Father Abraham, there is no other piece of art which does it so well. It is, as characterized in 'The Lincoln Statue' by W. F. Collins, the statue of

> one who trusted, one who knew
> The common heart.

Of all the Lincoln statues none has been more loudly praised or more widely condemned than that of George G. Barnard which stands in Lytle Park, Cincinnati, Ohio.

It was the result of a gift by Charles P. Taft and was completed in 1917. Unlike Saint-Gaudens, Borglum, and nearly all the other sculptors, Barnard chose to represent the smooth-shaven Lincoln of the life mask made in 1860 by Leonard W. Volk. He also chose, unlike others, to represent the body of Lincoln in all its angularity, without softening the effect in the slightest degree. For this purpose he selected as a model a Kentuckian, born within fifteen miles of Lincoln's birthplace, who had spent a great part of his life in splitting rails. His height and physique corresponded with those of Lincoln remarkably. Barnard said of this man:

> A study of this man's body showed it to be in harmony with the body of Lincoln. The Greeks had nothing like that. It was a genuine product of American soil, as typical in its way as the Indians. The legs were long and he had a back that seemed to bend without causing a corresponding cavity in front. I spoke of this to him and he said:
> 'I have been splitting rails all my life.'
> He was about forty years old. That was the natural explanation of his overdeveloped back and shoulder muscles. Lincoln had gone through the same exercise and the same result was noted in his form. He was probably the most powerful physical being known to the frontier life.
> I have seen the models of Europe — men of Greece and Italy — symmetrical and beautiful in a classic way; but nothing ever appealed to me like the form of this Kentuckian. It affected the spirit like the passing of a storm through the sky.

Since we have noticed the philosophy of art which produced the Saint-Gaudens Lincoln in the grand manner, perhaps Barnard's philosophy should be quoted as an explanation of his statue. In speaking of the 1860 life mask, he says:

For one hundred days I sought the secret of this face in the marvelous constructive work of God. Here is no line, no form, to interpret lightly, to evade or cover. Every atom of its surface belongs to some individual form, melting into a larger form and again into the form of the whole. The mystery of this whole form nature alone knows — man will never fathom it, but at least he should not bring to this problem forms of his own making.

Art's virtue is to reveal, not to obscure. It is a power to make plain things hidden. Art is not nature, the mask of Lincoln not sculpture. The mask controls its secrets, Lincoln's life revealed them, as the sculptor must reveal the power and purpose of this wondrous mask.

Barnard's Lincoln is not beautiful, unless there is literal fact in the line of Keats —

> Beauty is truth, truth beauty...

It possesses a rugged majesty and original power, however, which are not seen in other Lincoln statuary. This ungainly, crude figure, with hard yet tender face and sublime seriousness has impressed many as the one great Lincoln statue. It is the Lincoln of the frontier, of the debates and the circuit, the American type and the symbol of democracy.

Lyman Whitney Allen's poem 'Barnard's Statue of Lincoln' expresses at once an appreciation and the best explanation of the entire work.

> This is a symbol of democracy —
> A towering figure risen from the soil
> And keeping the earth mould, yet so informed
> By Spiritual power that they who gaze
> Perceive high kinship bearing similar stamp
> To One of eld from whom was learned the way
> Of wisdom and the love that goes to death.
> And this is commonalty, glorified —
> A root out of dry ground, but watered

THE SCULPTORS AND PAINTERS OF LINCOLN

By those inherent and ancestral streams
Whose springs are in the furthest heavenlies.
And this is nature's haunting miracle —
The lowly dust builded to pinnacles,
The earth-bound soul consorting with the stars.
Unshapely feet — but they were such as trod
The winepress of God's judgment on a land,
Were such as clomb, striding through storm and night,
The perilous steeps of right, leading a host.
Ungainly hands — but they were such as plucked
Thistles and planted flowers in their stead,
Were such as struck hell's irons from a race
And open swung barred gates of privilege.
Unsightly back — but it was such as bore
The bruises of a nation's chastisement,
For see, the double cross welted thereon,
The emblem of a statesman's Calvary!
Uncomely face — but it was such as wore
The prints of vigil and the scars of grief,
A face more marred than any man's, save One,
And save that One a face more beautiful.

It is impossible to discuss all the Lincoln memorials here. These three are, perhaps, the strongest, but there are several others, each remarkable in its own way. The O'Connor statue, representing the Lincoln of the 'Farewell Address,' which stands before the Capitol of Springfield, Illinois, is remarkable for the intimacy and ease of manner which it attains by avoiding the grand majesty which so many affect. The seated statue by Daniel C. French, which is in the National Lincoln Memorial at Washington, is as genuinely appealing as the traditional 'man of sorrows' with something of the intimacy of the Borglum and O'Connor statues. Although it does not seem to possess any rare subtlety or originality, it does after a fashion more nearly portray the Lincoln of all phases than does any other. It is quite suited, as such, to hold its place in the National Lincoln Memorial. It does not attain, however, the place which the Saint-Gaudens has so long held as the most popular statue.

Nothing, since the death of Lincoln, has so clearly shown the state of public opinion concerning the hero as the controversy which arose over the statue which was to be presented to England by the American people. In 1914 the International Committee that was formed to celebrate the Hundred Years' Peace between Great Britain and the United States, wishing to place in London a permanent memorial of the amity of the two nations, proffered a statue of Lincoln to the British Government. The offer was accepted and an especial site was assigned for it near Westminster Abbey on Parliament Square. It was at first intended to send a replica of the Saint-Gaudens statue, but in 1917 Charles P. Taft offered to pay for a replica of the newly completed Barnard statue. This offer was gratefully accepted by the American and British committees.

Then the controversy arose. The fight against the Barnard statue was led by F. W. Ruckstuhl, of the *Art World*, who called it a 'woeful, wallowing Willie, mourning for mother and complaining of a colic,' and again, 'a stoop-shouldered, consumptive chested, chimpanzee-handed, lumpy-footed, giraffe-necked, grimy-fingered clodhopper, wearing his clothes in a way to disgust a ragman.' It is interesting to note that such language was common in the mouths of Lincoln's partisan opponents when he was alive. Old photographs were brought out to prove that Lincoln's hands were not large and that he dressed in the height of fashion. Eulogies were dug up to prove that he was graceful and fully aware of the elegance and niceties of conduct.

To the defense of Barnard came a large number of artists and authors, among others, Charles Dana Gibson, John Sargent, and Frederick MacMonnies. Ex-Presidents Taft and Roosevelt agreed, for once, that Barnard's statue was the real Lincoln. Robert Lincoln, however, said: 'The result is a monstrous figure which is grotesque as a likeness of President Lincoln and defamatory as an effigy.'

In the midst of the controversy several other statues were suggested by particular admirers. Among the most prominently mentioned were those of Borglum, Patrick, French (the statue which is now at Lincoln, Nebraska, and not the seated statue of the Lincoln Memorial), and Ball. In order to determine the opinion of the public in general, a popular referendum was conducted by the *Independent*. The results as published in the *Independent* for December 29, 1917, were as follows:

Saint-Gaudens	9820
Patrick	3356
Borglum	2841
French	1467
Ball	1356
Barnard	1207

The final solution was that a replica of the Saint-Gaudens statue went to London to be placed in Parliament Square, and a replica of the Barnard statue went to Manchester to be placed in Platt Fields.

There are inevitably two Lincolns. The Saint-Gaudens and Barnard statues are best examples of the continual conflict in interpretation. Saint-Gaudens produced a noble statue in the grand manner, and that is praise enough when we consider how many artists attempted the grand manner only to fail. Robert Underwood Johnson, in his poem 'Saint-Gaudens: an Ode,' has fitly eulogized the great sculptor thus:

> Yet shall the future be not all bereft;
> Not without witness shall its eyes be left.
> The soul, again, is visible through Art,
> Servant of God and Man. The immortal part
> Lives in the miracle of a kindred mind,
>
> That found itself in seeking for its kind.
> The humble by the humble is discerned;
> And he whose melancholy broke in sunny wit
> Could be no stranger unto him who turned
> From sad to gay, as though in jest he learned
> Some mystery of sorrow. It was writ:
>
> *The hand that shapes us Lincoln must be strong*
> *As his that righted our bequeathed wrong;*
> *The heart that shows us Lincoln must be brave,*
> *An equal comrade unto king or slave;*
> *The mind that gives us Lincoln must be clear*
>   *As that of seer*
> *To fathom deeps of faith abiding under tides of fear.*
>
> What wonder Fame, impatient, will not wait
>   To call her sculptor great
> Who keeps for us in bronze the soul that saved the State!

The Lincoln of Saint-Gaudens is the Lincoln that we generally wish to remember, the statesman, the hero, the prophet; but the other legend, the Lincoln of the frontier, the symbol of democracy, the strong man, the honest, sincere, hard-working countryman, yet has its appeal and will not likely fade away.

IX

Conclusion

IF THE study of Lincoln literature reveals nothing more, it
certainly reveals the extent to which this extraordinary
human being has captured the imagination of two generations of poets, dramatists, novelists, historians, and biographers. There is no evidence that interest is flagging.
New interpretations and studies come from the press
every month of the year, and by the time a student considers himself up to the moment, several new studies have
been announced. After considering a large portion of the
material in every field of art, there is one striking conclusion; namely, that history and literature are more nearly
agreed in the evaluation and interpretation of Lincoln
than might be supposed on reading the more ephemeral
productions in the field of literature or the partisan
diatribes in biography. The better literary treatments are
correlated with the better biographies, and the two often
overlap in spirit as well as manner.

The bases for estimates of Lincoln are often at variance,
but the estimates themselves are in most respects the same
in their general terms. With the exception of bitter parti-
sans who cannot forget Sherman's march through Georgia — for which Lincoln was, of course, partly responsible — and the destruction of an established social régime
based on slavery, which is remembered through a haze

of romance as remarkable as that of the Lincoln legend, students of Lincoln agree that he was the great man of the age. Some would have him placed above every other mortal genius. He was the most individual man who ever lived. Singular and solitary he remains, as in his lifetime, at once familiar and remote, common but impressive, plain but mysterious, unmeasured and unsolved. No solution or measurement has yet been found satisfactory. Admiration is still the common ground upon which we stand. There is as yet no version which can be accepted as a true picture of both the private and the public Lincoln. Sandburg combined with Stephenson may be recognized as the best version of the private Lincoln; Charnwood, perhaps, has the best of the public Lincoln. But the Lincoln who lives in the mind of the average American is not greatly dependent upon the interpretation of the biographers, for he is largely a myth.

We like to have our great men summed up in a name or a story, even though we know that they can never be. 'Honest Abe,' 'Father Abraham,' and 'The Emancipator' are yet the indices to the popular Lincoln, but these very names are changing in meaning with every year. As time passes, Lincoln gathers more securely the significance of his period about him and becomes more and more a national mythos. The certainty with which this mythos will continue to live depends upon how much Lincoln is able to stand reinterpretation. Judging from the past, we may assume an indefinite life for it.

The remarkable thing about the mythos is that, if history and biography are to be trusted, Lincoln was a worthy man to be made into a symbol of justice, mercy, spiritual and intellectual strength, or a symbol of democracy and freedom. The biographers and historians may not be able to make every fact fit into this picture, even though the mass of facts fits naturally; but the mythos is undisturbed because it has seized upon the best of the Lincoln story as poetic truth.

Without growing sentimental we may lay claim as Americans to having lived and created more legends during two hundred years than any other civilized nation, and we do not need to rely on our own opinion about the matter. With due thanks for all criticism to those who visit the United States for six weeks and then write a book, still we do have universal testimony to the poetic appeal of Washington, Jefferson, Hamilton, and the daring experiment which they and their associates inaugurated. Whatever hesitancy may be occasioned by the acute realization of the blatancy of our Fourth of July, our shortcomings as a democracy, or our unoriginality as artists, we need not flee to Europe for romance or be ashamed to admit that we worship a hero born and reared in the crudest portion of our civilization. The testimony of Michael Pupin to the appeal of a Franklin or a Lincoln to a boy in Serbia or that of John Drinkwater to the world appeal of Lincoln must make an American wonder at his own modesty in acclaiming his country's heroes.

The legend of Washington has been dealt with roughly in the hands of his recent biographers. There was the silly cherry-tree episode, which typified an impossible boy, and there were the stories of the man, which went to enormous lengths to produce the picture of an impregnable hero. There were the omissions and exaggerations that go to make up every legendary figure. All these have been removed, and yet the heroic Washington who attended the Continental Congress dressed in his regimentals remains unfathomed by the debunkers. Washington is yet an enduring symbol, for he is a legend created, not alone by 'Parson' Weems and Gilbert Stuart, but also by the American people.

In the same manner Benedict Arnold has become a legendary villain. No matter how much biographers may try to remove the impression that Arnold was an evil man, his one act has enshrined him in the popular fancy as the symbol of forces which worked against the ultimate liberation of the colonies, and as such a symbol he cannot be anything but an evil figure in the American legend. In a less complete way Aaron Burr has likewise been villainized. From a purely logical standpoint the intricacies of popular fancy in weaving such legends are impossible to comprehend. The difference between the act of Benedict Arnold and the acts of United States officials who betrayed forces and resources of their government into the hands of the seceding States is not a difference in kind, but rather in significance, as they are interpreted in American history.

History is a strange creation. From the almost unlimited supply of facts coherent histories can be assembled that will present truthfully the individual opinions of an unlimited number of historians. Given a sufficiently large sequence of facts to choose from, an historian can prove anything that seems true. Yet, in the minutiae of modern historical research there are numerous gaps. No one has ever attempted to write a history of even the briefest period of a government or a chapter of a man's life without realizing that not a tithe of the facts of day-by-day and hour-by-hour events can ever be known. And yet, we are told that the realm of history is the realm of facts. So the enormous mass of individual histories is — a partial account of partial fact.

CONCLUSION

Histories of the Civil War continue to be written without bias or favor. The biographies of its great leaders are again rewritten without bias or favor. An eminent historian, W. E. Dodd, produces a study, *Lincoln or Lee*, in which he seeks 'to study and to assess... without bias or favor, hoping thus to strengthen the appeal of History to a generation too little prone to think and assess.' In this work the slaves of the entire South are 'three million negroes singing and frolicking at their work,' and it is said of R. E. Lee that he could have spoken Lincoln's 'Second Inaugural Address.' Archibald Rutledge, in 'A Southerner Views Lincoln,' conceives that 'with the stroke of a pen, Lincoln destroyed a noble civilization, and established, as far as the race question is concerned, something like a permanent chaos,' and that Lincoln prided himself on his lowly origin with 'the sullen pride of a commoner.' And yet another, Edgar Lee Masters, in *Lincoln the Man* attempts to remove every vestige, not merely of greatness, but also of decency from the man Lincoln, and does not hesitate to employ the basest innuendoes in order to darken the picture. So even in works that range from history to partisan diatribes public men are assessed with as much bias as we expect to find in fiction. The Lincoln of poetry in all of his glory is no farther removed from fact than the Lincoln set forth by his detractors.

It can be shown from ample, if incomplete, evidence that Lincoln had great executive ability or that he had none; that he was a great judge of men or that he was a very poor judge of men; that he was handsome or that he was extremely ugly; that he was awkward or that he was graceful; that he was carefully dressed or that he was slouchily and poorly dressed; that he was very democratic or that he was very aloof; that he told questionable

stories or that he did not tell them; that he was religious
or that he was indifferent; that he loved his wife exceedingly well or that he could scarcely bear with her; that
he was merely a drifter who waited until public opinion
could not be denied or that he knew always the proper
time to do the proper thing; that he preserved the Union
or that the Union was preserved in spite of his countless
deficiencies and errors; that he was the greatest general
and strategist of the Union or that by meddling he prevented great generals from achieving victory; that he was
soft-hearted or that he was iron-hearted; that he was a
tyrant or that he was the best and most just ruler that
ever lived; that he was the most popular and loved man in
the North during his presidency or that he was the most
unpopular and hated; that he was predominantly melancholy or that he was predominantly happy; that he was
very much bent on freeing the slaves or that he was indifferent to their status; that he was a ludicrous and un-
inspiring figure or that he was all but majestic; and so on.

Any and all of these conceptions are amply documented
by biography and criticism without including the work of
a single writer south of the Mason and Dixon Line.

In the immense mass of Lincoln literature there is an
historical lie for every historical truth. As each new student of the material holds the entire or a portion in solution, a new figure is precipitated. The result is never the
same. *The* biography of Lincoln has not yet appeared, and
it is unlikely that it will ever appear. But if it is charged
that the legend-making propensities of the people of the
United States have once and for all buried the real Lincoln
under a mass of untruths, it must be considered that the
same forces have clothed him in truths that the facts of
his life could never have otherwise attained. Such is the

manner in which legend works; and though many of the untruths may long survive to puzzle the diviners of the facts, the truths will never be tarnished by them.

Myth and legend may be said to have attained their last stage when they have become so patently questionable that a theorist finds it necessary to deny their entire significance and reinterpret them in the light of higher criticism. Many men recognized, a few years after the death of Lincoln, that the man they had known had passed from the realm of fact into the realm of legend and myth.

In 1872, when the unrestrained adulation of the martyr President was at a peak, there appeared a brochure by a native of Illinois, D. B. Turney, entitled *The Mythifying Theory, or Abraham Lincoln a Myth.* With a back-hand slap at the Straussian system in general the author began, 'I can come a thousand times as near the proof that Mr. Lincoln never existed, as all the skeptics combined can that Christ never was.' First of all, there was the evidence in the very name of the mythical figure, *Ab* — a father; *Abram* — a high father; *Abraham* — the father of a great multitude. Or better yet, *Ab* — father; *ra* — restore; *ham* — the children of Ham. There it was, the history of the mythical ruler and emancipator, all in the mythical name. Passing to the second feature of the name, the author produced a multitude of evidences that it was a symbol of other important phases of the life of the supposed Lincoln. The conclusion of a further and more lengthy examination, which proceeds in all preposterousness, brought the following result:

He was a myth. This we see from the name; Abraham — father of a great multitude; Lincoln — liberator slain. He made the slaveholders relinquish their slaves, and died by the hands of a conspirator. 'If he were not a mere myth, but a real person, how could his whole story be thus recorded in his name?... But these are not all the points in connection with his name, which show Abraham Lincoln to have been a myth. Can a man who makes any pretensions to the first principles of reason, believe that there ever was such a thing as a real nation whose people had to call the name of the second officer in the government, in pronouncing that of the first?... What could be more unreasonable? Now see! ABR HAMLIN COLN. This proves the myth.

In 1894 a second critic, Bocardo Bramantip, arose to attack the myth in a carefully reasoned dissertation, *The Abraham Lincoln Myth*, dated the year of our Lord 3663. He first attacked the myth in its barest form as being evidently the product of folk-imagination and literary interpolation and polishing:

About the year 1860, on the eve of the great Civil War in America, there suddenly appeared as a great public leader a man of obscure origin, named Abraham Lincoln.

Although previously wholly unknown to the great mass of the people, he was chosen President of the Republic, and as the principles he represented were looked upon with abhorrence and fear by nearly one-half the nation, his election precipitated a rebellion. But he showed himself from the very outset to be a man of destiny — the greatest of statesmen and the wisest of rulers. During the course of the war, and as it is commonly stated, on the first day of January, 1863, he issued a Proclamation emancipating the slaves everywhere throughout the territory in possession of the rebels. This was practically tantamount to universal emancipation. Thus was the slavery of the African race in America abolished. He suppressed the Rebellion and saved his country.

Elected to the Presidency a second time, shortly after his inauguration, while attending the theater on a Good Friday Night, he was assassinated by an actor who, after committing this horrible crime, leaped upon the stage exclaiming, 'Sic semper tyrannis — the South is avenged!' But although the theater was crowded with people devoted to the President, his murderer was allowed to withdraw unmolested. From the moment of his assassination Abraham Lincoln was looked upon as a martyr, and by the African people in America as their 'Moses,' who had led them out of bondage. Such is the popular tradition....

The story of his assassination suggests, in all its details, the hand of the novelist or a playwright. The time chosen for the tragedy, a Good Friday night; the place, a crowded theater; the assassin, a professional actor of tragedy; the murderer's dramatic leap upon the stage, brandishing the weapon of death and exclaiming in dramatic tones, 'Sic semper tyrannis!' (which it may be remarked, was simply the legend of the State of Virginia); the vast audience paralyzed with amazement or fear — all the accessories seem like skillfully arranged settings for the tragic climax of a romance or a drama... the story looks artificial and suspicious on its face.

In the method of Huxley, the author proceeds to argue that one could not imagine this to happen in the year 3663; that the nineteenth century was generally afflicted with hero-worship and this is only one of many legends; that in 3663 there is no document known to have been written or printed earlier than three centuries after the death of Lincoln (it is reasonable to suppose that there will be no paper of today existing then); that the similarities of the existing records show that they had a common 'groundwork,' and nothing is known of the originator or originators of this groundwork; that the story is wholly irreconcilable with the Constitution of the United States, in that, arguing *a priori*, the tenth article does not permit a president so to act, and, arguing *a posteriori*, the thirteenth amendment, which was not adopted until two years after the supposed proclamation, provided for the abolition of slavery, which the myth would have us believe was abolished in 1863. The only conclusions possible, of course, are that the story is pure allegory, having as its substratum of truth the triumph of liberty in its 'irrepressible conflict' with slavery; or that under the influence of the desire of one of the major political parties whose conception of the proper interpretation of the Constitution was very liberal, upon the slender foundation of a few historic facts there was gradually built up the legend as it stands, the purpose being to have a sacred precedent for extending the power of the Chief Executive; or that the entire story is a forgery of the twentieth century.

There may be a deep significance in such drolleries. For Abraham Lincoln certainly lived, and just as certainly the mythical elements are in his story. How shall we deny to this man either his existence or his significance? His existence may some day be denied, but his significance never.

The seriousness of the Straussian system or Huxley's higher criticism as a menace to a national religion of Lincolnism is at the present day not even interesting, for we are near enough to Lincoln to know that the myth is grounded on fact. The seriousness of Lincolnism as a national religion is, however, another matter. If we may believe John Drinkwater, Lincoln has already passed out of the realm of national heroes into a higher sphere in which he symbolizes for all the world the ideal of spirituality, morality, intellectuality, and democracy.

Lincolnism has not been without its unfortunate aspects as a national religion. There are odes, epics, novels, short stories, dramas, essays, masques, moving pictures, Lincoln numbers of magazines, Lincoln calendars, Lincoln music, Lincoln memorials, Lincoln temples, and many

CONCLUSION

Lincoln statues and paintings that perpetuate the grandeur of an American legend which is of deep spiritual and poetic meaning to the world at large. But there are also the endless misinterpretations and fictions created and used for questionable purposes. The interest shifts in these from the personality, intellect, and purposes of the man to exaggerations of phrases and incidents and to lies tacked to his name which are used as bait in the turbid waters of politics and sectarian projects. Lincoln the hero and prophet is debased into a petty talisman, the cure-all for modern social and political ills. The Lincoln tariff myth served in its time to convince the gullible of the righteousness of a partisan policy. 'We are doing just what Lincoln would do if he were living' became a familiar catchword. The democracy of Abraham Lincoln as expressed in the 'Gettysburg Address' was the magic solvent which campaigning mayors swore to apply in all the problems of civic government. Capital found in him its prophet, and socialism seized upon stray sentences as incontrovertible proof of his social philosophy. The significance of the utterances of Lincoln does not merit this degradation to trivial purposes, but it is the logical fate of the folk-hero to become, in a measure, what his various admirers want him to be.

The legend has elaborated its own truth about Lincoln, and it is that Lincoln was authentically the prophet of a new world. A few unreconstructed Southerners and Copperheads are yet picking over the facts of the 'irrepressible conflict' for any and every fact that may be used as proof that Lincoln was a villain, but, far from negating the legend, they gain for it, by their unfriendly bias, an increasing number of supporters. So-called accurate histories of the rebellion, for want of imagination, fail to grasp the true significance of Lincoln because they fail to see beyond the facts. We must comprehend that — to paraphrase Shelley — there is this difference between a history and a legend, that a history is a catalogue of detached facts, which have no other connection than time, place, circumstance, and cause, and effect; the other is the creation of actions according to the unchangeable forms of human nature, as existing in the mind of the creator, which is itself the image of all other minds. The one is partial, and applies only to a definite period of time, and a certain combination of events which can never again recur; the other is universal, and contains within itself the germ of a relation to whatever motives or actions have place in the possible varieties of human nature. Time, which destroys the beauty and use of the history of particular facts, stripped of the poetry which should invest them, augments that of legend and forever develops new and wonderful applications of the eternal truth which it contains.

An historical fact which has satisfactory proofs and antecedents may become a myth through interpretation. When a figure becomes symbolic, it is no longer simply historical. A figure may, on the other hand, never have existed and yet become as worthy a myth as one based on fact. In either case it is not the elements which go to make the myth, but rather the truth that they are combined to reveal, which makes the significance of the whole. Surely the crude border chieftain engaged in petty ambuscades and plundering expeditions that historians find in King Arthur after the garments of legend are stripped off him is less significant than the mythical king whom legend-makers have made into a type of justice, honor, and chivalry. No less is William Tell or Robin Hood, the figment of a ballad-monger's brain, the symbol of liberty and

CONCLUSION

truth because he did not exist. Although the living beauty of Cleopatra might be disappointing to an American whose preference in matters of feminine beauty has been influenced by the Ziegfeld Follies, yet as a symbol of feminine seductiveness she is forever enshrined in the hearts of men. In each of these cases the fact, if there ever was any, has been transcended.

So in the case of Abraham Lincoln, these very workings of the poetic mind have made — within a period of recorded history, printing presses, and modern methods of research — a myth. Emerson said in his eulogy on Lincoln that 'in a period of less facility of printing, he would have become mythological in a very few years.' It would seem that in some ways the facility of printing has in reality made possible the more permanent and immediate establishing of the myth. Certainly the universal character of the legend would not have been possible of attainment in a period of less than a hundred years without printing.

If, as historians, we are not able to study the history of Lincoln in the spirit of Emerson's 'Essay on History,' we should be able to grant that in gaining a sympathetic view of the Lincoln of American legend it is necessary that we

> attain and maintain that lofty sight where facts yield their secret sense, and poetry and annals are alike. The instinct of the mind, the purpose of nature, betrays itself in the use we make of the signal narrations of history. Time dissipates to shining ether the solid angularity of facts. No anchor, no cable, no fences, avail to keep a fact a fact. Babylon, Troy, Tyre, Palestine, and even early Rome are passing already into fiction. The Garden of Eden, the sun standing still in Gibeon, is poetry thenceforward to all nations. Who cares what the fact was, when we have made a constellation of it to hang in heaven an immortal sign?

THE END

A CLASSIFIED BIBLIOGRAPHY

I. ANTHOLOGIES

ANONYMOUS. The Lincoln and Hamlin Songster, or the Continental Melodist, etc.... Philadelphia, 1860.

—— The Lincoln and Johnson Union Campaign Songster. Philadelphia, 1864.

CARNEGIE LIBRARY SCHOOL ASSOCIATION. Washington and Lincoln in Poetry. New York, 1927.

HARRINGTON, MILDRED (compiler). Our Holidays in Poetry. New York, 1929.

HOWE, M. A. DEW. (ed.). The Memory of Lincoln. Boston, 1899.

MURDOCH, JAMES E. (ed.). Patriotism in Poetry and Prose. Philadelphia, 1866.

OLDROYD, OSBORN H. (ed.). The Poet's Lincoln: Tributes in Verse. Washington, 1915.

PLOTTS, J. N. (compiler). Poetical Tributes to the Memory of Abraham Lincoln. Philadelphia, 1865.

SCHAUFFLER, R. H. (ed.). Lincoln's Birthday: A Comprehensive View of Lincoln as Given in the Most Notable Essays, Orations, and Poems, in Fiction and in Lincoln's Own Writings. New York, 1909.

STIDGER, WILLIAM L. R. (ed.). The Lincoln Book of Poems. Boston, 1911.

WILLIAMS, A. DALLAS (ed.). The Praise of Lincoln: An Anthology. Indianapolis, 1911.

WRIGHT-DAVIS, MARY (ed.). The Book of Lincoln. New York, 1919.

II. POETRY

(Poems which may be found readily in the anthologies are not listed here unless they have been cited in the text. All poems not found in the anthologies are listed.)

BIBLIOGRAPHY

ALDRICH, JULIA CARTER. A Memory of 1865. Wauseon, Ohio, 1914.

ALLEN, LYMAN W. Abraham Lincoln: A Poem. New York, 1896.

—— An Epic Trilogy, 3 vols. Vol. II, The Emancipator. New York, 1929.

AMES, A. S. Abraham Lincoln. Education, 40:247, 1919.

ANONYMOUS. General Emancipation Ballad and Emancipation Ode. [n.p.], 1863.

—— Abraham Africanus I: His Secret Life as Revealed under the Mesmeric Influence. New York, 1864.

—— A Lincoln! Per Omaggio l'autore. [n.p., 1865?]

—— Lincoln. Outlook, 85:311, 1907.

—— Lincoln. American Magazine, 65:358–59, 1908.

ARTHUR, SAMUEL J. Lincoln's Legacy. Boston, 1923.

BANGS, J. K. Lincoln's Birthday Poem. Lippincott's Magazine, 87:239, 1911.

BEIDLER, JACOB H. Lincoln. Chicago, 1896.

BELL, GEORGE W. Abraham Lincoln: A Poetical Interpretation. Cleveland, Ohio, 1913.

BENÉT, STEPHEN VINCENT. John Brown's Body. Garden City, New York, 1927.

BENJAMIN, S. G. W. Ode on the Death of Abraham Lincoln. Boston, 1865.

BERNARDI, JACOPO. Ad Abramo Lincoln. Pinerlo, Italy, 1862.

BIRCH, EDMUND P. The Devil's Visit to 'Old Abe.' New York, 1862.

BIRD, MARK B. The Victorious. Kingston, Jamaica, 1866.

BLANCHARD, RUFUS. Abraham Lincoln: The Type of American Genius. Wheaton, Illinois, 1882.

BOKER, GEORGE H. Our Heroic Themes. Boston, 1865.

BOUNDY, THOMAS. Liberty's Martyr. Jermyn, Pennsylvania, 1897.

BROTHERSON, F. B. M. Poems. (See 'March 4th, 1865' and 'Abraham Lincoln.') Peoria, Illinois, 1880.

BROWNELL, HENRY H. Ode to Abraham Lincoln. Atlantic, 16:491, 1865.

BRYANT, WILLIAM CULLEN. Poetical Works, edited by Parke Godwin, 2 vols. New York, 1883.

BIBLIOGRAPHY

BURDICK, M. L. Lincoln. Lippincott's Magazine, 71:268, 1903.

BURKE, JOHN. Stanzas to Queen Victoria and other Poems. (See 'Death of Abraham Lincoln.') New York, 1866.

BUTLER, CHARLES H. Our Leader. Washington, 1909.

BYNNER, WITTER. Lincoln. Harper's Weekly, 58:11, 1914.

CARMAN, BLISS. Man of Peace. Collier's, 42:16, 1909.

CHENY, JOHN V. Lincoln. Independent, 52:378, 1900.

—— Lincoln. Atlantic, 103:227–28, 1909.

CHURCHWELL, GEORGE W. Tribute to the Memory of Abraham Lincoln. New York, 1909.

CLARK, THOMAS C. Abraham Lincoln: Thirty Poems. Chicago, 1934.

COATES, F. E. Hero Poem. Century, 77:544, 1909.

—— His Face. Harper's Monthly, 122:419, 1911.

COHEN, S. Abraham Lincoln. Atlantic, 129:770, 1922.

COOKE, E. V. Beatitude. Good Housekeeping, 80:11, 1925.

CORMICAN, PATRICK J. A Tribute to Abraham Lincoln. Washington, 1923.

COWGILL, FRANK B. Trilogy of Lincoln Verse. Los Angeles, 1932.

DOLE, NATHAN H. Banner Memories. North American Review, 189:174–79, 1909.

DUNAND, CHARLES. La Mort du Président Lincoln. Sens, chez l'auteur, 1868.

DUNBAR, PAUL L. Complete Poems. New York, 1913.

EDDY, FREDERICK B. On St. Gaudens' Statue of Lincoln. Outlook, 97:311, 1911.

FERREIRA, F. A Mort de Lincoln. Canto Elegiaco. Rio de Janeiro, 1865.

FLETCHER, JOHN G. Lincoln. Some Imagist Poets. Boston, 1917.

FREEMAN, JAMES R. Abraham Lincoln; A Poem. Eau Claire, Wisconsin, 1909.

FRENCH, BENJAMIN B. A Letter and Short Poem, on the Death of Abraham Lincoln. Albany, New York, 1870.

FULTON, DAVID B. Poem, Abraham Lincoln. Brooklyn, 1909.

GILDER, RICHARD W. On the Life Mask of Abraham Lincoln. Century, 33:37, 1886.

GRAVESTEIN, KATE E. Liberty and Lincoln. Chicago, 1916.

BIBLIOGRAPHY

GRENIER, ÉDOUARD. The Death of President Lincoln (translated by Mrs. C. L. Botta). New York, 1918.

GUITERMAN, ARTHUR. He Leads us Still. Independent, 97:205, 1919.

GUNN, BENJAMIN J. Life of Abraham Lincoln in Verse. Great Bend, Kansas, 1914.

HAGEDORN, H. Lincoln. Current Literature, 46:448, 1909.

HALPINE, CHARLES G. Poetical Works (see 'Ancient Abe'). New York, 1869.

HANAFORD, PHEBE A. Our Martyred President. Boston, 1865.

HAYDEN, CAROLINE A. Our Country's Martyr. Boston, 1865.

HAYS, M. E. Abe. Education, 44:289, 1924.

HILL, C. W. Lincoln. Good Housekeeping, 83:13, 1926.

HODGES, L. M. Lincoln. Harper's Weekly, 53:29, 1909.

HYLTON, JOHN D. The Praesidicide: A Poem. Philadelphia, 1868.

JAMES, JAMES. The Two Epistles. Albany, New York, 1864.

JANVIER, FRANCIS DeHAES. The Sleeping Sentinel. Philadelphia, 1863.

JONES, EDWARD S. The Sylvan Cabin. San Francisco, 1915.

JORDAN, C. B. Lincoln Legend. Survey, 34:43, 1915.

KAUFFMAN, R. W. Abraham Lincoln. Harper's Weekly, 53:29, 1909.

KEMP, H. H. Lincoln; A Retrospect. Independent, 64:413, 1908.

LAUGHLIN, E. O. Lincoln Circuit. Ladies' Home Journal, 41:26, 1924.

—— Nancy Hanks. Literary Digest, 102:34, Sept. 21, 1929.

—— Emancipated. Literary Digest, 110:29, July 18, 1931.

LIEBFREED, EDWIN. Lincoln. [n.p.], 1921.

LINDSAY, NICHOLAS VACHEL. Collected Poems. New York, 1925.

LONGACRE, W. F. Pillars of Hercules. Independent, 70:387, 1911.

LORD, JAMES J. Lincoln Monument Dedication Poem. Danville, Illinois, 1907.

LOWELL, JAMES RUSSELL. Harvard Commemoration Ode. Cambridge, Massachusetts, 1865.

—— Poetical Works. Boston and New York, 1887.

BIBLIOGRAPHY

MacKaye, Percy. Ode on the Centenary of Abraham Lincoln. New York, 1909.

McCloskey, G. V. A. Lyrics (Three Lincoln Poems). New York, 1919.

MacMaster, Homer E. Abraham Lincoln Looks Across the Mall. Boston, 1932.

March, George O. Fin de Siècle, Lincoln's Birthday Exercises. Lebanon, Ohio, 1900.

Markham, Edwin. The Coming of Lincoln. Arena, 41:483, 1909.

—— Lincoln and Other Poems. Garden City, New York, 1924.

—— Lincoln Triumphant. Ladies' Home Journal, 43:8, 1926.

—— Ann Rutledge. Ladies' Home Journal, 43:167, 1926.

Masters, Edgar L. Spoon River Anthology. New York, 1915.

—— The Great Valley. New York, 1916.

Mathews, Stella T. The Life of Abraham Lincoln in Verse. Seattle, 1923.

Meader, Stephen W. Their Lincoln. Ladies' Home Journal, 35:20, 1918.

Meany, E. S. Abraham Lincoln. Overland Monthly, 53:226–27, 1909.

Moore, H. T. Lincoln Memorial. St. Nicholas, 58:275, 1931.

Neis, Anna Marie. Lincoln. Boston, 1915.

Newell, Robert H. Lincoln the Martyr President. New York, 1865.

Newkirk, Garrett. Lincoln Life Sketches in Verse and Prose. New York, 1920.

Nims, George W. Abraham Lincoln Souvenir. Boston, 1903.

Noyes, Isaac P. Ode on Lincoln. Washington, 1907.

Oppenheim, James. The Lincoln Child. Monday Morning and Other Poems. New York, 1909.

Osmaston, Francis P. B. Springfield and Concord. London, 1907.

Parmenter, Catherine. Lincoln Memorial. St. Nicholas, 61:front, 1934.

Pearce, John T. Last Days of Lincoln. Chicago, 1904.

Phifer, Lincoln. Silent Village. Christian Century, 50:186, 1933.

Powers, R. M. Bread and Milk. St. Nicholas, 49:348–49, 1922.

BIBLIOGRAPHY

PRESSFIELD, H. February 12, 1809. Sunset Magazine, 54:54, 1925.

RAY, HENRIETTA C. Lincoln. New York, 1893.

REBELLE, A. YOUNG. Abram: A Military Poem. Richmond, 1863.

RHODES, JACOB. The Nation's Loss. Newark, New Jersey, 1866.

RILEY, JAMES W. Lincoln. Reader Magazine, 5:307, 1905.

ROBINSON, EDWIN A. The Master. The Town Down the River. New York, 1910.

ROGERS, HENRY A. Loyal Legion Hymn. Boston, 1918.

ROMIG, EDNA DAVIS. Lincoln Remembers. Philadelphia, 1930.

SANDBURG, CARL. Cornhuskers. New York, 1918.

—— Good Morning America. New York, 1928.

SERMENT, JACQUES H. Sur une Gravure; Stances; à Abraham Lincoln. Paris, 1865.

SEYMOUR, MAYCE F. The Lincoln Memorial. Boston, 1927.

SHERWOOD, A. Lincoln and Darwin. World's Work, 17:11128–32, 1909.

SMITH, L. C. Footprints through the Glen (two Lincoln poems). Rochester, New York, 1907.

SNIDER, DENTON J. Lincoln in the Black Hawk War. St. Louis, 1910.

—— Lincoln and Ann Rutledge. St. Louis, 1912.

—— Lincoln in the White House. St. Louis, 1913.

—— Lincoln at Richmond. St. Louis, 1914.

SPICER, A. H. Nancy Hanks's Lullaby. Ladies' Home Journal, 45:23, 1928.

STAPLES, ERNEST L. A Man of Destiny: Being the Story of Abraham Lincoln; an Epic Poem. Shelton, Connecticut, 1902.

STEDMAN, EDMUND C. Hand of Lincoln. Outlook, 88:259–60, 1908.

STODDARD, RICHARD H. Abraham Lincoln: An Horation Ode. New York, 1865.

—— Abraham Lincoln's Birthday. New York Mail and Express, Feb. 12, 1898.

STREET, ALFRED B. In Memoriam. Albany, New York, 1870.

TAYLOR, BAYARD. The Ballad of Abraham Lincoln. Boston, 1870.

314

BIBLIOGRAPHY

THOMPSON, EDWARD W. When Lincoln Died and Other Poems. Boston and New York, 1909.

THOMPSON, MAURICE. Lincoln's Grave. Cambridge and Chicago, 1894.

THORN, JAMES S. Abraham Lincoln. New York, 1925.

VILLERS. La Mort du President Lincoln. Paris, 1867.

WALLER, MARY E. Our Benny. Boston, 1909.

WATKINS, LUCIAN B. The Old Log Cabin. Fort D. A. Russell, Wyoming, 1910.

WEBSTER, JACKSON C. The Foe Unmasked... the Character of the Martyr President. New York, 1865.

WESTALL, JOHN. In Memoriam. Fall River, New York, 1865.

WHITAKER, R. Lincoln and Darwin. Independent, 66:404, 1909.

WHITE, ROBINSON. Poems. Washington, 1930.

WHITMAN, WALT. Drum Taps. New York, 1865.

WHITTIER, JOHN GREENLEAF. Poetical Works. Boston and New York, 1888.

WILEY, A. A. Lincoln Memorial. Ladies' Home Journal, 42:27, 1925.

WRIGHT, CARRIE D. Me an' Abe: A Narrative Poem of Abraham Lincoln's New Salem Days. Chicago, 1930.

III. FICTION

ALTSHELER, JOSEPH A. In Circling Camps. New York and London, 1921.

ANDREWS, MARY R. S. The Perfect Tribute. New York, 1906.

—— The Counsel Assigned. New York, 1912.

—— Passing the Torch. Ladies' Home Journal, 41:3-5, 1924.

ATKINSON, ELEANOR. The Boyhood of Lincoln. New York, 1908.

—— Lincoln's Love Story. New York, 1909.

BABCOCK, BERNIE S. The Soul of Ann Rutledge. Philadelphia, 1919.

—— The Soul of Abe Lincoln. Philadelphia, 1923.

—— Booth and the Spirit of Lincoln. Philadelphia, 1925.

—— Little Abe Lincoln. Philadelphia, 1926.

—— Lincoln's Mary and the Babies. Philadelphia, 1929.

315

BIBLIOGRAPHY

BACHELLER, IRVING A. Eben Holden: A Tale of the North Country. New York, 1900.
—— A Man For the Ages. Indianapolis, 1919.
—— Father Abraham. Indianapolis, 1925.
BOYD, LUCINDA. The Sorrows of Nancy. Richmond, 1899.
BROWN, KATHERINE H. The Father. New York, 1928.
BUTTERWORTH, HEZEKIAH. In the Boyhood of Lincoln. New York, 1892.
CATHERWOOD, MARY H. Spanish Peggy: A Story of Young Illinois. Chicago, 1899.
CHITTENDEN, LUCIUS E. Lincoln and the Sleeping Sentinel. New York, 1909.
CHURCHILL, WINSTON. The Crisis. New York, 1901.
COBB, PERCIVAL B. The Martyr's Return. Wantagh, New York, 1915.
DAVIES, MARIA T. The Matrix. New York, 1920.
DIXON, THOMAS. The Clansman. New York, 1905.
—— The Southerner. New York, 1913.
DWYER, J. F. Bust of Lincoln. American Magazine, 73:386–96, 1912.
EGGLESTON, EDWARD. The Graysons: A Story of Abraham Lincoln. New York, 1888.
GALE, OLIVER M., and WHEELER, HARRIET M. The Knight of the Wilderness. Chicago, 1909.
GERRY, MARGARITA S. The Toy Shop. New York, 1908.
GILBERT, A. Matterhorn of Men. St. Nicholas, 40:308–13, 1913.
GREENE, HOMER. A Lincoln Conscript. Boston, 1909.
GRIERSON, FRANCIS. The Valley of Shadows. Boston, 1909.
GUITERMAN, ARTHUR. Lincoln Stories. Woman's Home Companion, 33:44–45, 1906.
HARRIS, JOEL CHANDLER. On the Wing of Occasions. New York, 1900.
JUDSON, E. Z. C. The Parricides. New York, 1865.
KIRKLAND, JOSEPH. The McVeys. New York, 1888.
LITTLE, RICHARD H. Better Angels. New York, 1928.
LONGSTRETH, T. M. As We Forgive Those. St. Nicholas, 50:338–47, 1923.

BIBLIOGRAPHY

BIBLIOGRAPHY

MARQUIS, DON. No Matter What they Think. Collier's, 87:11–13, 1931.

MAULE, MARY K. A Prairie Schooner Princess. Boston, 1920.

MEADER, STEPHEN W. Longhanks. New York, 1928.

MORROW, HONORÉ W. Benefits Forgot. New York, 1917.

—— The Lost Speech of Abraham Lincoln. New York, 1925.

—— Forever Free. New York, 1927.

—— With Malice Toward None. New York, 1928.

—— The Last Full Measure. New York, 1930.

—— Dearer Than All. Good Housekeeping, 98:34–37, 1934.

PAGE, THOMAS NELSON. The Red Riders. New York, 1924.

PERRY, J. R. Man at Washington. Harper's Weekly, 53:22–23, 1909.

ROBERTS, O. Our Townsman. Collier's, 42:17, 1909.

SCOTT, MILTON R. Supposed Diary of President Lincoln. Newark, Ohio, 1913.

SINGMASTER, ELSIE. Gettysburg. New York, 1907.

—— November the Nineteenth. Pictorial Review, 25:8–9, 1924.

STODDARD, W. O., JR. How Lincoln Came to School. Atlantic, 129:205–06, 1922.

TARBELL, IDA M. Back There in '58. American Magazine, 63:3–13, 1907.

—— He Knew Lincoln. New York, 1907

—— Father Abraham. New York, 1909.

—— In Lincoln's Chair. New York, 1920.

THORPE, F. N. Ann Rutledge; True Story of the Life Romance of Lincoln. Harper's Weekly, 53:22–26, 1909.

WADE, MARY H. Abraham Lincoln; A Story and a Play. Boston, 1914.

WALDMAN, M. If Booth Had Missed Lincoln. Scribner's Monthly, 88:473–84, 1930.

WRIGHT, CARRIE D. Lincoln's First Love: A True Story. Chicago, 1901.

IV. DRAMA

ANONYMOUS. The Royal Ape: A Dramatic Poem. Richmond, 1863.

ARMSTRONG, LOUISE V. W. The Old History Book. New York, 1928.

317

BIBLIOGRAPHY

BATES, ESTHER W. Shadow of a Great Man. Boston, 1930.

BUNGE, MARTIN L. D. Abraham Lincoln: A Historical Drama. Milwaukee, 1911.

BUSCH, WILLIAM. Cogitationes Vespertinae (see The Young Republic). Chicago, 1872.

—— Americanus. St. Louis, 1874.

CARPENTER, S. D. The Irrepressible Conflict. Madison, Wisconsin, 1862, and New York, 1914.

DALTON, TEST. The Mantle of Lincoln. New York, 1926.

DAVIES, WILLIAM W. Transfusion. Louisville, Kentucky, 1923.

DILLMAN, WILLARD F. Pageant of Abraham Lincoln. [n.p.], 1921.

DIXON, THOMAS. A Man of the People: A Drama. New York, 1920.

DOWNEY, STEPHEN W. The Play of Destiny as Played by Actors from the Kingdom of the Dead. New Creek, West Virginia, 1867.

DRINKWATER, JOHN. Abraham Lincoln: A Play. Boston and New York, 1919.

GALLUP, CLARENCE M. Abraham Lincoln: A Play. Providence, 1931.

GAMMANS, HAROLD W. Spirit of Ann Rutledge. New York, 1927.

LANGDON, WILLIAM C. The Masque of the Titans of Freedom. Urbana-Champaign, Illinois, 1918.

LEE, JULIAN. Lincoln Yesterday and Today. Chicago, 1933.

LEVINGER, ELMA E. A Child of the Frontier. New York, 1925.

LUBY, WILLIAM A. J. Wilkes Booth; or, the National Tragedy. Kalamazoo, Michigan, 1880.

RENLÖM, EDWARD. Lincoln's Anfang, Glück und Ende. Coburg, Germany, 1865.

ROGERS, JAMES W. Madame Surratt. Washington, 1879.

SANFORD, ANNE P. (compiler). Lincoln Plays. New York, 1933.

SCHNAKE, FRANZ A. F. Abraham Lincoln. Omaha, Nebraska, 1899.

TORRIE, HIRAM D. The Tragedy of Abraham Lincoln. Glasgow, 1876.

VESTAL, DEWITT C. Assassination. San José, California, 1879.

BIBLIOGRAPHY

WADE, MARY H. Abraham Lincoln: A Story and a Play. Boston, 1914.

ZINK, WALTER M. Lincoln and Humanity. Buffalo, New York, 1916.

BIBLIOGRAPHY OF ADDITIONAL WORKS USED

ABBOT, LYMAN. Abraham Lincoln's Agnosticism. Outlook, 84:654–55, 1906.

—— Abraham Lincoln's Religion. Outlook, 113:330–31, 1916.

—— Review of *The Soul of Abraham Lincoln*. Outlook, 124:656, 1920.

ADAMS, CHARLES FRANCIS, JR. Charles Francis Adams. New York, 1900.

ADAMS, HENRY. The Education of Henry Adams: An Autobiography. New York, 1918.

—— Letters of Henry Adams, edited by W. C. Ford. Boston and New York, 1930.

ADDERUP, ANDREW. Lincolniana; or, the Humors of Uncle Abe. New York, 1864.

ALGER, HORATIO, JR. Abraham Lincoln, the Backwoods Boy. New York, 1883.

AMERICA-JAPAN SOCIETY. Essays on Lincoln by Japanese Students, Special Bulletins for February, 1927–29. Springfield, Illinois.

ANONYMOUS. The Life of Abraham Lincoln, Wigwam Edition. New York, 1860.

—— The Life and Martyrdom of Abraham Lincoln. Philadelphia, 1864.

—— Abraham Lincoln: A Legacy of Fun. London, 1865.

—— Lincoln's Anecdotes. New York, 1867.

—— Only Authentic Life of Abraham Lincoln. New York, 1864.

—— Old Abe's Jokes, Fresh from Abraham's Bosom; Containing all His Issues, Excepting the Greenbacks, to Call in Some of which this Work is Issued. New York, 1864.

—— Book of the Prophet Stephen, Son of Douglas. New York, 1864.

ARNOLD, ISAAC N. Lincoln and the Overthrow of Slavery. Chicago, 1866.

BIBLIOGRAPHY

—— The Life of Abraham Lincoln. Chicago, 1884.

AVARY, MYRTA L. Recollections of Alexander H. Stephens. New York, 1910.

BALLARD, COLIN R. The Military Genius of Abraham Lincoln. London, 1926.

BANCROFT, GEORGE. Memorial Address on the Life and Character of Abraham Lincoln... Delivered in the House of Representatives at Washington on the 12th of February, 1866. Washington, 1866.

BARNARD, GEORGE G. Barnard's Lincoln. Cincinnati, 1917.

BARRETT, J. H. Life of Abraham Lincoln. Cincinnati, 1860.

BARTLETT, DAVID V. G. Life of Abraham Lincoln. Dayton, Ohio, 1860.

BARTON, WILLIAM E. The Paternity of Abraham Lincoln. New York, 1920.

—— The Soul of Abraham Lincoln. New York, 1920.

—— Abraham Lincoln and his Books. Chicago, 1920.

—— The Life of Abraham Lincoln, 2 vols. Indianapolis, 1925.

—— The Women Lincoln Loved. Indianapolis, 1927.

—— Abraham Lincoln and Walt Whitman. Indianapolis, 1928.

—— The Lineage of Lincoln. Indianapolis, 1929.

BEECHER, HENRY W. Sermon on the Death of Abraham Lincoln. Manchester, 1865.

BELL, LANDON C. Lincoln Myths Are Passing — But Slowly. Columbus, 1930.

BEVERIDGE, ALBERT J. Abraham Lincoln, 1809–1858; 2 vols. Boston and New York, 1928.

BLACKNALL, O. W. Lincoln as the South Should Know Him. Raleigh, North Carolina, 1915.

BRADFORD, GAMALIEL. The Haunted Biographer. Seattle, 1927.

BRAMANTIP, BOCARDO. The Abraham Lincoln Myth. New York, 1894.

BROOKS, NOAH. Personal Recollections of Lincoln. Harper's Monthly, 35:222–30, 1865.

—— Abraham Lincoln and the Downfall of American Slavery. New York, 1894.

BROWNE, FRANCIS F. Every Day Life of Lincoln. Chicago, 1913.

320

BIBLIOGRAPHY

BROWNING, ORVILLE H. Diary; edited by T. C. Pease and J. G. Randall, vol. I. Springfield, Illinois, 1925.

BRYANT, WILLIAM C. Prose Writings; edited by Parke Godwin, 2 vols. New York, 1901.

BULLARD, F. LAURISTON. Tad and his Father. Boston, 1915.

BURR, ANNA R. Weir Mitchell, his Life and Letters. New York, 1929.

CABOT, JAMES E. A Memoir of Ralph Waldo Emerson, 2 vols. Boston and New York, 1887.

CARPENTER, FRANCIS B. The Inner Life of Abraham Lincoln: Six Months at the White House. New York, 1929.

CATHEY, JAMES H. Truth is Stranger than Fiction; or, the True Genesis of a Wonderful Man. [n.p.], 1899.

CHARNWOOD, GODFREY RATHBONE BENSON. Abraham Lincoln. New York, 1917.

—— Some Lincoln Problems. Anglo-French Review, reprinted in Living Age, 307:528–37.

CHINIQUY, CHARLES. Fifty Years in the Church of Rome. Chicago, 1885.

CHITTENDEN, L. E. Recollections of President Lincoln and his Administration. New York, 1891.

—— Personal Reminiscences, 1830–90. New York, 1893.

CHOATE, JOSEPH H. Abraham Lincoln. New York, 1901.

CLARK, J. S. Life and Letters of John Fiske. Boston and New York, 1917.

CLARK, LEON P. Lincoln. New York, 1933.

COGGINS, J. C. Abraham Lincoln a North Carolinian, with Proof. Gastonia, North Carolina, 1927.

CONWAY, MONCURE D. Autobiography, 2 vols. Boston and New York, 1904.

COX, KENYON. Augustus St. Gaudens. Atlantic, 101:298–310, 1908.

CURTIS, GEORGE W. (ed.). The Correspondence of John Lothrop Motley, 2 vols. New York, 1889.

DODD, WILLIAM E. Lincoln or Lee. New York and London, 1928.

DRINKWATER, JOHN. Lincoln, the World Emancipator. Boston, 1920.

—— The World's Lincoln. New York, 1928.

BIBLIOGRAPHY

ELIOT, GEORGE. George Eliot's Life as Related in her Letters and Journals, edited by J. W. Cross, 3 vols. Edinburgh and London, 1885.

EMERSON, RALPH WALDO. Works, 12 vols. Boston and New York, 1903–04.

—— Journals, edited by E. W. Emerson and W. E. Forbes, 10 vols. 1909–14.

FARNHAM, C. H. A Life of Francis Parkman. Boston, 1901.

FROTHINGHAM, PAUL R. Edward Everett, Orator and Statesman. Boston and New York, 1925.

GARRISON, WILLIAM L. The Words of Garrison: A Centennial Selection. New York, 1905.

GODWIN, PARKE. A Biography of William Cullen Bryant, 2 vols. New York, 1883.

GORHAM, GEORGE C. Life and Public Services of Edwin M. Stanton, 2 vols. Boston and New York, 1899.

GRIDLEY, JAMES N. Lincoln's Defense of Duff Armstrong. Springfield, Illinois, 1910.

GRIERSON, FRANCIS. Abraham Lincoln, the Practical Mystic. New York, 1918.

GUROWSKI, ADAM. Diary, 3 vols. Boston, 1862–66.

HALE, EDWARD E. James Russell Lowell and his Friends. New York, 1901.

HAPGOOD, NORMAN. Abraham Lincoln, the Man of the People. New York, 1899.

HAWTHORNE, NATHANIEL. Complete Works, Riverside Edition, 13 vols. Boston and New York, 1914.

HAYCRAFT, SAMUEL. History of Elizabethtown. Elizabethtown, Kentucky, 1921.

HAYNE, PAUL H. Letter to Mrs. Margaret Preston. MS. in Duke University Library.

HERNDON, WILLIAM H. Abraham Lincoln, Miss Ann Rutledge, New Salem, Pioneering and the Poem: A Lecture Delivered in the Old Sangamon County Court House, November, 1866. Springfield, Illinois, 1910.

HERNDON, WILLIAM H., and WEIK, JESSE W. Herndon's Lincoln, 3 vols. Chicago, 1889. (Cited as Herndon.)

HILL, FREDERICK T. Lincoln the Lawyer. New York, 1906.

BIBLIOGRAPHY

HITCHCOCK, CAROLINE H. Nancy Hanks; the Story of Abraham Lincoln's Mother. New York, 1899.

HOBSON, JONATHAN T. Footprints of Abraham Lincoln. Dayton, Ohio, 1909.

HOLLAND, JOSIAH G. Life of Abraham Lincoln. Springfield, Massachusetts, 1865.

HOLLOWAY, EMORY. Whitman: An Interpretation in Narrative. New York and London, 1926.

HOWARD, JAMES Q. Life of Abraham Lincoln. Columbus, Ohio, 1860.

HOWE, M. A. DEW. The Life and Letters of George Bancroft, 2 vols. New York, 1908.

HOWELLS, MILDRED. Life in Letters of William Dean Howells. Garden City, New York, 1928.

HOWELLS, W. D., and HAYES, J. L. Lives and Speeches of Abraham Lincoln and Hannibal Hamlin. New York, 1860.

JACKSON, MARY N. A Fair Rebel's Interview with Abraham Lincoln. New York, 1917.

JAMES, WILLIAM. The Letters of William James, edited by his Son, Henry James. Boston, 1926.

JORDAN, DAVID S., and KIMBALL, SARAH L. Your Family Tree. New York and London, 1929.

KENNEDY, WILLIAM S. Oliver Wendell Holmes. Boston, 1883.

—— John G. Whittier, the Poet of Freedom. New York, 1892.

KRANS, HORATIO SHEAFE. Lincoln Tribute Book. New York, 1909.

LAMON, WARD H. Life of Abraham Lincoln. Boston, 1872.

—— Recollections of Abraham Lincoln, 1847–1865, edited by Dorothy Lamon Teillard. Chicago, 1895.

LANIER, SIDNEY. Letter to his Father. Copy of MS. in Duke University Library.

LATHROP, ROSE H. Memories of Hawthorne. Boston and New York, 1897.

LAWRENCE, MILLARD. The Life of Honest Abe, Done up Brown in Jazzistory. Milwaukee, Wisconsin, 1929.

LEA, J. HENRY, and HUTCHINSON, J. R. Ancestry of Abraham Lincoln. Boston and New York, 1909.

LEACOCK, STEPHEN B. Lincoln Frees the Slaves. New York, 1934.

323

BIBLIOGRAPHY

LEARNED, MARION D. Abraham Lincoln: An American Migration. Philadelphia, 1909.

LEWIS, LLOYD. Myths After Lincoln. New York, 1929.

LILLY, WILLIAM E. Set My People Free. New York, 1932.

LINCOLN, ABRAHAM. Complete Works, edited by J. G. Nicolay and John Hay, 2 vols. New York, 1894.

LINDSAY, NICHOLAS VACHEL. The Litany of Washington Street. New York, 1929.

LINN, WILLIAM A. Horace Greeley. New York, 1903.

LOWELL, AMY. Tendencies in Modern American Poetry. New York, 1917.

LOWELL, JAMES R. Prose Works, 8 vols. Boston, 1891.

LUBBOCK, PERCY (ed.). The Letters of Henry James. New York, 1920.

LUDWIG, EMIL. Lincoln (translated by Eden and Cedar Paul). Boston, 1930.

MARTIN, JAMES M. A Defence of Lincoln's Mother, Conversion and Creed. Minneapolis 1921.

MASTERS, EDGAR L. Lincoln the Man. New York, 1931.

MAYNARD, NETTIE COLBURN. Was Abraham Lincoln a Spiritualist? Philadelphia, 1891.

McCALL, SAMUEL W. Thaddeus Stevens. Boston and New York, 1899.

McCARTHY, CHARLES H. Lincoln's Plan of Reconstruction. New York, 1901.

McCLURE, ALEXANDER K. Abraham Lincoln and Men of War-Times. Philadelphia, 1892.

——— 'Abe' Lincoln's Yarns and Stories. Chicago, 1901.

MILLER, FRANCIS T. Portrait Life of Lincoln. Springfield, Massachusetts, 1910.

MILTON, GEORGE F. The Eve of Conflict: Stephen A. Douglas and the Needless War. Boston, 1934.

MINOR, WILMA F. Lincoln the Lover. Atlantic, 142:838–56, 143:1–14, 215–25, 1928–29.

MOORE, FRANK. The Rebellion Record: A Diary of American Events, 11 vols. New York, 1864–68.

MORROW, HONORÉ W. Mary Todd Lincoln. New York, 1928.

MORSE, JOHN T., JR. Abraham Lincoln, 2 vols. Boston and New York, 1893.

BIBLIOGRAPHY

—— Life and Letters of Oliver Wendell Holmes, 2 vols. Boston and New York, 1893.

NICOLAY, JOHN G., and HAY, JOHN. Abraham Lincoln: A History, 10 vols. New York, 1890.

NORTON, CHARLES E. Letters, edited by Sarah Norton and M. A. DeW. Howe, 2 vols. Boston and New York, 1913.

OLDROYD, OSBORN H. The Mystic Number Seven in the Life of Abraham Lincoln. Washington, 1930.

PENNEL, ORRIN H. The Religious Views of Abraham Lincoln. Alliance, Ohio, 1904.

PERRY, BLISS. Walt Whitman: His Life and Work. Boston and New York, 1906.

PERRY, J. R. The Poetry of Lincoln. North American Review, 193:213–20, 1911.

PETERS, MADISON C. Abraham Lincoln's Religion. Boston, 1909.

PHILLIPS, WENDELL. Speeches, Lectures, and Letters, 2 vols. Boston, 1892.

PICKARD, S. T. Life and Letters of John Greenleaf Whittier, 2 vols. New York, 1899.

PIERCE, EDWARD L. Memoir and Letters of Charles Sumner, 1845–60, 4 vols. London, 1893.

PRATT, SILAS G. Lincoln in Story. Chicago, 1901.

RANDALL, J. G. Constitutional Problems under Lincoln. New York and London, 1926.

—— Lincoln's Task and Wilson's. South Atlantic Quarterly, 29:349–68, 1930.

RHODES, JAMES FORD. History of the United States from the Compromise of 1850, 9 vols. New York, 1893–1922.

RICE, ALLEN T. (ed.). Reminiscences of Abraham Lincoln. New York, 1885.

ROBINSON, LUTHER E. Abraham Lincoln as a Man of Letters. New York, 1918.

ROTHSCHILD, ALONZO. Lincoln, Master of Men. Boston and New York, 1906.

—— 'Honest Abe.' Boston and New York, 1917.

RUSSELL, WILLIAM H. My Diary North and South, 2 vols. London, 1863.

BIBLIOGRAPHY

RUTLEDGE, ARCHIBALD. A Southerner Views Lincoln. Scribner's, 83:204–13, 1928.

ST. GAUDENS, HOMER. St. Gaudens, the Master. Century, 78:212–28, 611–26, 1909.

SANDBURG, CARL. Abraham Lincoln: The Prairie Years, 2 vols. New York, 1926.

SCHURZ, CARL. Abraham Lincoln, an Essay. Boston and New York, 1891.

SCOTT, MILTON R. Essay on Lincoln: Was he an Inspired Prophet? Newark, Ohio, 1906.

SCRIPPS, JOHN L. Life of Lincoln. Chicago and New York, 1860.

SCUDDER, H. E. James Russell Lowell: A Biography, 2 vols. Boston and New York, 1901.

SEITZ, DON C. Lincoln the Politician. New York, 1931.

SHAW, ALBERT. Abraham Lincoln: His Path to the Presidency, a Cartoon History. New York, 1929.

—— Abraham Lincoln: The Year of his Election, a Cartoon History. New York, 1929.

STEARNS, F. P. Sketches from Concord and Appledore. New York, 1895.

STEPHENSON, NATHANIEL W. Abraham Lincoln and the Union. New Haven, Connecticut, 1918.

—— Lincoln: An Account of his Personal Life, Especially of its Springs of Action as Revealed and Deepened by the Ordeal of War. Indianapolis, 1922.

—— (compiler). An Autobiography of Abraham Lincoln. Indianapolis, 1926.

STODDARD, WILLIAM O. Abraham Lincoln. New York, 1888.

STOREY, MOORFIELD. Charles Sumner. Boston and New York, 1900.

TARBELL, IDA M. The Life of Abraham Lincoln, 2 vols. New York, 1895.

—— In the Footsteps of Lincoln. New York and London, 1924.

THAYER, WILLIAM M. The Pioneer Boy and How he Became President. Boston, 1863.

—— The Character and Public Services of Abraham Lincoln. Boston, 1864.

BIBLIOGRAPHY

—— From Pioneer Home to White House. Norwich, Connecticut, 1882.

TRACY, GILBERT A. Uncollected Letters of Abraham Lincoln. Boston and New York, 1917.

TRAUBEL, HORACE. With Walt Whitman in Camden, 3 vols. Boston, 1906–14.

TROWBRIDGE, J. T. My Own Story, with Recollections of Noted Persons. Boston and New York, 1903.

TURNEY, D. B. The Mythifying Theory; or, Abraham Lincoln a Myth. Metropolis, Illinois, 1872.

TYLER, LYON G. Barton and the Lineage of Lincoln. Holdcroft, Virginia, 1930.

VICTOR, O. J. The Private and Public Life of Abraham Lincoln (In Beadle's Lives of Great Americans Series). New York, 1864.

WALSH, WILLIAM S. Abraham Lincoln and the London Punch. New York, 1909.

WARREN, LOUIS A. Lincoln's Parentage and Childhood. New York and London, 1926.

WEED, THURLOW. Autobiography, 2 vols. Boston and New York, 1883–84.

WELLES, GIDEON. The Diary of Gideon Welles, 3 vols. Boston and New York, 1911.

WEIK, JESSE W. The Real Lincoln. Boston, 1922. (See also Herndon and Weik.)

WETTSTEIN, C. T. Was Abraham Lincoln an Infidel? Boston, 1910.

WHITMAN, WALT. Complete Prose Works. Philadelphia, 1892.

—— The Wound Dresser: A Series of Letters Written from the Hospitals in Washington During the War of the Rebellion, edited by R. M. Bucke. Boston, 1898.

WHITNEY, HENRY C. Life of Abraham Lincoln. New York, 1908.

WILSON, RUFUS R. Lincoln in Caricature. [n.p.], 1903.

INDEX

INDEX

Booth, John Wilkes, 4, 6, 37, 48, 51, 164, 262

Borglum, Gutzon, statue of Lincoln, 288, 291, 292, 293

Boswell, James, 12–13

Boyd, L., 47

Bradford, Gamaliel, *The Haunted Biographer*, 50–51

Bramantip, Bocardo, *The Abraham Lincoln Myth*, 302–303

Brooks, Noah, 132 n.; story of Lincoln's visions, 185–186

Brown, John, 102, 203, 224; Lincoln's characterization of, 208

Brown, K. H., *The Father*, 126 n.

Brownell, Henry Howard, 36, 37

Browning, Orville H., *Diary*, 209

Bryan, William Jennings, 222

Bryant, William Cullen, 64, 67–68; 'The Death of Abraham Lincoln,' 36, 214; opinion of Lincoln, 67–69

Buchanan, James, 55

Burke, Edmund, Lincoln's opinion of Burke's biography, 11

Burr, Aaron, 298

Butler, Benjamin F., 70

Butterworth, Hezekiah, *In the Boyhood of Lincoln*, 47 n., 109

Bynner, Witter, 'A Farmer Remembers Lincoln,' 43, quoted, 245

Byron, Lord, 62

Caesar, Augustus, Lincoln compared to, 223–224

Caesar, Julius, Lincoln compared to, 16, 165

Calvin, John, 168

Cameron, Simon, 31, 64

Carman, Bliss, 'The Man of Peace,' 41

Carpenter, Francis B., 216; *The Inner Life of Abraham Lincoln*, 5, 284–286; 'The First Reading of the Emancipation Proclamation,' 284

Cass, Lewis, 134 n.

Catherwood, M. H., 47, 160 n.

Charlemagne, Emperor, Lincoln's genealogy traced to, 112

Charnwood, Lord, 29, 61, 208, 272, 296;

comment on Herndon, 12–13; *Abraham Lincoln*, 19–20; Lincoln's opportunism, 29–30

Chase, Salmon P., 65, 71, 124–125, 176, 177, 188, 222; on Lincoln's Divine guidance, 172

Chaucer, Geoffrey, 264

Child, Lydia Maria, 73

Chiniquy, Father Charles, *Fifty Years in the Church of Rome*, quoted on Lincoln's associating himself with Moses and Christ, 173–176

Chittenden, L. E., 129; on Lincoln's Divine guidance, 176–177

Christ, Jesus, Lincoln compared to, 37, 41, 113, 145, 165, 169, 174–178, 180–182, 192, 301

Churchill, Winston, *The Crisis*, 45, 46, 192–193, 241

Collins, W. F., 'The Lincoln Statue,' 288

Conklin, J. C., 80–81

Conway, Moncure D., 74

Coolidge, Calvin, 112

Cox, Kenyon, address on Saint Gaudens, 287

Cranch, Christopher Pearse: 'The Martyr,' 6, 35

Crane, Ichabod, 236

Crockett, David, 116, 131, 141

Curtis, George William, 79, 80, 100

Dalton, Test, *The Mantle of Lincoln*, 50

Darwin, Charles, 42, 43, 191

Davies, Maria Thompson, *The Matrix*, 48, 112, 115

Davis, Henry Winter, 31

Davis, Jefferson, 134

DeVere, Aubrey, 81

De Vermandois, Isabel, Lincoln's genealogy traced to, 112

Dickens, Charles, fondness for story of Lincoln's dream, 188

Dixon, Thomas, 222, 224; *The Southerner*, 47, 48, 110, 115, 193, 217, 220–221, 240; *The Clansman*, 47, 193, 220–221; *A Man of the People*, 50, 217, 221

INDEX

Dodd, W. E., *Lincoln or Lee*, 299

Douglas, Stephen A., 32, 46, 55, 62, 65, 88, 191, 223, 232; Lincoln's Peoria reply to, quoted, 206–207

Drinkwater, John, 297, 304; *Abraham Lincoln: A Play*, 21–22, 49, 50, 129, 221–222, 224, 271–280; *Lincoln, the World Emancipator*, 203

Dunbar, Paul Laurence, Poem, quoted, 220

Eggleston, Edward, *The Graysons*, 45–46

Emerson, Ralph Waldo, 61, 78, 80, 90, 92, 97, 98, 101, 125, 129, 165, 179, 229, 268; opinion of Lincoln, 82–87, 236–237; eulogy of Lincoln, 307; 'Essay on History,' quoted, 307

Everett, Edward, opinion of Lincoln, 87–89

Fell, J. W., 106

Fessenden, William P., 176

Fields, James T., 73, 75, 90

Fields, Mrs. James T., 179

Fiske, John, 100

Fletcher, John Gould, 257; 'Lincoln,' 43, quoted, 258–260, 261

Ford's Theater, scene of assassination, 164, 278

Franklin, Benjamin, 297

Frazier, Sir James George, *The Golden Bough*, 4

Frémiet, Emmanuel, quoted on Lincoln's features, 282–283

Frémont, John C., 59, 68, 70–71, 72, 73, 85, 130, 209, 217, 222

French, Daniel C., statue of Lincoln, 291–292, 293

Gale, O. M., *The Knight of the Wilderness*, 47 n.

Gammans, H. W., *Spirit of Ann Rutledge*, 50, 162

Garrison, William Lloyd, 66, 73, 217; opinion of Lincoln, 71–72

George, Lloyd, 21

Gerolt, Baron, 84

Gibbons, James Sloane, 'We Are Coming, Father Abraham, Three Hundred Thousand More,' 126 n.

Gibson, Charles Dana, 293

Gilder, Richard Watson, 'To the Spirit of Abraham Lincoln,' 38, quoted, 39; 'On the Life Mask of Abraham Lincoln,' 38

Godwin, Parke, 67, 68

Grandison, Sir Charles, 126

Grant, Ulysses S., 80, 102, 183, 232, 243, 278

Gray, Fred, 95

Gray, Nat, 95

Greeley, Horace, 31, 68 n., 86; opinion of Lincoln, 64–67; Lincoln's reply to 'Prayer of Twenty Million,' 211

Green, H., *A Lincoln Conscript*, 47 n.

Grierson, Francis, *The Valley of Shadows*, 46, 183–184; Lincoln's mysticism, 183–185

Griffith, D. W., 47

Guiterman, Arthur, 'He Leads Us Still,' 43

Gurowski, Adam, *Diary*, 102

Hackett, James, Lincoln's letter to, 60

Hale, Edward Everett, 65

Hamilton, Alexander, 70, 297

Hanks, Dennis, 107 n., 115, 122, 152; description of Nancy Hanks, 107

Hanks, John, 121 n., 122, 131, 132 n., 142; version of slave market story, 135–137

Hanks, Lucy, 111 n.

Hanks, Nancy, 42, 43, 48, 118, 119; legendary aspects of, 105–113

Hapgood, Norman, *Abraham Lincoln, the Man of the People*, 17–18

Harris, Joel Chandler, 'The Kidnaping of President Lincoln,' 239–240

Harte, Bret, 37

Hawthorne, Nathaniel, 78, 236; opinion of Lincoln, 89–92

Hawthorne, Mrs. Nathaniel, 89

Hay, John, 92, 185, 190; See Nicolay and Hay for references to *Abraham Lincoln: A History*

331

INDEX

INDEX

INDEX

INDEX

Taft, Charles P., 292

Taft, William H., 293

Tanner, Corporal James, 165 n.

Tarbell, Ida M., biography of Lincoln, 17, 104; *Father Abraham*, 126 n.; quoted on Lincoln's associating himself with Christ, 173

Taylor, Bayard, 'Gettysburg Ode,' 38; *The Ballad of Lincoln*, 38

Taylor, Benjamin Franklin, 'The President's Dream,' 189-190

Taylor, Tom, tribute to Lincoln, 7

Taylor, Zachary, 131

Teillard, Dorothy Lamon, comment on Lamon's *Lincoln*, 9-10

Tell, William, 306

Thayer, William M., 107; *The Pioneer Boy*, 8, 57, 106; *The Character and Public Services of Abraham Lincoln*, 57-58

Thompson, E. W., poem comparing Lincoln with Christ, 181-182; 'We Talked of Lincoln,' 242-243

Thompson, Maurice, 'At Lincoln's Grave,' 38; quoted, 129-130, 246

Torrie, Hiram D., *The Tragedy of Abraham Lincoln*, 49-50, 142-143

Traubel, Horace, 94

Traylor, Sampson, 241

Trowbridge, J. T., *My Own Story*, 125 n.

Turner, F. J., 7, 17, 40; 'The Significance of the Frontier in American History,' 7, 17, 40, 230-232; *The Frontier in American History*, 331

Turney, D. B., *The Mythifying Theory, or Abraham Lincoln a Myth*, 301-302

Twain, Mark, 51

Tyler, Lyon G., *Barton and the Lineage of Lincoln*, 111 n.

Untermeyer, Louis, comment on Robinson's 'The Master,' 257; quoted on Whitman's Americanism, 264

Vestal, D. C., *Assassination*, 49

Victor, J. O., 'dime novel' biography, 58, 106

Volk, Douglas, 286 n.

Volk, Leonard W., life mask of Lincoln, 281, 289

Wade, Benjamin, 31

Walsh, William S., *Abraham Lincoln and the London Punch*, 55

Ward, Artemus, 225, 252, 276

Warren, L. A., *Lincoln's Parentage and Childhood*, 118

Washington, George, 5, 6, 68, 88, 123, 124, 265, 266, 297-298.

Webster, Daniel, 32, 251, 287

Weed, Thurlow, 65

Weems, Mason L. 'Parson,' 5, 8, 11, 57, 106, 298

Welles, Gideon, 71, 177; on Lincoln's Divine guidance, 172; story of Lincoln's dream presaging victory, 188-189

Wheeler, H. M., *The Knight of the Wilderness*, 47 n.

Whitman, Walt, 7, 35, 43, 47, 165, 229, 240, 263-264, 265, 269; 'Oh Captain! My Captain!', 35, 189; quoted, 214-215; 'When Lilacs Last in the Door-Yard Bloom'd,' 35, 260, 267; quoted, 269-271; opinion of Lincoln, 94-97, 268; *Specimen Days*, quoted, 96-97; *Drum Taps*, 214, 267-268; 'Death of Abraham Lincoln,' 239; 'Hush'd Be The Camps Today,' 268; comment on photographs, portraits, and statues of Lincoln, 283-284

Whittier, John Greenleaf, 73, 79; 'Emancipation Group,' 38, 214; opinion of Lincoln, 73

William the Conqueror, 112

Williams, A. Dallas, *The Praise of Lincoln*, 44

Williams, F. H., *The Burden Bearer*, 40, 194

Wilson, Rufus R., 55

335